AUTHORS SERIES • VOLUME VII

THE NORWEGIAN-AMERICAN HISTORICAL ASSOCIATION

Waldemar Ager

AUTHORS SERIES • VOLUME VII

Immigrant Idealist A Literary Biography of Waldemar Ager, Norwegian American

By

EINAR HAUGEN

1989
The Norwegian-American Historical Association
NORTHFIELD • MINNESOTA

The figure that appears on the cover and title page of this book is one of the twenty-four letters in the older Germanic runic alphabet used in the Scandinavian countries from about 200 to 800 A.D. In addition to representing the sound "m," approximately as in modern English, it also has a name, meaning "man" or "mankind." It thus serves here as a symbol for the humanities.

To
Clarence Clausen
and
Clarence Kilde

Foreword

WALDEMAR AGER, as editor and author, was one of the most original and influential men of letters among Norwegian Americans. He was an idealist who tirelessly and valiantly did battle for the causes he believed in, the two major ones being temperance and Norwegian-American cultural growth. The foremost expression of the latter would be an independent immigrant literature.

The present volume, *Immigrant Idealist: A Literary Biography of Waldemar Ager, Norwegian American* by Einar Haugen, is a well-informed and sensitive scholarly statement about Ager's own contributions to this literature. He produced many volumes of fiction—short stories and novels—and wrote numerous polemical articles, editorial opinions, and reports. But the study moves substantially beyond a consideration of Ager's literary products and situates him and his life's work in the larger context of the immigrant world, its place in an evolving pluralistic American society, and its relationship to Norway. We are pleased to publish this volume as the seventh in our Authors Series.

Einar Haugen is Victor S. Thomas Professor Emeritus of Scandinavian and linguistics in Harvard University. He is a member of the Association's publications board and is recognized for his many publications within his field and the related areas of Norwegian-American history and literature.

In editing this volume for publication I had the competent assistance of Mary R. Hove, which I wish to acknowledge with warmest thanks. She also prepared the index.

St. Olaf College   ODD S. LOVOLL

Preface

I HAVE DEDICATED this book to Clarence Clausen, not only because he is my oldest living friend, but also because I learned a great deal from him during our three years together in graduate school at the University of Illinois. Over the years it has been good to know that he was there, at St. Olaf College, and when he asked me to write a sketch of Ager's life, it was a pleasure to consent.

I have also gratefully dedicated it to Clarence Kilde because he entrusted me with the Ager collections that he had gathered over many years. Without his devotion to Ager's memory it would have been impossible to compose this book.

Beyond these two I owe a great deal to the staff of the Norwegian-American Historical Association Archives at St. Olaf College, including Professor Lloyd Hustvedt, Charlotte Jacobson, and Ruth Hanold Crane. They have helped me find the materials I needed, including pictures and other memorabilia. I also had valuable assistance from the Rølvaag family, especially Solveig Zempel, and the faculty of Norwegian, especially Margaret O'Leary. Odd S. Lovoll, as the editor of the Norwegian-American Historical Association, was a helpful resource at every turn. Finally I wish to mention my hosts Ella Valborg Tweet and Helen Wilbur. On my visit to Eau Claire Peggy Hager was my ever-present helper, guiding me to a valuable interview with Ager's son, Eyvind. Howard Lutz was also a useful intermediary. While Eyvind was the only member of the Ager family I met, I had epistolary contact with his sister Hildur.

In Norway the staff of the University Library in Oslo was most generous, above all Johanna Barstad, who furnished me with bibliographies and access to the Norwegian-American collection, and enabled me to copy hundreds of pages from the microfilmed files of *Reform*. On a visit to Fredrikstad and

Gressvik to see Ager's early home, I benefited from the guidance and hospitality of Finn Andersen and his wife. In Oslo Herborg Handagard gave me access to a bibliography of her father's writings and kindly xeroxed his letters from Ager (1897–1935).

A special thanks goes to my wife, Eva, who has read the chapters as they were ready and has corrected my more egregious errors.

Finally, a personal note: I learned to know and admire Waldemar Ager when I was still a young man. He came to Sioux City, Iowa, to speak and was a guest in my parents' home. Later, in Madison, Wisconsin, he was the guest of my wife and me. These brief encounters and my ardent reading of his writings are ever present in the background of this book.

July 22, 1987   EINAR HAUGEN

x

Contents

Illustrations

Immigrant Idealist

Unless otherwise indicated, all illustrations come from the collection of the Norwegian-American Historical Association.

LITERARY BIOGRAPHY OF WALDEMAR AGER

Introduction

WALDEMAR AGER (1869–1941) was the founder of a movement to develop a Norwegian-language literature among immigrants in the United States. From the 1890s to the 1920s he was the central figure in what he insisted on calling a "Norwegian-American" literature. As he saw it, this was a secular literature that had its roots in Norway and bloomed in America. By using the Norwegian language it maintained a link with the early lives of the emigrants in their native land, but by drawing its observations from the American lives of the immigrants it was a true reflection of their experiences in their new homeland. As long as one maintained the Norwegian language and the native culture embodied in it, there would be no break in the continuity of the immigrants' lives. They could grow right into the new land and make their contribution to it, not only as hewers of wood and drawers of water, but as partners in the building of a new American civilization.

This idealistic view of America and its potentiality for incorporating elements of non-English culture was probably widespread among immigrants from various countries. It conflicted with the usual Anglo-American concept of assimilation, which required that immigrants give up any allegiance not just to a foreign government but also to a foreign culture and language. Immigration was a one-way process whereby foreigners were to become Americans, but Americans did not in any way accept foreign languages or customs. Immigrant experience was to be a conversion, a transformation, in which the immigrant shed the "old Adam" and came forth in a new guise as a good American citizen.

Ager fully accepted the notion of becoming an American citizen, a new political creature, but he saw no disloyalty in maintaining alongside an American life a Norwegian culture which did not involve resistance to the democratic

1

institutions of America. Nor did he object to learning English, but he wished to maintain within his family and in his church and his friendships the language of his ancestors. The difficulty was that American life was forever nibbling at his base, luring away his children and exerting a subtle influence on him, an influence that was intensified by the crises of World War I. These factors will be explored at some length in the following account of his life. The aim of this study is to present a full-length portrait of an important figure in the development of an American immigrant group. Not every aspect of his life can be considered, for he was fluent and active in many fields, as journalist, speaker, and author. The stress will be on his literary career, with glances at other relevant areas.

He came to America when immigration from northwestern Europe was at a peak, in the mid-1880s. While Norwegians had been trickling into the United States since 1825 and had already discovered the Midwest as their mecca well before the Civil War, the end of the war opened the floodgates and turned Norwegians loose by the thousands. During the 1870s and 1880s the emigration was so heavy that it carried with it more than the natural increase of the population. In 1814 Norway had less than a million inhabitants; an estimated 750,000 left the country during the century of immigration. In the top year of 1882 more than 28,000 Norwegians emigrated. It is commonly said that only Ireland had a heavier proportion of emigrants.

The early emigrants were drawn mostly from the farming population and they sought out the open, arable lands in the upper Midwest, from 1840 streaming into Wisconsin, Iowa, Minnesota, and the Dakotas. They organized Lutheran churches which conducted services and instructed the children in Norwegian. Hundreds of congregations were founded, books and newspapers were published, and for some decades one could speak of a "Norwegian America." From the 1880s emigrating families were outnumbered by individuals, many of them urban, seeking work, often in American cities. Cities like Chicago and Minneapolis became magnets for the new migration, along with many smaller towns like Eau Claire, Wisconsin, where Ager would settle.

In the climate of settlement secular literature did not flourish. The leaders of the Lutheran churches held that the reading of anything but the Bible and the hymn book was a frivolous exercise, not conducive to the goal of salvation. If journals were started, they should be guided by the clergy. This pattern was broken early by persons of a more worldly persuasion, but it was not until the 1860s and 1870s that major newspapers sprang into being. Such journals as the weeklies *Skandinaven* and *Decorah-Posten* were founded in 1866 and 1874 respectively in Chicago and in Decorah, Iowa. But there were also numerous minor efforts, often with special interests, like *Reform*, the temperance weekly which became the voice of Waldemar Ager after it moved to Eau Claire, Wisconsin, in 1888. In an age before the automobile, electricity, radio, and television, these newspapers all fulfilled a purpose by informing a widespread clientele about news not only from the homeland overseas but also from the life of fellow countrymen in America.

Such journals also became the early repositories of letters, travel accounts, poetry, and even fiction, either translated or original, often reprinted from Norwegian sources. While not the first Norwegian-American writer, O. A. Buslett in Wisconsin was a pioneer, described as "poet, storyteller, dramatist, and reformer." His first story "Fram" (Forward) appeared in 1882; he became an early friend of Ager, who would later characterize him as one who "had a lyre in one hand and a dissecting knife in the other."[1] Another early author, H. A. Foss, wrote *Husmandsgutten* (The Cotter Boy, 1889), a best-seller, though it could hardly be classified as great literature. Peer Strømme was an author-pastor-lecturer who made his mark by writing *Hvorledes Halvor blev Prest* (How Halvor Became a Pastor, 1893). All these were earlier than Ager's first book, which came only in 1894. But Ager was the first to launch the idea that Norwegians in America had the makings of a literature of their own, distinct from that of the motherland but still reflecting their own lives in a language they all knew from childhood. For a generation he would be not only its leader but also its chief glory.

It should perhaps be made clear just what Norwegian is or was. While it is by definition the language of Norway, the term can be ambiguous. The picturesque land of Norway, the northernmost and almost the westernmost country of continental Europe, became a distinct entity some thousand years ago, in the ninth century A.D. The language spoken, usually called Old Norwegian, was a branch of the Scandinavian languages, which included Danish and Swedish as well as Icelandic, with which Norwegian was most closely allied. Norway had its own government until 1450 A.D., when it was dynastically united with Denmark, an arrangement that lasted for nearly four hundred years. In effect, Denmark became dominant and Norway fell into a dependency which accepted the language of the Danish court as its written language. Although the union with Denmark was broken in 1814 and a new union with Sweden established, this had no effect on the language. Norwegian was still written identically with Danish, but Norwegians spoke a multitude of rural dialects, and the urban elite had created a Dano-Norwegian speech form that was radically different from Danish. This was the language of Ager: speech that was urban Norwegian, a written language that was Danish. To him these two forms were quite simply spoken and written Norwegian.

During his lifetime Ager was certainly the best known Norwegian American, widely heard and read by all segments of Norwegian-American society.

3

Immigrant Idealist

His newspaper of opinion was noticed, quoted, and argued with, and he himself had his fingers in innumerable pots, particularly those that concerned prohibition and the cause of the Norwegian language. Since his death in 1941 silence seems to have fallen over his figure, in part because, as someone has said, "his work is frozen in a foreign language." This book will be an attempt to rescue him from the oblivion that seems to have settled on his work and personality. He was a good man and a great one, whose idealism inspired him to do everything he thought best for his fellow countrymen. He should be honored, not forgotten. He was one who kept faith with his ancestors by projecting an America he loved and wished would live up to the future it ought to have.

4

WALDEMAR AGER
A CHRONOLOGY

1869   Born March 23, Fredrikstad, Norway, to Martinius Mathisen Ager of Eidsberg and Fredrikke Marie Johnsdatter Stillaugsen, known as Mathea, of Fredrikstad.

1871   Family moves to Græsvig (now Gressvik), across the Glommen (now Glåma) river from Fredrikstad.

1873   Enters school at age four and a half.

1882   Family having moved to Christiania (Oslo), Waldemar leaves school at age thirteen to find employment.

1883   Father Martinius emigrates to America to settle in Chicago as a custom tailor.

1885   Mother Mathea and three children emigrate to Chicago; Waldemar begins as apprentice printer at *Norden*, a Norwegian-American weekly newspaper.

1887   Joins the Harmony Total Abstinence Society, becomes its secretary.

1891   Becomes editor of *Templarbladet*, a four-page temperance monthly published in Milwaukee, Wisconsin. Becomes a naturalized citizen of the United States.

1892   Moves to Eau Claire, Wisconsin, to work as a printer in the office of *Reform*, a weekly Norwegian newspaper advocating temperance and prohibition.

1894   *Paa drikkeondets konto: Fortællinger og vers* published in Eau Claire at *Reform*'s printshop. Father Martinius dies in Chicago and is buried in Mt. Olive Cemetery. Mother moves to Eau Claire.

1896   Promoted to business manager and co-editor of *Reform*.

1899   Marries Gurolle Blestren from Tromsø; wedding trip to New Orleans. *I strømmen, en fortælling* published in Eau Claire.

1900   First visit to Norway since emigration.

1901   *Afholdssmuler fra boghylden* published in Eau Claire.

1903   Becomes editor of *Reform*.

1905   Starts and edits *Kvartalskrift*, journal of Det Norske Selskab i Amerika.

1906   *Fortællinger for Eyvind* published in Eau Claire.

1907   *When You are Tired of Playing: Stories for Eyvind* translated by J. J. Skørdalsvold and published in Eau Claire.

1908   Becomes a member of the Eau Claire Public Library Board. *Hverdagsfolk*, short stories, published in Eau Claire.

5

1910   *Kristus for Pilatus. En norsk-amerikansk fortælling* published in Eau Claire.

1911   *Presten Conrad Walther Welde*, Norwegian title of *Kristus for Pilatus*, published in Christiania by Aschehoug publishers.

1912   First Eau Claire citizen to appear in *Who's Who in America.*

1913   Mother Mathea dies in Chicago and is buried in Mt. Olive Cemetery.

1914   Second visit to Norway: director of Wisconsin exhibit at Constitution Centennial, Christiania.
Edits *Afholdsfolkets festskrift*, published in Eau Claire.

1915   Edits *Norge i Amerika*, a reader, with G. Bothne,
published in Christiania by Dybwad publishers.

1916   *Fortællinger og skisser* published in Eau Claire.
Oberst Heg og hans gutter published in Eau Claire.

1917   *Paa veien til smeltepotten*, a novel, published in Eau Claire.

1918   *Udvalgte fortællinger* published in Minneapolis by Holter publishers.

1919   Fiftieth birthday, honored by friends with a gift of a thousand dollars; buys cottage on Lake Chetek.

1921   *Ny samling. Fortællinger og skisser* published in Eau Claire.

1923   Awarded Order of St. Olaf by King Haakon of Norway. *Det vældige navn. Et drømmebillede fra verdenskrigen* published in Eau Claire.

1924   *Christ before Pilate: An American Story* published in Minneapolis by Augsburg Publishing House.

1926   *Gamlelandets sønner*, a novel, published in Oslo by Aschehoug publishers.

1929   Receives honorary Doctor of Letters (Litt. D.) from St. Olaf College, Northfield, Minnesota.
Hundeøine, a novel, published in Oslo by Aschehoug publishers.

1930   *Under forvandlingens tegn. Fortællinger og saadant* published in Eau Claire.

1931   *I Sit Alone*, translation of *Hundeøine* by Charles Wharton Stork, published in New York by Harper's.

1934   Third and last visit to Norway, lecture tour sponsored by Nordmanns Forbundet, with daughter Valborg.

1938   *Skyldfolk og andre*, short stories, published in Eau Claire.

1939   Receives St. Olaf medal from King Haakon.

1941   Dies August 1, and is buried in Lakeview Cemetery, Eau Claire.

1

Apostle of Temperance

IN 1892 an ambitious and idealistic young Norwegian American named Waldemar Ager arrived in Eau Claire, Wisconsin. The town was the thriving center of the lumbering industry in northwestern Wisconsin, strategically and scenically located at the confluence of the Chippewa and the Eau Claire rivers. At the time, Wisconsin was the leading lumber-producing state. The whine of sawmills was heard everywhere as lumber interests were busy cutting down the abundant forests of northern Wisconsin. In the woods as in the mills there was plenty of work for willing hands, among them French Canadian, Irish, and Norwegian immigrants. Norwegians from the wooded areas of eastern Norway already had experience in the industry and so were attracted to Eau Claire.

But Waldemar Ager was not seeking a lumbering job, even though he hailed from Fredrikstad on the east coast of the Oslofjord, where lumbering was also a major pursuit. He came in expectation of a job as a printer in the Fremad Publishing Company, which was managed by the editor of the newspaper *Reform*, Ole Br. Olson.[1] Ager was twenty-three years of age, and he had spent seven years in Chicago since his emigration in 1885. His qualifications and antecedents will be examined in the next chapter; suffice it to say here that Olson picked him because he was a declared teetotaler and because he had demonstrated not only that he was a skillful typographer but also that he had budding talents as a temperance agitator.

On June 23, 1892, Ager began his Eau Claire career by gathering a group of young Norwegians and organizing a branch of the Good Templars. There were twelve charter members, four men and eight women, who took the pledge of temperance and signed their names to the charter. Officers were duly elected, including as vice-president Miss Johndine Blestren, whose sister

7

Ager as a young man, with temperance pin

Gurolle would later become Ager's wife. As this fact suggests, such organizations were not just serious and dour-faced puritanical gatherings. For the
young immigrants they formed social outlets of a secular order, where they
could hear recitations of poetry and prose, sing songs, and indulge in so-called
"circle dances," an innocent form of folk dancing. They brought together
young men and women and offered opportunities for more permanent connections. The minutes of the first meeting report that "Wm. Ager gave a declamation and Miss Amelia Olson performed a number on the piano."[2] After some
discussion the name "Excelsior" was adopted for the group, a significant reminder of the high ambitions of the charter members.

Five years later there were fifty-five members in good standing, and an account in the newspaper *Reform* praised the members for having struggled
against disapproval and modest means to maintain their organization. "There
is hardly any Norwegian temperance society or lodge that has kept its work
going for so long a period." The writer defends its value, not only as an example for others, but as a school for its members. "Young people have developed
their talents through debates, speeches, song, music, and declamations. The
Temple has also had a handwritten newspaper which is alternately edited in

8

"Excelsior" Temperance Lodge, Eau Claire, founded by Ager. Ager on right, his wife-to-be second from left in back row

Norwegian and English." Biographies of the current officers show that the members were born in the 1870s, some in Norway and some in America.[3] "Excelsior" was Temple No. 23 in a larger organization founded in Chicago in 1891 called The Norwegian-Danish Grand Temple; Ager was secretary of the latter organization.

Temperance societies were still a new and unfamiliar form of organization for Norwegian immigrants. They offered the newcomers alternatives to the Lutheran churches that had sprung up among them and they provided a warm, supportive atmosphere to offset the temptations of the American saloon. Lutheran pastors were suspicious of the temperance movement, either because they shared the Norwegian State Church attitude that favored moderate drinking or because they took the low church (Haugean) position that all secular societies were bad because they were not devoted to prayer meetings. Ager, with a Methodist upbringing, stood foursquare on the side of the independent temperance organizations.

Ager's daily work was also in the cause of temperance, helping Ole Br. Ol-

9

Ole Br. Olson, editor of Reform *until 1903. Courtesy Eyvind Ager.*

son as he did to get out his newspaper. *Reform* had existed under that name since 1888. In 1890 a shareholders' corporation (at $10 per share) was formed and named Fremad (Forward) Publishing Company. The newspaper represented a merger of *Arbeideren* (The Worker, 1886) and Olson's Chicago newspaper *Afholdsbladet* (Temperance Journal, 1880), which moved to Eau Claire in 1888. On its masthead *Reform* bore a vicious-looking serpent that entwined a school, a church, and the United States Congress, symbolic of the power of the saloon. Ager was not only the typographer but also a frequent contributor. Soon he was listed as business manager, working hand in glove with Olson as editor. They were both excellent speakers and deeply committed writers.

During these years Ager was busy "improving his mind," filling in the blanks in his scanty education. A notebook of his, apparently started in 1891, is a compendium of literary quotations from such great authors of Scandinavia and Germany as Ibsen, Welhaven, Kierkegaard, and Goethe. He prefaced it by a verse of his own:

> "One can read, one can learn
> From all the books in the world—
> Fumbling in the search for knowledge.
> But all our research only strengthens

10

Our longing for what we seek —
Truth and Beauty, these we hunt
Trying hard to catch them.
When we no longer have strength,
We may still be far away;
No one knows it, no one knows —
I have tried it, I am weary."[4]

This bit of neo-romantic despair was far from expressing Ager's joy in the classics, from which he was accustomed to extract lessons for the bibulous. In 1894 he gathered together some of his contributions to the temperance cause in a little volume titled *Paa drikkeondets konto* (Charged to the account of the evils of drink).[5] Like most of his books this was printed in *Reform*'s print shop and published by the Fremad Publishing Company.

While present-day readers will hardly find anything very instructive in its contents, the book proved to be an excellent launching pad for Ager's career as an author. Olson prefaced it with a flowery introduction: "At last I have persuaded him to publish a book." Only twenty-five at the time, Ager had been held back by fear of criticism and commercial failure. But Olson was convinced that his young protegé "has the potentiality of becoming something as an author." Readers of his newspaper had already noticed Ager's articles and short stories, and they had wondered who he was: "He certainly writes well."

In Olson's eyes the most gratifying of Ager's traits was that he wrote as a confirmed temperance man. "He has never tasted a drop himself, and yet he has felt the pain. He hates drinking, but he hates almost worse the great host of nice people who are indifferent to all the miseries that the legalized poisoning of humanity brings about." "He doesn't dream of greatness," avers Olson, "and yet who does not dream a little when his first book appears — but I know that he wishes to be of use." He ends by citing Ager's versified motto:

"Although I know not what I can do,
One thing to me is amply clear:
I shall have no rest till I pursue
The fray of life without a fear."[6]

The idea that the book is to be a weapon in his hand may seem rather daunting to the general reader, who perhaps does not need or wish to be bludgeoned into abstinence. But reviewers greeted the book enthusiastically. It contains eight stories, followed by some fourteen poems.

The verses are of little interest; Ager would never again publish poetry, aside from occasional newspaper contributions. They bear such transparent titles as "A Drunkard's Death" and "The Prodigal Son." In "Viking Blood" he

11

Masthead of Reform, *1893*

contrasts the belligerent stance of remote ancestors with present-day inaction against the demon rum. One verse may be paraphrased:

> "Handsome women handed him
> A glass of sparkling wine;
> First refused, he tasted then,
> A cautious sip, a slow descent,
> His first steps into vice."[7]

The idea of this poem, that social pressure for conformity is behind the evil of drinking, also runs through his stories, which are the real meat of his contribution.

The first section, "Leaves from a Diary," presents sketches from urban Norwegian-American life, based on Ager's observations from his days in Chicago, or possibly from his reading. In the first episode the narrator is riding the cable car when a sudden stop jerks the passengers out of their somnolence: a drunk has been run down. In all their faces one can read only relief that they were not the victim; they have the same "assumed sad expression as a husband announcing his rich father-in-law's demise at the newspaper." "They say he 'should have been more careful' and are filled with an inexpressible sense of well-being. Of course they don't know him. But what if it had been someone's husband, or son, or if it had been me?"

Other episodes pass in review: a tattered old woman who is mercilessly teased by bystanders; a home that is set on fire by a drunken father who tips a burning lamp; a drunkard's corpse fished out of the river; an old friend whose face is lined and furrowed by drink and who begs for his friendship; a scene from his own life when his drunken father taunted him to take his first drink. The sketches end with a scene observed in a performance of *Othello*, in which Iago shrewdly plies Cassio with liquor to gain his treacherous ends. The moral Ager draws is that a civilized but cynical indifference allows the perils of drinking to exist; saloons are attractive, pleasant places, and those who defend them pose as "friends of freedom."

The story "Johannes" is almost a short novel, beginning with the title character's marriage proposal, awkward but sincere. Ager follows him and his wife into their happy home in the newly-constructed Norwegian area of Chicago west of Humboldt Park. The serpent enters their Eden in the form of a Yankee capitalist who establishes a saloon for his son in their neighborhood. It is purely a matter of business, but eventually the saloonkeeper, one George Adams, manages to attract Johannes by flattering him. There is a project for a new streetcar line, and Johannes takes to spending time in the saloon in the evenings. His wife disapproves, even to the extent of fetching him home; but he abuses her and resents her attentions. "Over there it was always cozy. One could sit in comfort, smoke one's pipe, and discuss the questions of the day. They were especially concerned about the laboring man's cause, and many a sharp attack was directed at the capitalists with their trusts, monopolies, combinations, and all that kind of thing." Johannes loses his home, and the only thing that saves him is that he joins a temperance lodge; he gets his old job back, and can look forward to a happy future.

The next five stories are little more than schematic accounts of the terrors of intemperance. Only the last tale is really noteworthy. "For the Sake of the Spleen" is a charming and amusing story about old skipper Næss. Back in Norway he was a promising young lad, a sailor who won the heart of his captain's daughter and married her after taking his mate's examination. He got a ship of his own, sailing to England, and commanded it for twenty years. But a sailor's life has its temptations, and he starts drinking. He also meets with reverses, as steamers were taking over the traffic from the wooden vessels he commanded. "They dirty the heavens with their smoke," he says, "and they muddy the waters and make fun of the Lord, who has given men all kinds of winds to sail by." He loses his ship and is given command of a coastal steamer. But he lacks the tact to please his passengers: in his blunt seaman's language he tells one of his men: "Ola, pick up that old lady by her rear end and help her get on land!" He is so impossible that he has no choice but to emigrate. He turns up on a quiet street in the Norwegian neighborhood in Chicago. Here he has trouble navigating in the still unpaved streets, needing the help of his wife and two daughters. With the aid of a daughter's suitor, the women succeed in getting him to attend a meeting of the temperance lodge. He is talked to, but rejects their teachings as hypocrisy. But then he falls ill, and the doctor who attends him speaks severely to him. After this he rejects drinking and joins the lodge, on the plea that he does so "for the sake of his spleen."

The skipper's character is pictured in a vivid, concrete way, with the use of lively colloquial dialogue. He comes through as a real person, stubborn and amusing. There is a sprinkling of English words, as might be expected in a Norwegian-American environment. In these stories Ager clearly expresses a feeling of sympathy with the problems of the characters. Nowhere does he

13

condemn the drinkers, nor does he preach at them in religious terms. They were good, hard-working men, devoted to their wives and children except when temptation overcame them. And even in the midst of his tracts Ager is irresistibly amusing.

Especially in the last story Ager reminds one of his great Norwegian contemporary, Hans Aanrud (1863–1953). Aanrud had begun writing short stories about the farm people of his boyhood in eastern Norway in 1887. He published collections of these in 1891, *Fortællinger* (Tales), and 1892, *Fra Svipop til Venaasen*, and gradually won status as a children's classic. Much of what is said of him would also apply to Ager. Thus A. H. Winsnes speaks of Aanrud's "good-natured irony," and his "delicate blend of keen observation and intensity."[8] Aanrud's stories began appearing only after Ager left Norway, but he must have known them and learned from them. Aside from Ager's concern about drinking, the two were like-minded. Both of them were also admirers of the Norwegian novelist Jonas Lie.

Ager had no need to fear his critics: his sales ran up to four printings. His scrapbook contains some thirty-five reviews, all laudatory. One journalist wrote: "Temperance literature is, unfortunately for the good cause, as a rule anything but brilliant. This book is an exception. It is written with an unmistakable poetic and stylistic talent" (*I ledige Timer*). Another wrote that "in comparison with most 'Scandinavian' literature so far produced in America, this is a linguistic pearl" (*Dakota*). A third agreed that Ager had "a promising talent as an author" (*Heimdal*). A fourth praised "the author's humor, his witty ideas that often come quite surprisingly" and "his keen perception" (*Fergus Falls Ugeblad*). A fifth commended him for "a much better and more correct language than we find in most Norwegian-American writing" (*Scandia*).[9]

The most searching review was by Ager's friend and fellow prohibitionist J. J. Skørdalsvold, a teacher with bachelor's degrees from Augsburg College and the University of Minnesota. He averred that "it really takes a great gift to be able to produce anything remarkable in this area." In a lengthy article appearing in *Reform* he maintained that "no one over here has used the language as Ager has in these stories. It is simple and clear, quiet and sober. But all of a sudden the tempo speeds up, with such surprising turns of expression as only a genius can produce. . . . Several of the stories are literary productions of high quality." He comments on the fact that Ager's anger is directed "at the pharisees of our time, those who as upright citizens and good churchgoers are to blame for the torments of their fellows."[10]

Even if some of the critics are discounted as over-enthusiastic well-wishers, there is no doubt of their surprise and delight at detecting literary quality amid the propaganda. They had genuine interest in recognizing Ager's talent and he would have abundant opportunity to confirm their judgment.

14

None of these reviews came from Norway. The only overseas recognition it has been possible to find was a belated review in a temperance journal over the signature "Idar." He conceded that the writer was "a thoughtful soul" and that his "Leaves from a Diary" showed "a not inconsiderable stylistic ability."[11] Ager admitted that "I had not intended to create anything of literary value. The theme is not appropriate for that. I have to write about something that I either love or hate if I am to write anything. Both hate and love make one blind, and one makes mistakes; but then one has at least the satisfaction of having expressed one's opinion, even if one is left with the books unsold." This was in a letter to his newfound friend and colleague, O. A. Buslett, dated December 1, 1894.[12] In a later letter to the same correspondent he expressed his conviction that the time would come when people would show respect for Norwegian-American authors: "The snobbish contempt that is now shown toward the honest attempts to create a literature of our own will surely not last forever."[13]

2

Roots of Personality

WHAT KIND OF PERSON was this man Waldemar Ager? How did he happen to burst upon the peaceful community of Eau Claire, Wisconsin?

Waldemar Theodor Ager was born on March 23, 1869, in the town of Fredrikstad, Norway, on the eastern shore of the Oslofjord. In the census of 1865 it had a mere 4,820 inhabitants, but it was evidently growing rapidly, for by 1890 the population had more than doubled to 12,451. As a good seaport it became an important exporter of timber, drawing its raw materials from the heavily forested region to the east. From birth Ager was surrounded by timber, so that it was not entirely fortuitous that he chose to settle in Eau Claire.

Ager was descended from a long line of craftsmen and always regarded himself as a craftsman. His parents were Mathea (1835–1913) and Martinius (1834–1894) Ager. Mathea was born in Fredrikstad; her baptismal name was Fredrikke Marie Mathea Johnsdatter Stillaugsen. Her father John was a sailor from the nearby community of Onsø, and was described as a ship's carpenter. Martinius, whose full name was Martinius Mathiesen Ager, was born in Eidsberg, another nearby community; he became a non-commissioned officer and a tailor by trade. His father Mathis (1782–1874), also a non-commissioned officer, had taken part in the Swedish wars of 1807–1808 and 1814. His name and that of his brothers was Mathiesen, but when they entered the army, the story goes, they had to add proper family names to the patronymic. They arbitrarily picked agricultural names: one brother chose Eng, "meadow," another Myra, "marsh," while the third chose Ager, "field."

Ager's parents were married in 1857 and lived for a time in Christiania (now Oslo), where Martinius served as a police officer, part of the time connected with the local penitentiary. In 1866 they returned to Fredrikstad, where Waldemar was born; he was their second child by that name, the first having

16

Martinius Ager and four brothers in 1874 at their father's funeral in Glemninge, Norway. Brothers were pallbearers. Seated from left: Hans Peter, Alexander; standing: Martinius, Johan, Ole Jørgen.

17

died. When Ager visited Fredrikstad in 1934, he noted that the house he was born in was gone, so "I can't prove that I was born at all." His jocose reflection was that as a "Norwegian-American scribe I had only 'barely' managed to exist, and the difference between existing and barely existing is not worth making much fuss about."[1]

In 1871, when Waldemar was two years old, they moved across the wide mouth of the Glommen (Glåma) river to the suburb of Græsvig (now Gressvik). They built a house and set up a country store, and Waldemar was sent to Åle school. Here Waldemar spent significant early years of his life, and he forever regarded it as his home. "We were called Gressvikings," he later reminisced, "not to be confused with those Vikings who ravaged the coasts of England, Scotland, Ireland, and France, and in the year 1000 discovered America. We ravaged nothing and discovered nothing — at least nothing of any concern." Ager recalled how his parents had "struggled and skimped to get the store paid for." "We children understood that it was really for us they worked and strove."[2]

Memories of Gressvik are clearly embodied in two of Ager's novels, his first and his last. The town he calls Flovig in *I strømmen* (In the Stream, 1899) is really Gressvik.[3] The poetic depiction of the river Glåma, on whose banks Ager played, provides a backdrop for the realistic picture of the town. "Toward the south lie the sawmills and the planing mills in a row along the shore. . . . Toward the east the Flo lake spreads itself large and still, while over on the other side the boat slips and warehouses of the city are silhouetted in sharp, jagged contours. Below one's feet the houses are crowded down to the shore. The larger houses are higher up and press down on the smaller ones, as if they were struggling to push the small, shabby cottages out to sea." "Everywhere there are neat little workers' dwellings sprinkled down just as chance would have it, in glorious confusion. Each house appears determined to occupy its unique place in the world, even if it consists of only a living room and a kitchen. The streets bend aside and make themselves as narrow, crooked, and imperceptible as they can."

In *Hundeøine* (I Sit Alone, 1929), his last novel, Ager reminisces even more intimately about himself and his family.[4]

"The earliest memories of my childhood home are connected with a big room and a floor painted yellow. This floor must have been very large, for we held races on it, my brother and I, each of us driving a pair of old greased boots by the laces, kicking them in front of us on the floor, while we ourselves pushed along behind on the seats of our trousers." "There were a big table and a smaller one, besides a sewing machine, whose whir was the last thing we heard in the evening and the first we heard in the morning. The stove with its many stories — how plainly I can see it before me! — and the woodbox. That was

18

Waldemar Ager as a boy in Norway

my place most of the time. Also it was my job to see that it was well filled. Many a glorious winter evening did I spend in that corner. . . . After father left us for America a shadow came over the home. We were always expecting a letter from him, and in the evening mother would often turn her head so the tears shouldn't fall on her work."

"Of the kitchen, too, I have memories. When the fire burned on the hearth, and mother stood watching the porridge, I watched her. She was always so busy sewing for others that she didn't get much time to devote to us. . . . I was grateful if I could stand beside her and hold her by the skirt when I longed for her. Also it was a splendid skirt to hide my eyes in, if someone had been bad to me or I had been bad and repented. There was both consolation and for- giveness in mother's dress." In a later chapter he writes: "It was at this time that father left for America. For many years he had tried to support his family by various trades, but it had not gone well with him. Anyhow, mother had been forced to take in sewing as far back as I can remember. . . . I am aglow, I feel warm streams shooting up between my shoulders when I think of times alone with mother. Just to sit and look at her while she was using her needle! So fast it went, an infinity of stitches that no one could count. Her hands worked fast and they had to work fast. I perceive now that each of these count-less stitches was a tiny bread crumb, and we needed so many."

"Children are children. We never lacked food and we poor youngsters had all the fun in the world. To school and from school. We laughed at everything and got fun out of everything. Poor we all were, but I can remember nothing else than that we were happy most of the time. We knew there were rich chil-dren on the other side of the fjord, but we didn't envy them. Rather we felt sorry for them because they had to go in Sunday clothes on weekdays and couldn't go barefoot in summer, and we had heard furthermore that they strug-gled with frightfully hard lessons over at their schools."

"They come thronging upon me, these incidents of my youth, and I gladly let them pour over me. This is my form of worship, for I too have lived and have much to thank God for, if I only will and can—as I sit far out here on the prairie this winter day—feel the sun of my childhood warming me between the shoulders."

Some of Ager's later adventures in *Hundeøine* are not directly biographical; for example, his father did not vanish in America. But warm memories of home and mother are genuine.

While the Agers were born and baptized as Lutherans, they (or at least Mathea) joined the Methodist church in Fredrikstad. One Ole Peter Peterson had been converted in America, in either Boston or New York, and returned to his native town in 1849 to found a Methodist congregation, the first in Nor-way. Mathea joined in 1875 in the pastorate of one Johan Pettersen. Martinius had a drinking problem, possibly intensified by economic difficulties, and Waldemar was on one occasion a witness to a scene of violence. While in a drunken stupor Martinius struck his wife so that her nose bled. In 1882 the mother and three children left for Oslo, while the father emigrated to Chicago in 1883. Tickets that may have been promised never arrived, and the family scratched out a living as best they could. Waldemar, who had begun school at the unusually early age of four and a half had to leave at the equally early age of twelve and a half. He worked as an errand boy at a bookbinder's, and he tried his hand at a tailor's shop and as an apprentice painter. At the age of fourteen he joined a young people's temperance society.

In 1885 the mother decided to follow her husband to Chicago, possibly aided by relatives in Oslo. She sailed with Waldemar and his siblings Johan and Camilla, by way of England as was usual in those days, to New York. Ager later described their arrival in Chicago. He stood on a street corner "with an old-country satchel in my hand and a two-years-older sister beside me." "I had a scanty supply of English words that I had thought would be sufficient to lead to our parents' house on West Chicago Avenue." But he quickly discov-ered that anyone who had a handsome sister did not need to know English to

Ager family at Martinius's tailor shop on West Ohio Street in Chicago. From left: Waldemar, holding Martha; his father Martinius (1834–1896); his mother Mathea (1836–1913); sister Camilla and daughter Hannah; brother Johan's wife Alida holding May; John; Johan, holding Esther. Courtesy Eyvind Ager.

find his way in Chicago. "Men rushed up, offering to carry our baggage." But Ager was disappointed to realize that the men spoke only with his sister, though he had always thought of himself as the more important of the two![5]

Martinius Ager had set up his own tailor shop on Erie Street, and Waldemar made his first home with his parents. A picture of the family reveals him as a dapper young man. In what seems like a burst of Americanization fervor he took the name of William. His brother Johan took the name John Cornfield, while his sister married one William Cameron. Ager often expressed great fondness for his sister. Ager's mother joined the First Norwegian-Danish Methodist Church, and later on they joined the new church on Logan Square, First and Immanuel Methodist Church. The minister there was one Ole Jacobson, pietistic, arrogant, and inclined to be abusive of others. On a Sunday morning with Martinius present he denounced him and excluded him from membership, presumably for his drinking. Waldemar, sitting beside him, felt the shudders in his father's body. Martinius lived only to 1894, when he died of a strangulated hernia. After this Mathea moved to Eau Claire to keep house

21

for her still unmarried son Waldemar. Only when he married did she return to Chicago to live with her other son John.

Mathea lived well into the new century, until December 25, 1913. She was clearly the unifying force in the family, deeply beloved by Waldemar and an important influence on him. She is described as an intelligent woman who read widely and was possessed of an excellent narrative gift and a deep sense of justice. Her life is said to have brought many trials; according to the obituary in her son's newspaper "it was made a via dolorosa for her by drink." "Thanks to her patience and her faith, her prayers were heard and she won out." She joined a temperance society in Chicago and even entertained its meetings in her home. "She hated the liquor traffic with all her heart and never lost an opportunity to implant that hate in her children." A Methodist pastor who knew them in Chicago described her as "one of the most unusual women I have met in my life." She was deeply religious without showing herself as a pietist, sharp of mind without being bitter, brilliant without showing off.[6] When she died, her husband was exhumed and laid beside her, so that they were united in the grave.

Chicago had by the time Ager arrived become something of a center for Norwegian settlement and social activity. Two major Norwegian newspapers had been established: the long-enduring *Skandinaven*, a bastion of radical Republicanism, founded in 1866, and the less viable *Norden*, more church-oriented, founded by bookseller I. T. Relling in 1874. Waldemar found a job as an apprentice with the latter newspaper, where the editor was his later colleague and friend Peer O. Strømme. In an essay of 1907 Strømme remembered Ager as apprentice and recalled that while he was a diligent worker, he refused to follow the traditional practice of bringing a pail of beer to slake the thirst of the older employees.[7] In 1887 he joined a total abstinence society, The Harmony Total Abstinence Society, and made a solemn pledge never to touch alcoholic liquors.

Here he must have met Ole Br. Olson, who edited *Afholdsbladet* (The Temperance Journal), which he had founded in 1880. Ager soon began contributing to it, but his first known and acknowledged article is a poem entitled "Den kloge Mus" (The Wise Mouse), which appeared in *Reform* on December 31, 1889. It is a parable about a mouse that sniffed at its trap and got caught. Just so, the glass is a seductive trap for men.[8] In the barely four years he had been in Chicago he must have won a circle of like-minded friends, for on March 23, 1889, they celebrated his twentieth birthday with a poem. Signed C. P. N., this printed tribute commemorated their unity in the noble cause, to be sung to the patriotic tune "Mens Nordhavet bruser" (While the North Sea Foams). The last stanza may be paraphrased as follows:

22

Mathea Ager, Waldemar's mother

"Your battle we know is for the good cause,
a goal that you must keep in mind.
Oh, would that we might see the enemy some day
Biting the dust before your banner.
Then when you dance your last step,
Your brow will be adorned by a laurel wreath."[9]

Ager also contributed to *Templarbladet* (The Templar Journal), which was
founded in Milwaukee in 1891. In its first volume there is a poem by him enti-

tled "Den barmhjertige Samaritan" (The Good Samaritan), and a series of narrative sketches entitled "Paa de berusende Drikkes Konto" (Charged to the Account of Intoxicating Drink).[10] He edited *Templarbladet* from 1891–1894. He later said, "I had no temperance papers that I could clip things from, so I had to make up a song or story to fill up the issues."

On October 28, 1891, he took out American citizenship, "renouncing and abjuring all allegiance and fidelity to the King of Sweden and Norway," and signing himself "William Ager." On June 1 of the same year he had taken out an insurance policy with the temperance lodge Broderbaandet (The Brotherhood Bond) No. 32 in Chicago. Both commitments were sincere and whole-hearted.

In 1892 he left his family in Chicago and struck out on his own. One reason was that a doctor advised him to leave the malaria-ridden area where they lived. Another must have been his acquaintance with Ole Br. Olson, who had moved to Eau Claire in 1888 and founded *Reform*. He needed a printer, and who could be better suited than Ager?

In Chicago he had mastered the craft of printing. He had made himself noticed by being obviously bright and by having, for one with little formal education, a remarkable talent for reading and writing. He had the right passion for temperance, thanks to his bitter experience with an alcoholic father and his deep affection for his Methodist mother. He had already been writing for a temperance journal and participating in the temperance movement. He came to America at the peak of Norwegian immigration in the most exciting era of Norway's cultural coming of age. A young man with sixteen years of Norwegian experience would not forget his roots, at the same time that he could become a loyal American citizen. He had the makings of the ideal Norwegian American.

3

Formative Years: 1892–1899

FROM 1894 Ager is listed as a regular contributor to *Reform*, and in 1896 he got the title of *bestyrer* (manager). His role in the editing of the newspaper was growing. Articles by him appeared from time to time over the abbreviation "Wm. A." or his favorite pseudonym "En enfoldig Sjæl" (A Simple Soul). In 1895 and 1896 he contributed articles from Chicago, though he was now living in Eau Claire. One is reminiscences of the Chicago Columbian Exposition: he comments on the Norwegian Viking ship, which now "looks shrunken and abandoned" on a foundation of old timber and covered by old canvas.[1] In another letter from Chicago he discoursed on such varied topics as death, dogcatchers, poverty, and Gustave Doré's paintings.[2] In an article titled "The Emperor's New Clothes" he dismissed the political talk of gold and silver raised by William Jennings Bryan, calling it "nonsense."[3]

As these tidbits indicate, Ager could be quite polemical; he wielded a sharp pen. In 1897 he took part in a controversy with a writer named O. A. Tveitmoe, who wrote in *Rodhuggeren* (The Radical, literally The Root Cutter).[4] *Rodhuggeren* was a Populist weekly which appeared from 1883 to 1888 in Fergus Falls, Minnesota.[5] Tveitmoe had called for the creation of a socialistic colony on the Pacific coast, where the "wage slaves," "the factory animals" who accumulate wealth for their masters, and the "stooped and browbeaten farmers struggling with a desperate debt" could join him.

Ager landed hard on Tveitmoe: "In recent times a whole chorus has arisen from those who howl about the great misery of farmers and workers. With delight they revel in hunger, tears, bowed backs, aches, and sweat. They just can't make the farmers and workers miserable, poor, and unhappy enough." Ager thought that most of this sympathy was wasted: "If socialists had a little more respect for honest work, they would enjoy more respect themselves. As

25

long as they regard a wage earner as a slave and a factory laborer as an animal they can cultivate their ideals on paper and build their new societies on sand." Ager regarded himself as a wage earner, a believer in honest work, thrift, and contentment. "I have always worked for wages myself. Though they have been modest, they have always sufficed. I have done my work with interest and have never regarded it as slavery. It is only when I have been without work that I have been dissatisfied. But in this statement I suppose they will see on me the mark of the beast."[6]

The controversy was taken up by the well-known Norwegian-American writer H. A. Foss. In *Nye Normanden* (The New Norseman) in Minneapolis he charged Ager with being a "phrasemonger and a deceiver," for hiding his identity as "En enfoldig Sjæl" and pretending to be a laborer rather than an office worker.

To this insinuation Ager could indignantly reply: "I have in principle never signed my name to a newspaper article, and I have written a good many. An article will have to stand on its own feet; my name makes little or no difference. Those of *Reform*'s readers who know me are quite aware of who writes under the signature of 'Wm. A.' or 'En enfoldig Sjæl.' . . . I have always regarded myself as a wage earner. Remember: I do not associate all kinds of imaginable misery with that term. At the age of twelve and one half I had to end my schooling and do manual labor in a sawmill. Later I learned the craft by which I have made my living. My daily wage at *Reform* is $1.65. It was less before, and as I usually work ten to eleven hours daily and one night a week and do all the kinds of work that occur in a printshop, I may even flatter myself that I am a rather capable worker." He rejected Foss's efforts to portray him as a capitalist and an enemy of the cause of labor. "I will certainly never sink so low that I would oppose the legal and honest demands of oppressed workers seeking a more equitable ordering of the relation between capital and labor. But I think that without doing harm to the cause of labor one can raise one's voice against the kind of friendship to labor that consists of turning earth into a hell to gain an ear for a new, imaginary heaven."[7]

Ager here spoke in an American tradition that favored labor while opposing socialism. He spoke as the self-made man, though representing also his ancestors' tradition of craftmanship.

In his editorial writing he also revealed a strong pacifist bent. In 1898 the United States was ready to go to war over the sinking of the *Maine* off Cuba, in what became the Spanish-American War. "We are to have war, they tell us now. We must have vengeance on the Spaniards for the destruction of the *Maine*. . . . What is war? War is to kill as many of our opponents as possible with as little loss as possible. . . . Who is to do the killing? We, of course — or else we get someone to do it for us, farm boys and workers preferred. We send them off to kill Spaniards for us — a lot of them. And wish them God's blessing for this deed, — give them flags, drums, and patriotic songs to entertain them — and a pension if they return. If they return — . For if they don't return, they get only honor . . . the honor of being killed in the attempt to kill others." Picking up on the widespread criticism of the yellow press, he notes ironically that the bravest soldiers are the editors: "They fume and foam and call for war. How willing these patriots are to sacrifice their heart's ink and risk their paper!" People "want to see blood flow. Spanish blood and lots of it. . . . Not like cannibals who kill their enemies to eat them, but as a civilized nation that kills in order to kill."[8]

Another of Ager's concerns, which he now voiced for perhaps the first time, was the problem of maintaining Norwegian culture and language among the immigrants. As early as 1897 he began to worry: "Common opinion seems to be that the Norwegian language is only for 'the old man' and 'the old woman' in this country, and that every young person who wants to get ahead must let him- or herself slip entirely over into the American language." By studying a volume of Scandinavian-American biographies he found that all who had won distinction had a solid education in the Norwegian language. If young people are to build character, he contended, they need a mother tongue and a nationality. It is a sin not to teach one's children the ancestral language. Ager cites a mother he overheard telling her child in English to "shut your mouth," a phrase picked up in the streets. Children learn only contempt for their parents: "They gather on street corners instead of in schools, churches, and temperance societies."[9] This theme was to become a major one in Ager's writing, alongside the issue of temperance.

Another opponent Ager found it necessary to tackle was the controversial "father of Norwegian teaching," Rasmus B. Anderson (1846–1936), who had been professor of Scandinavian languages at the University of Wisconsin and American minister to Denmark. Anderson in his later years moved away from his liberal past to become a critic of modern Scandinavian literature.[10] In his newly acquired publication *Amerika*, Anderson launched a campaign against what he called "swinishness" in literature. Ager became concerned when he attacked the translation into Norwegian which Ager had made of the world-famous novel *Quo Vadis* (1896) by the Polish writer Henryk Sienkiewicz, a historical romance about Nero's Rome. Anderson charged that the novel was immoral, which Ager maintained only showed that Anderson was "zealous without understanding." The only basis for Anderson's claim that Ager could detect was a description of one of Nero's orgies, from which a Christian nobleman flees. This, said Ager, was in fact one of the best chapters in the book, a powerful sermon on the value of Christianity as an antidote to the evils of paganism.[11]

27

Immigrant Idealist

One of Anderson's favorite targets was Ibsen's *Ghosts*. Ager wondered how Anderson could imagine that either *Ghosts* or *Quo Vadis* would awaken "impure, sensual lusts," any more than the nude statues in a museum. Even the Old Testament has its strong scenes. "I have some aversion to the virtue that needs too much support—the virtue that drags itself forward on cane and crutches to sniff out vice in others and proclaims its own virtue in the market-place. What is the difference between a whore and a woman who forever cries, 'Tempt me not'?"[12]

Ager was well prepared for literary discussion, for he had been busy reading the masterpieces of literature. Under the title *Afholdssmuler fra boghylden* (Abstinence Crumbs from the Bookshelf) he published a number of articles reflecting his reading. In 1901 he collected them in a little volume with the same title; it had only limited circulation and was never reprinted.[13] As the title indicates, the articles all have a common theme, but they are interesting as evidence of Ager's pursuits in these early years. In an introduction he points to the bookshelf as "an arsenal, where all can go and have access to whatever weapons they can find." "There are adequate weapons for the cause of temperance in literature, and they have been neglected." He knows that his treatment is not professional, but "that would take months, and I have had only hours to spare." What stands out in this casual work of Ager's is the idealism it reflects; it may also be regarded as a preparation for his own literary career.

He begins by comparing Falstaff, a creation "of the world's greatest dramatist," with Jeppe, by Ludvig Holberg, whom Ager here calls "Scandinavia's greatest." "They both belong to an age in which there were no fanatical temperance advocates, an age when drinking was not regarded as either a sin or a shame." "Before the temperance cause came on the scene, poets praised drinking in their poetry and ridiculed drunkards on the stage." "Most ridiculous of all were the drunkards who could not afford to drink as much as they wished." "Those who rode to hell at a gallop were entertained by those who laboriously proceeded on the same path with a cane and a crutch." "While Falstaff is a nobleman, Jeppe is a poor, ignorant peasant." In one's laughter at Falstaff there is an element of repulsion. But for Jeppe the laughter is mixed with sympathy. "Jeppe is shown as a human being."

In his later essays Ager took up the "wine poets" of eighteenth-century Denmark and Norway, some of them even clergymen. "The worst thing about the drinking songs was that they were very good." He discussed Goethe's *Faust*, with its depiction of Mephistopheles, as well as many plays of Ibsen: *Hedda Gabler*, where the character Eilert Løvborg is described metaphorically as having "vine leaves in his hair" (with a regretful side glance at Ibsen's unsympathetic portrayal of temperance advocates!); *Rosmersholm* with the gifted but

28

alcoholic Brendel; *Ghosts* and Osvald's accursed Alving heritage; and *An Enemy of the People* with its dishonest majority mob.

Ager also made excursions outside Scandinavia, citing Zola's story of "The Shoulders of the Marquise," whose décolletage graced the Third Republic; Daudet's story of "A Game of Billiards," which lost a war for France; *The Merchant of Venice*, in which Shylock demanded his pound of flesh (like the American saloon interests); the Crusades, when mobs were reluctantly driven to unselfish actions because "God willed it"; and the English painter William Hogarth, whose paintings depicted the horrors of gin ("The Gin House"). Ager also took up such Norwegian authors as Jonas Lie and Arne Garborg, who portrayed examples of "cultivated drinking"; and finally Henrik Wergeland and his allegory of the thistle gatherer, who gathers thistledown for his grandmother's pillow, an image of the apparently fruitless labors of the idealists.

In each instance Ager found a conflict that somehow reminded him of the struggle with alcohol.

Although this book was not widely circulated, it did get some acclaim from fellow editors. B. B. Haugan placed him first on the list of Norwegian writers in America. *Superior Tidende* proclaimed him a genius. His former chief Peer Strømme declared that there was not a single boring line in the book: it is "written with talent and genuine humor. One is fascinated and gets angry, and one laughs and profits from it. But I do not think he has been fair to all of the writers."[14]

Until 1899 Ager had remained a bachelor, after 1894 sharing a home with his loving widowed mother. But on July 5, 1899, he married a member of his temperance lodge, the "Excelsior." She was Gurolle Blestren, a younger sister of the Johndine Blestren mentioned earlier. Gurolle had come from Norway with her parents, who became residents of Eau Claire, when she was only ten years old. She was born in the far north of Norway in the city of Tromsø, on February 10, 1873. At the time of their marriage she was twenty-six and he was thirty. They celebrated their wedding by taking a trip to New Orleans, one of Ager's very few visits to the South.

As far as anyone can tell, it was also the only time he took his wife with him on a trip. As would become his custom, he reported on the journey in *Reform*, but both then and later he never mentioned Gurolle. She shortly became so busy raising their children and taking care of the household that this was apparently the only time she went with him. Even here, on what he titled "En Ferietur" (A Vacation Trip), the only evidence of her presence is a program of the opera *Martha* that survives in the Ager files. On it she has written that she heard the opera in Memphis.

Ager reported many amusing observations on the trip. He was surprised, perhaps a bit shocked, on seeing girls who kissed their acquaintances "and are

29

Gurolle Blestren Ager as a young woman

not ashamed at being kissed." He found the women's flowery hats entertaining: "The car looks like a greenhouse. Every lady's hat is modern, and every modern lady's hat is a flower bed in which red and white roses sprout beautifully amid reeds of the sea, and lilies-of-the-valley and forget-me-nots have grown amid ostrich feathers and birds' wings."[15]

In Memphis he was impressed by the air of southern gentility: blacks were courteous and helpful, whites dignified and thoughtful, "as if they were every moment meditating on Ibsen." "There was none of the brute force and selfishness that one sees in the West." On the train from Vicksburg to New Orleans he pondered the problem of the Negroes. He reflected current prejudices in expressing the opinion that slavery had ultimately been to their benefit: it taught them to obey and to work. But "a people that has learned to obey will also learn to command when its time comes." "When I saw the blacks working along the railroad and observed their powerful bodies, which looked as if they were made of cast iron, the broad shoulders, strong white teeth, and powerful pates dripping with sweat while they wielded the spade and the hoe, it dawned on me that the South belongs to the blacks. They are conquering it with their bare fists and will gradually force the whites northwards."

30

Leaders of the Norwegian Temperance Movement in America around 1900. Seated from the left: E. E. Løbeck, Ole Br. Olson, T. K. Thorvilson; standing: Ager and Gustav Eide.

31

Immigrant Idealist

In New Orleans he encountered an old and "moldy" city, which he found unusually interesting. But he was chiefly impressed by a statue of General Lee and the museum called Memorial Hall. Here he thought of the bitterness of a "lost cause." In his opinion, "No cause can be absolutely bad when a whole nation believes in it, fights for it, and gives its life for it." "The gray brigades marched past their general — and down below the ground, for that is where most of them went." His last observation was that a number of Scandinavian names occurred in the rolls of the Confederate army, but he did not have time to investigate them.[16] In later years he would look more closely into the Norwegian participation in the Northern armies.

This was very much what Gurolle Ager got to see on her wedding trip. She apparently played no part in her husband's public life and remained strictly a homebody. Both of them apparently accepted her private role as a mother and a homemaker. Her most obvious contribution to Ager's life was the nine children she bore from 1900 to 1917. They were Eyvind Blestren (born 1900), Gudrun Fredrikke (1904), Trygve Martinius (1906–1975), Valborg Hansine (1907), Solveig Camilla (1909), Magne Oterbak (1910–1963), Roald Sneve (1913), Hildur Johndine (1915), and Borghild Gurolle (1917–1981). There were four sons and five daughters, all of whom survived their father. Their second names are derived from either the family or close friends. Eyvind married Inga Peterson and Trygve, Elvira Gullixson, while Magne and Roald remained unmarried. Gudrun married Milo Bergh, Valborg, Arnt Oyen, Solveig, John W. Best, Hildur, Albert B. Nicolai, and Borghild, Richard Berge. Some still live in nearby towns, others are widely scattered.[17]

Ager believed firmly in the value of the family. In a 1987 interview, the oldest son, Eyvind, recalled that most of the women they knew in his youth had the same traditional view of a wife's place as his mother. He also confirmed that the New Orleans "vacation trip" was in fact a wedding trip. Interviews by Clarence Kilde with the other children add details about the family life. Solveig praised her mother's skill as a storyteller: at night she would sit on the edge of the bed and narrate, on occasion even making up her own stories. Son Magne was so fond of her retelling of "De tre bukkene bruse" (The Three Billygoats Gruff) that he got the family nickname of "Bucky." Mrs. Ager survived her husband by ten years; during this time she lived with her son Roald.

Daughter Solveig confirmed Ager's role as a family man who came home regularly for lunch and supper before going back to the office to work. He was gone much of the time, but she still spoke warmly of him: "He loved and understood music; he could play the flute himself. And he loved to draw pictures." Daughter Gudrun also stressed their father's affectionate nature. After being interviewed she enthusiastically spoke of her enjoyment at reliving

32

"those cherished memories of a dear, loving father," whom she appreciated as "a person of great wisdom, wit, and talent, a great humanitarian."[18]

Of the children Eyvind, the oldest, was closest to his father; he worked for some years in the printshop as a typographer and later as a traveling agent for the Sons of Norway. He also mastered Norwegian, speaking nothing else to his father. Trygve was the only one who became a journalist; he was a reporter for the *Minneapolis Tribune*, and for a time worked for the Norwegian Information Service in Washington. He also compiled a scrapbook of his father's work. The knowledge of Norwegian declined in the younger children, the last four being confirmed in English. Interest in their father's work also declined as they became more scattered and found their own niches. Of the youngest ones only Hildur has shown a vivid interest in his work, translating and publishing a collection of his stories.[19]

4

In the Stream: 1899

AGER'S AMBITIONS went well beyond the sketches he had included in *Paa drikkeondets konto* in 1894. After five years he was ready to try his hand at a full-length novel. This time the scene is laid in Norway.

The setting corresponds in detail to the little town where Ager grew up, and one suspects that the characters and the story are reflections of people he had known in his boyhood. He calls it Flovig, but the description identifies it as the Gressvik in which he had lived from his third to his thirteenth year. The title *I strømmen* alludes to the river Glåma that flows past the town into the sea, but also to the fate of the leading character, Johannes Lidahl. Metaphorically it may even refer to the overflowing force of the liquor traffic.

The first chapter is a mood-setting piece which describes the source of the river, far up in the country. It is an imaginative depiction of the river's gradual growth in size and importance as it flows through the land. It is personified as "meeting in loving embrace" with other brooks, "creating" lakes and waterfalls, and "hastening toward its death" in the great ocean outside. At Flovig it finds its first outpouring in a *flo*, a huge pool or body of water.

In Flovig "nearly all the people had their income from the sawmills and planing mills. They lived by lumber, saw only lumber, and handled only lumber. . . . They had become lumber persons. But there were two kinds of lumber, finished and unfinished. Just so there were two kinds of people— finished and unfinished. All according to their class and position at the mills." Their cottages were scattered along the shore, up in the hills, and among the knolls. "They were neither good nor bad. They gave in marriage and took in marriage, did many good deeds, and sinned in moderation."

The symbolism of the irresistible current that finds its death in the sea and its last calm by the community of Flovig is a kind of counterpart to Bjørnson's introductory chapter in *Arne* (1858) on how the mountain became decked with trees. But here the symbolism leads to death, not to growth and life, since Ager was no doubt thinking of the often irresistible pull of demon rum. But it makes a charming and poetic introduction to his story.

The novel begins by describing the home of Mrs. Lidahl, formerly the trusted housekeeper of Mrs. Engelsen, the millowner's wife. Lidahl is a mill-worker, whose job it is to sharpen saws. Mrs. Lidahl is a passionate house-cleaner, whose immaculate home is felt as a reproach by her neighbors. Her former mistress often visits her, and they agree that their husbands fall short of their ideals of cleanliness, Lidahl because of his job, the millowner because of his smoking. After their marriage the first thing Mrs. Lidahl did was to take all her husband's clothes out and beat them thoroughly. "When he got them back the day after, whole and clean, he felt an indescribable void. The wind seemed to blow right through them, and he felt estranged — something had been taken from him, an injustice had been done." When it became known that he had taken to drink, the women of the neighborhood blamed it on the ambitious-ness of his wife: "He was a martyr." "He didn't want to be of a better class than he was. They understood perfectly that he was fighting for the right of poor people to their dirt and their rags."

Lidahl's drinking goes from bad to worse, even bringing about the death of a newborn daughter. This leads him into a religious crisis, and he stops drinking for a time. Mrs. Lidahl finds her chief comfort in Georg and Mathilde, who are growing up as model children. The girl Mathilde is just starting school. On her first day she observes a one-armed boy who is being tormented by the other children and feels sorry for him. She learns that he is the son of Erik Jansen, the town drunkard, popularly known as "Gamle-Erik," Old Erik, Norwegian for "Old Nick." The son is "Vesle-Erik," Little Erik. In a small, re-stricted community like Flovig, says Ager, "where geographic conditions and gossip made it easy for people to keep an eye on each other, they needed a kind of thermometer to determine the moral value of their neighbors." It was well known that Foreman Mikkelsen was the godliest man, while Erik Jansen was at the lower end of the thermometer.

One night Georg comes across a bundle outside their house that proves to be Gamle-Erik, dead drunk. They take him in, Mrs. Lidahl cleans him up, and he shows enormous gratitude. He is moved to talk freely, and even does his best to speak "politely." He praises Mrs. Lidahl as a real lady: "If I had a wife like that, I'd be in the American Congress or the Norwegian Storting today." They get the sad story of how his boy lost his arm: he, the father, had acciden-tally cut it off with an axe. The scene is a dramatic depiction of Erik's despera-tion, but also shows that he is not without his perceptive moments: "Have you noticed that there is a difference between a shiny coffee urn and a dirty one: the shiny one sings, while the dirty one gurgles and whines."

The next day Little Erik is sent up to the Lidahls' to thank them for what they have done for his father. The kindness he meets at the Lidahls' and the friendliness of their children even encourages him to resist a tormenting schoolmate. Erik is forced by his mother to go out begging. On his return, there is a visitor in his home, a pilot from neighboring Buvik, one of Erik Jansen's boon companions. The men are playing cards, with a bottle of whiskey between them. In his befuddlement the pilot forces a drink on the unwilling boy.

Georg Lidahl and Little Erik become fast friends, united in opposition to the teasing and disdainful boys. Ager devotes some space to the children's games, especially their playing marbles and trading buttons, which they use as money. Erik is happy playing with Georg and Mathilde; he even plans to teach Mathilde an English song he has learned: "Throw out the lifeline." But one day Mrs. Lidahl detects vermin on Georg and immediately blames it on Erik. Mathilde whispers it to a friend, and when Erik comes to school, no one will sit beside him. When it dawns on Erik what the reason is, he picks up his things and leaves school, never to return. He tries to reestablish the relationship to the Lidahls, but is rejected. When his mother forces him to go begging again, he seeks out a woman who had been kind to him. She counsels him to return home, but he seeks lodging in the mill, and when he is chased out of there, he spends the night in a box. He catches a cold that turns into influenza, and he is put to bed. He dies while Mathilde is with him, bringing him flowers—a sad victim of ill treatment by the "good" people and total neglect by the "bad" ones.

Ironically enough, Little Erik's funeral is well attended. The boys who had tormented him even help to adorn his grave, making an informal monument for him. Father Erik, overwhelmed by remorse, drinks himself into a fit of delirium tremens. Lidahl feels that "as Christians they ought to do something about it. . . . Something had to be done, and Lidahl talked his wife into going. She generally had to do most of what Lidahl hated to do himself."

But Mrs. Lidahl surprises Jansen's wife by not preaching religion at her; she starts scrubbing the floor! She and a neighbor woman "decided that with the help of God they would have all the dirt out by four o'clock." They attack the dirt "with true berserk fury; it looked as if a tornado had raged." They share "a secret joy" over their battle with the arch enemy, "who was driven from spot after spot and fled down the hillside in a dirty black stream of muddy water." Even the wife, Mrs. Jansen, is caught up in their zeal; she starts to clean herself up, and when they get her properly dressed and coiffed, they are surprised to find that she is quite presentable. Erik is similarly inspired, gets religion and

36

joins not only the Good Templar Lodge but even the Methodist Church. "People couldn't believe their eyes: their moral thermometer was upset. They no longer had a lowest point; their security was gone and they were unhappy because they no longer had a fixed standard to refer to."

The final episode seems almost tacked on after this climax. It concerns the relation of Lidahl to his foreman, Mikkelsen, the top of the moral thermometer. Mikkelsen has been getting hints of the owner's dissatisfaction with his work: "He reached for his pocket flask oftener than usual; he felt more exposed to colds than before." He suspects that Lidahl is a candidate for the foreman's job, and so he plays a trick on him. He conceals a flask in Lidahl's locker. Lidahl has been abstinent for a long time and now appears to be a religious person. But when he discovers the mysterious flask, the old temptation is rekindled. He soon begins to drink again.

About the same time, Mikkelsen's son comes home from the capital, where he has been studying painting. One day in winter when the river is frozen over, Lidahl seizes the chance to cross it in order to go to town and get his flask refilled. Mikkelsen's son has also set out; his goal is a young people's dance where he expects to see his sweetheart. But the ice has thawed, and neither of them reaches town safely. The younger man's terror is vividly described; when he is found he has become mentally deranged. Lidahl's wife goes in search of her husband, but he is nowhere to be found; she thinks of following him into the water, but is held back by Mrs. Engelsen. Mathilde sits up waiting for her parents to return. She even composes some verses to go with a pair of stockings she has knitted for her father. Eventually the mother learns the bitter truth: Lidahl has drowned. She comforts herself with some words from the Bible: "As thy day is, so shall thy strength also be."

The novel is well constructed and holds our interest to the end. In spite of a certain sentimentality in the depiction of Little Erik, it is a realistic slice of life from small-town Norway, as no doubt observed by Ager in his boyhood. Such subject matter was especially characteristic of Norwegian literature in the 1880s as it was practiced by writers like Bjørnson, Kielland, and Jonas Lie. Like some of their novels, *I strømmen* deals with a theme from the life of the working class. Although its major aim is to portray the evils of drink, it is far more than a temperance treatise. It affords many glimpses of a narrow small-town society, smug and self-satisfied, gossipy and malicious, but on occasion also kind and helpful. Religion is not a major theme: in fact, most of the religious people are clearly hypocritical. The one strong central figure is Mrs. Lidahl, who in spite of her passion for cleanliness comes off well in comparison with her often indecisive husband. There is much emphasis on the cruelty of children toward anyone who is "different." There are passages of great humor amid the tragic events. One feels strongly an ironic sense, a passionate detachment that presumably reflects the author's attitude toward the society of his own childhood.

The novel was extensively reviewed in the Norwegian-American press and as was its usual practice with Norwegian-American products, they gave it almost uniform praise. Reviewers were quite aware of its value as a temperance tract, but they were even more impressed by its literary qualities. It became a kind of breakthrough for Norwegian-American literature.

To take just a few of the many encomia: O.A. Buslett, himself a pioneer among Norwegian-American writers, regarded it as "without reservation . . . the best book written on this side of the Atlantic" — in Norwegian, of course. *Decorah-Posten*'s reviewer: "As far as I can see, this is one of the most important books written by Norwegians on this side of the ocean." *Fram*: "A significant book, no doubt the best literary work produced by a Norwegian American." *Republikaneren*: "Among all the books appearing on the Norwegian-American market this will absolutely stand as one of the best." *Nye Normanden*: "One of the most valuable contributions to Norwegian-American literature." Even *Ungdommens Ven*, a religious publication, in spite of wishing that Ager had left out some things, declared that "it is the best any Norwegian has written in America." Peer Strømme wrote in *The Minneapolis Times*: "He is destined to take a place in the front rank among Norwegian writers of fiction."

Most reviewers made a point of complimenting Ager for his Norwegian style. Buslett wrote: "It is written in good Norwegian without affected or foreign phrases." *Decorah-Posten*: "Ager has a fluent pen and he rarely stumbles on words." *Fram*: "Ager has a splendid mastery of the language, which together with his keen perception enables him to produce stories that remind one of Alexander Kielland's best." *Nordvesten*: "The language is unusually good." *Folkevennen*: "The book is written in a masterful language, even though some of the dialogues are couched in the everyday speech that one is used to hearing in a little coastal town; but so far from harming the book, this contributes to increasing the interest and awakening respect for Mr. Ager as an author."

Different reviewers found various things to praise in the book's contents. Buslett was most affected by the chapter that described the drowning of the two men. *Decorah-Posten* praised the characterizations, but admitted that only one character was really memorable, Little Erik, "who wins the reader's sympathy." Buslett regretted the Bjørnson influence on the opening chapter, but *Scandia* praised the chapter as containing "real poetry." *Folkebladet* was also impressed by the character studies, "which are drawn with great psychological assurance." Strømme found that "the tragedy of ignorance and poverty is brought out in strong relief," but objected to "some unexpected exhibitions of poor taste in the author's descriptions of indecency and filth." *Reform* devoted a whole page to promoting the book, which sold for a modest 70 cents, reprinting all the reviews.[1] Some years later Ager reprinted the book serially in *Reform*.[2]

Ager probably appreciated most of all the review written by his friend in Norway, the author and temperance man Idar Handagard, who would later write a rather full essay on him. His review in *Menneskevennen* began by discussing the deplorably low literary quality that characterized temperance works in general. They were mostly moral sunshine tales aimed at turning drinkers into abstainers. He held this to be an obsolete way of attacking the problem; the modern view was that a weaning process must be applied to society as a whole, with assistance from legislation. He found in Ager's book this modern view, which demanded that one try to understand the motivations of not only the drinker but also the maker and seller of liquor. Ager's book was a "novel attempt to describe people instead of vices." He was delighted also with Ager's "brilliant humor" and his awareness that poor people could be just as cruel to each other as the rich who were accused of oppressing them. Handagard felt that the American temperance movement worked within quite narrow limits, and he found it remarkable that Ager's book could have come from a Norwegian in America and "that he could write in as unprejudiced a way as he has." "Now if he would free himself from all narrow-minded concepts, his authorship would gain in clarity and his characterizations in truth and depth."[3]

It is safe to say that this is just what Ager aimed to do in his later books.

5

The Emigrant Returns: 1900

IN THE SUMMER OF 1900 Ager decided to join a group excursion to visit the land of his birth. At this point he had spent almost exactly the same number of years in America as in Norway. The participants in the tour, some three hundred in number and mostly Norwegian Americans, jocularly referred to the excursion as "Vikingtoget" (The Viking Foray). They sailed from New York on May 15, and the date of Ager's last travel letter was June 30, when he wrote from Fredrikstad. A full account of the journey was printed in *Reform*, running through several issues.[1] Years later Ager reminisced about the trip in an article in *Nordmanns-Forbundet*.[2]

This was Ager's first chance to return to his early haunts, and his report sums up his feelings on seeing Norway again, besides pointing forward to his later writing.

It appeared that shipboard accommodations had not improved much in the fifteen years since Ager emigrated. He left New York on the *Oceanic*, described as the "world's largest passenger steamer, a 17,000 ton, 720-foot boat, accommodating two thousand passengers." The first night on board was chaotic, with husbands and wives separated and many passengers forced to sleep on the deck. He reports with some amusement that "twenty-six of us had secured, by cunning and bribery, a specially arranged area above deck. The berths were merely boards nailed together, and they reminded one of the coffins in which victims of the bubonic plague were buried." Still, the area which they denominated "Club 26" remained "a bright memory." Here they passed the time chatting, listening to speeches, and at times attending divine services. Several Norwegian-American pastors were in the group, as well as a number of "old settlers."

Ager comments on the food: "It was edible. The bread was good, and the

40

butter did not have a bad taste, in fact, it had no taste at all." The steward staved off complaints with a standard witticism, "a really irritating one": "He would be very sorry if anyone should leave the ship on account of the food. Those who complained listened with bitterness in their hearts; but no one left the ship before it docked!" Among illustrious personages on board were the "king of meat packing," Mr. Armour from Chicago, and Mr. Gould, the financier from New York. But the most conspicuous passenger was "a medium-sized, slender man with a narrow, spiritual face and a huge mop of reddish-yellow hair under his cap." This was none other than the world-famous pianist Ignace Paderewski. Ager tried surreptitiously to snap a photograph of him, but failed.

The ship was headed for Liverpool, where the Norway-bound passengers took a train to Hull on the English east coast and embarked from there for Norway. In Liverpool Ager spent the night at an emigrant hotel, where he met a number of young Norwegians on their way to the United States. "They appeared to be greatly surprised to learn that anyone really wished to see their homeland again." He noted with some concern that they drank freely, and considered if this might not be a good place to establish a temperance mission.

Looking at women of the English working class, he got a very poor impression. "A worse collection of bad flesh, dirt, and rags I have nowhere seen. Bareheaded, messy, pale, so tattered and awful that it could ruin one's appetite for days. They were ugly, and they drank like fish. . . . Some stood drinking with their infants at their bosoms. A nation with such women is doomed." Ager happened to be in England on Queen Victoria's birthday, May 24, and he felt a repugnance at the endless processions and demonstrations by ragged urchins. They were often marked also by effigies of Paul Kruger, the leader of the South African Boers, who was hanged and otherwise lampooned. "The poor quarters empty their whole content of rags and patriotism into the fashionable districts. They lack everything except the ability to shout hurrah 'for the good Queen.' "

In Liverpool Ager and a few others took the opportunity to visit the local art gallery. Here Ager spent some of his time studying the painting of Christ before Pilate by the Hungarian Mihály Munkáczy (1844–1900). Titled "Ecce Homo," and painted in 1881, the picture fascinated Ager for its contrast with an earlier painting on the same theme by Gustave Doré. Doré, he says, had portrayed Christ as "a stranger, one not understood," in short as a God. But Munkáczy presented Him as "tense and suffering, skin taut, eyes burning, embodying terror, humiliation, and forgiveness," in short, as a human being, a man. Ager would later translate these impressions into the leading theme of his 1911 novel, *Kristus for Pilatus*. A reproduction of Munkáczy's painting adorns its cover, and in the novel it hangs in the study of the leading character, Pastor Conrad Welde, as it would actually hang in Ager's own office. The pastor is indeed a Christlike figure, who in the end is "crucified" by his Norwegian-American congregation.

The passengers had their first sight of Norway on the south coast outside the port of Kristiansand, where all they could see were the outermost barren skerries. "These naked islands spoke to us. They told us that they had seen us when we left, and that while they were waiting for us to return they had been washed by many a salty spray. We recognized them—and we nodded to them as our eyes filled with tears; the air was so still and attentive that we could not speak out loud. We wanted to tell them that we had been gone a long time, but now at last we were back; we glided past, and we began to sing."

In a later article he grew even more poetic: "In this marvelous early morning stillness something indescribably beautiful, something that mysteriously also belonged to us, or that we in a mysterious way belonged to, had clasped us between its gentle wings and drawn us to its bosom. Tell me it's foolish. That is superfluous. I already know that. But it is such foolish moments that make life worth living. It is in such foolish moods that one is born anew or that new life is created, even if one is old."

But not everything is roses and honey. Forward on the boat is one of the machinists, exchanging angry words with the passengers. He tells them that once they had left Norway, they should have stayed away; they should have used their money to help their relatives emigrate: send them money instead of becoming a burden to them. "His words were not foolish, rather they were the icy words of common sense. Those who quarreled with him understood his language but still could not understand him." On the other hand, Ager had a reminder of the financial advantages of tourism in a Norwegian newspaper clipping: "It is said that 300–400 Americans arrived yesterday in Christiania. . . . These Americans leave a sizable amount of money behind on their summer visits to Norway." He met some of the visitors on the way home later in the summer. Those who had visited kin were generally pleased, but those who were farmers were disappointed: their relatives had looked down on them because they had not become rich in America.

They went on from Kristiansand to sail up the Oslofjord; it was a Saturday night in early June, with the brightness of the northern summer. Flags were flying everywhere. Ager took note of this expression of Norwegian national feeling. Unlike 1885, when he had left, the flags were once again just red, white, and blue, excluding the mark of union with Sweden, an upper-left-hand quarter carrying the colors of the two nations. Its absence symbolized the aspiration to independence, five years before it was actually achieved. "Nothing was to remind us of the clenched fist across the border; it is a festive flag, a solemn flag, and it must be ours, completely ours, only ours." One gets the impression that Ager, who had left Norway at the early age of fifteen, only now got his first full baptism of the national fervor that was to characterize him for the rest of his life. "Norway, like a proud mother, revealed her hidden beauties piece by piece to us who had been gone so long."

Oslo had been Ager's last home before he and his mother left for America. The intervening years had wrought many changes. "One looks up spots that carry memories of boyhood days. One goes there and remains standing agape, staring like an idiot, rather than dropping some melancholy tear. New streets with tall, modern buildings cross one another, and there is nothing left of what one is looking for." Oslo had experienced a period of great urban growth, and he observed a general air of comfort and prosperity. "I have not seen a single ragged woman here." He noted that city people found their delight in hikes into the countryside, while country people were immigrating to the city. By this amalgamation he felt that Norway was "laying the foundation for a completely democratic form of government." He was impressed by Norwegian women, who seemed to him more "emancipated" even than American women. "They often have canes and they brandish them as they walk. A certain quick toss of the head and a mannish posture indicate that they are just as free as men."

But Oslo was not his goal. He quickly headed down the east coast of the fjord to Fredrikstad, the town where he was born. Here, too, there had been change, with a rapid growth that was due to the rise of industry, primarily lumbering and brickmaking. He described the city in some detail, noting its location near the great falls of the Sarpen River that promised to make this little town the most important industrial center in Norway outside the capital. He got the impression that much of the growth was due to an influx of Swedish laborers from districts across the border. These "are regarded as a kind of coolies who can live on little or nothing while they accumulate capital." For these Swedish workers, Norway was a "regular America" or a "Klondike"; but he believed that culturally and socially they were inferior. As one angry woman told him: "They buy a fat herring and sit looking at it one day while they eat their potatoes, and then they go for the herring the next day; so they can live for two days on one herring." Having in mind his Norwegian-American countrymen, he is a bit shocked to hear that the Swedes do not exhibit any patriotic feeling for Sweden. "In the eyes of the Norwegians this is downright villainous. They struggle to learn Norwegian, but apparently it is harder to learn a related language than one that is wholly strange."

Fredrikstad consists of two parts: an "old" town on the east coast of a bay and a "new" town on the west. The old town is dominated by the massive walls of the old fortress known as Kongsten, founded in 1570 and fortified by the Danish king Christian V. Here Ager recalls watching the soldiers marching up and down and playing war, while they courted their sweethearts in off-hours on the ramparts. He comments ironically, as the pacifist he now is, on how the heart is trained to beat faster at the sound of military marches. He describes the "old" town as a "rare sight, whose appearance has not changed in the last two centuries." "All is quiet, with grass growing long and green amid the cobblestones, and thick-walled buildings with curved roofs and tiny windows."

But Ager's most moving experiences were reserved for the "new" town to the west, which included the village of Gressvik where he had spent his boyhood. Here he used one opportunity to go fishing, and he vividly describes the charms of the landscape, untouched by tourists. "Strange how small everything looks: narrow roads and tiny distances. Was this due to my eye applying a larger dimension to my surroundings? Or have they grown in my dreams and my imagination away from reality? I shall never know."

He tells of looking up a "mountain" that had been a favorite spot of his childhood: "Out here I had once built a hut, where I was going to live alone for eight years just like Robinson Crusoe, and then write a book about it." It is interesting to note that the idea of writing was already in his mind. "It was my dream to escape to a desert island, but I never managed it. My hermit's life lasted only until I finished the hut. But I did think of moving out there for good whenever the world went awry and I was punished at home." He dreams of reliving his boyhood fantasy by doffing his jacket and heading out over the hills.

He recounts one of the memories that crowded upon him: "I had a fortress built of stones with a moat around it, behind a little hummock in our yard. It was protected by some empty bottles and at least one 'real' cannon. I recall how the neighbor boys destroyed it for me time and again. Each time I swore a horrible revenge and built it up once more, but did not dare to utter a word when I met the enemy. It is awful to be the injured party. But then the worst of my enemies died from a cherry stone in his stomach. Fate had intervened. Then I realized the seriousness of life for the first time: you could be bad for a while and not get punished; but then you got a cherry stone in your stomach and you died. When I was bad, I was spanked, and I accepted it gladly; but you could never be sure about a cherry stone. It was better to live with a sore behind than die for your sins from a cherry stone in your stomach."

After this touching but ironic story, he sighs: "But all this is irretrievably past. One has become grown-up, precociously wise, and thinks 'sensibly': no stupidities, no more bogeymen, no goblins. The sky that arches over all so clear and blue is empty air—into all eternity just empty air. Once it was a floor: we lived under it and the angels lived with God above it." "Memories stir until it grows painful; the house on the hill belongs to a stranger. It is many long years since it was my home. Better to get away. I recall some lines that make up the sad refrain of a Negro ditty:

44

The Emigrant Returns: 1900

Go away, go away,
And leave me alone—
For I'm a stranger
And a long way from home.

"A blue and white flower is growing right near my feet. I almost stepped on it. It is a wonderfully good old acquaintance, but I can't recall its name. That is bad—really bad, as when I meet a dear and well-known face and am asked, 'You do remember me?' I lower my eyes in confusion, I have forgotten the name. So now. I struggle in vain to bring back its name. It is nearly worse than with people; I know I have loved this flower, and I am indebted to it. In vain I hunt through my memory, naming all the flower names I can bring back from childhood. I have just turned to go away when it suddenly comes. We children called it 'night-and-bright-day,' a type of violet; the botanists may have another name for it, but none more beautiful." It is known in America as "wild pansy" or "johnny-jump-up."

He muses on the name of the tiny flower, "Not 'dark' night, just night and 'bright day.' We were most emphatic about the bright day; when we get older we often forget that after night comes the 'bright day.' We children knew it, knew it in all innocence and believed it. I place one of these little flowers in my wallet, with an almost religious solemnity. Now I shall never forget its name, and if I lose my faith in the bright day, I can restore it by gazing at the flower." He develops the idea in a passage that expresses his essentially optimistic philosophy: "This is no elegant flower; it is not large, it has no fragrance, and it is not sold in the marketplace. Nor can it measure up in beauty to the flowers of one color. It withers quickly, but it has a fragile little opinion about existence, and it is honest enough to express it in its own way. It told me a long story about the cold snow cover in the winter, and about spring when the snow melted and the sun broke through the earth so that it could emerge and struggle some inches up toward the great light that fractured the icy crust around its roots."

Ager concludes his account by telling of a banquet where he spoke and enjoyed the company of his fellow temperance people. He was glad to have been there and seen the heartening progress of their movement. It may well have been at this banquet that Ager met the man who was to become his closest friend in Norway, Idar Handagard (1874–1959). Their correspondence dates back to 1897, but Ager's first really intimate letter was written after his 1900 visit. By September 28 he was back home and the trip already seemed "like a dream." To Handagard he declared that "I shall never forget that you were the only one of the temperance people in Norway who found it worth their while to bother with a visitor. And the fact that the trip became so pleasant

45

is very largely due to you." He included snapshots and urged Handagard to visit him in America, promising him opportunities to lecture and earn his keep.[3]

As it turned out, Handagard never accepted Ager's invitation; according to his daughter Herborg, he was too busy acquiring a medical degree. He never practiced medicine, but became a respected author of popular medical treatises. He was also an ardent temperance advocate, and Ager confided some of his opinions and interests in their correspondence. Concerning his own *Paa drikkeondets konto*, which Handagard was the only Norwegian to review, he points out that he published it as "edification for believers" which as such might do some good. But he grants that his verses were bad: he lacked an ear. He expresses his disgust at the policies of President McKinley. He has begun to lose faith in the possibility of a political solution of the drinking problem. "The Christians wish to keep drink and the saloons. If they could vote hell out of eternity, they wouldn't do it. They won't do God's will and they won't even try to torment the devil."[4]

He reports with enthusiasm on his first-born son, Eyvind. "Excellent vocal qualities: like the nightingale he sings most beautifully after the fall of darkness. . . . And he works his legs like a bicyclist who has suddenly gone mad. He will surely become president of the cyclists' union and director of the water works, where he shows special skills."[5]

On this occasion, either in Norway or in America, Ager wrote his first autobiographical sketch, which Handagard would make use of in his 1903 account of Ager's life and work. In it, Handagard expressed his admiration for Ager's first book, which he held was still his best. "Here I finally found something of what I was looking for: a man who wrote humanely about a purely human effort and left out the religious phrases." "He observed people and he did not like their behavior; but he did not judge it. He just told what he saw, told it with a delicate scorn, a mild sorrow, and a repressed anger."[6] In his autobiography Ager emphasized that he "had never learned anything except what I could get for myself through reading. My only ability is an unusually good memory, so that I can benefit from books." "I don't know how I have gotten time for everything, but I could manage with little sleep, which gave me long evenings."[7]

46

6

To the Editor's Chair: 1900–1905

AFTER HIS RETURN from Norway Ager continued to write major articles for *Reform*. In 1900 he agitated vehemently for the Prohibition party and attacked both Democrats and Republicans because they had not been willing to support the cause.[1] He dissected a speech by William Jennings Bryan, who called for taking good care of young people but failed to mention the saloons and their influence on the young. This he called "colossal humbug and stupidity." He vigorously attacked *Skandinaven* in Chicago for "misleading information" about the prohibitionists. He continued to quarrel with Rasmus B. Anderson over what he saw as Anderson's persistent misrepresentations. Anderson had taken offense at Ager's insinuation that *Amerika* was edited "in the way the devil would prefer." Ager objected to Anderson's attributing the article to him as editor, since he had not written it. "Concerning your accusation of my having been brought up as a Methodist, I will readily confess that my mother is a Methodist. Is it your opinion that I should ask for forgiveness publicly because I have worked for total abstinence in spite of it? If it is a sin or a shame to have such a mother, I am in a bad way; for I love and admire her as much and as deeply as any son his mother."[2] Anderson had also twisted a letter Ager printed from Arne Garborg into support for atheism; Ager replied that Garborg had actually undertaken to make his recent writings an attack on free-thinking.

In an article titled "Words or Axes" he wrote admiringly of Carrie Nation, who attacked the illegal saloons in Kansas with an axe after the authorities failed to act. "I have been ashamed of the trouser-wearing sex ever since I read about you. Mostly because there are so many men in Kansas and because you are so old. A brave old grandmother you are—and wise, because you remembered that you had two arms and felt your responsibility."[3]

Immigrant Idealist

While Ager continued to be concerned about temperance and politics, a major interest in these early twentieth-century years was the creation of a Norwegian-American literature. He established a continuing exchange of letters with his only predecessor of any note, O. A. Buslett of Northland, Wisconsin. He discussed with him the value of criticism as an accompaniment to the work of authors. He maintained that "the best literary works are usually condemned by the critics. . . . We need *understanding*, I think; what sooner or later kills spiritual life is lack of understanding."[4] He further tells Buslett that he clearly detects such a lack in some of his own reviewers: "In my book there occurred such terms as 'Little Devil' and 'Old Nick.' Several nice Christian persons have refused to receive the book because these ugly words were found in it." In commenting on a book by Buslett he has read, he notes that "there is an undercurrent of irony—concerning a writer's position over here. This is something I can well understand. And yet I have begun in a more fortunate time than you. Among the temperance people I have a reliable flock of friends, who will support me regardless of how bad my product is." He goes on to say, optimistically: "We have a field before us. If it turns out that the Norwegian population here is to be swallowed up, then these literary efforts of ours are what will live the longest and be the best testimonials. Where there are new circumstances, and where something of a cultural life grows up, literature will be the thermometer because it is both art and history at the same time. I won't say that it will live because *we* produce it, but because something is produced by somebody." He argues that because Norwegian America does not produce great prophets is no reason for killing off the little ones. "The future will give literature the first rank. What is printed here will be tracked down, papers will be searched through, and forgotten things drawn forth."[5]

In a lengthy article in 1900 Ager pondered the fact that the early immigrants from Norway were much more easily Americanized than the more numerous later ones. Like most later observers, he attributed this situation to the growth of a Norwegian-American community, which sustained his hopes for the future. In a study of demographic statistics he found that while the Scandinavian-born constituted 5.52 percent of Wisconsin's population, they furnished only 5.36 percent of the convicted criminals. But their children furnished twice as many criminals, and he blamed this increase on inadequate home training in ethnic loyalty and the mother tongue.[6]

In August, 1901, one Pastor T. K. Thorvilson set forth an idea in the Norwegian-American press that a "Norwegian Society" should be founded for the promotion of the language and its culture in America.[7] Ager seized upon the idea with enthusiasm. He pointed to the failure of English-language publications as organs of Norwegian culture. He noted the lack of a Norwegian-American literature: "The pioneers have not yet found any poet for their saga.

We have themes enough and traditions of our own. . . . Here a Norwegian Society might accomplish something."[8] Ager saw, astute journalist that he was, an outlet for the urge he nourished to become the interpreter of the immigrants' literary aspirations, the poet of their saga. In January, 1902, Pastor Thorvilson returned to the theme, noting that there had been much discussion of the idea in the press, and proposed a committee of five named persons to make preparations. They were to be representative of the chief factions among the Norwegians, and he suggested Ager as the one who should convene the committee.[9] Thorvilson was born in Koshkonong in 1852 and was living in Eau Claire at this time, working actively for abstinence. He had even edited *Reform* in 1893, and published a tract on the evils of drink in 1900, *Drikke-ondet*.[10] His move may have been inspired by Ager; it was certainly discussed with him.

Ager commented, now over his initials "Wm. A.," that the proposal for a Norwegian Society seemed to have brought out all the forces of dissension that were typical of the individualistic Norwegians. Anderson in *Amerika* wanted to exclude all non-Lutherans, I. H. Kofoed, who represented the proponents of the new Norwegian language (*nynorsk*, then known as *landsmål*) in America, wanted to make it subservient to the interests of Norway's new language. Ager made the point that the society must be nondenominational and apolitical if it was to unite all who had an interest in preserving the Norwegian language.[11] The Reverend Henrik Voldal of the United Church supported Ager's views: "Let us form a Norwegian Society which is broad enough to include all good Norwegians who are reasonably agreed on the goal and the means for the preservation of our language and our Norwegianness in America."[12]

One unintended consequence of Ager's pro-Norwegian stance was a private collision with his friend Handagard, who was a user and active supporter of *landsmål*. Handagard not only sent Ager his own books in this new, rural language, but evidently tried to convince him that this was the only truly "Norwegian" language. What Ager wrote was really "Danish." In 1902 Ager wrote that he was annoyed because the language issue took him away from the temperance cause. "We have a titanic problem over here keeping our mother tongue from dying out. The only hold we have is the mother tongue and we must assume that the language of Norwegians is Norwegian." He goes on to explain that the descendants of Norwegian farmers have learned the Dano-Norwegian book language and regard it as a step forward. "*Landsmål* is a foreign language to me as a man from Smålenene." He concedes that it is a beautiful language and that he might even have gone in for it if he had remained in Norway. He comments on his own struggle to found a Norwegian Society: "My weakness is that I am a temperance man, which makes me impossible

49

Ager as a young editor, 1905

among the children of the world, and that I am not a member of the Church, which makes me impossible among the children of God." He suggests that Handagard should rather work to improve economic conditions and promote an American market for Norwegian products.[13]

In another letter Ager declared that "I love the Norwegian people as much as any other man on this side of the ocean." He asserted that "the *people* are worth more than the dialect and the orthography." "Here all our struggle must aim to preserve our *mother tongue*; otherwise we will sink into a bottomless melting pot." "If we begin to fight here about Norwegian and un-Norwegian, our hope of preserving the language is gone." He pleaded for a growing mutual understanding. The reasons he wished Handagard to visit him included a conviction that it would do him good to learn about America; he even hinted that Handagard might decide to stay here.[14]

The years from 1903 to 1905 were busy and significant years for Ager. In 1903 Ole Br. Olson died, and Ager was the obvious choice to replace him; by April 12, 1904, he was listed as editor on the masthead of *Reform*.

Early in 1903 a meeting of at least a hundred prominent Norwegian Americans was held in Minneapolis to organize a Norwegian Society. On January

28 they resolved to create the Norwegian Society in America (Det norske Sel-skab i Amerika) to "unite all Norwegian Americans around the worthwhile cause of Norwegian language, literature, and immigrant history." In the words of one enthusiastic observer, the theme of unity was emphasized by the presence of "Prohibitionists, Socialists, Democrats, Republicans . . . farmers, artists, clergymen, professors, physicans, musicians, workers, editors, salesmen, merchants, and students," as well as members of various religious groups.[15] Ager's dream had come true, and the omens were favorable. In short order he proceeded to launch a publication under his editorship called *Kvartalskrift* (Quarterly), beginning in January, 1905. It would continue to appear until 1922 with an abundance of worthwhile contributions, many of them by Ager himself.[16]

These were exciting years for patriotic Norwegians everywhere. Norway began attracting headlines because of the expressed determination of many Norwegians to break out of the ninety-year union with Sweden that had been imposed by the victors over Napoleon in 1814. Ever since the 1890s tension had been growing, and threats of direct confrontation aroused tremendous feeling both in Norway and in America. In 1905, Sweden grudgingly let Norway go. Norwegian Americans were ecstatic. For the first time in five hundred years Norway could again have its own king; Prince Carl of Denmark, whose choice was eventually ratified by popular vote, became their King Haakon VII.

Also in June, 1905, the Norwegian Society in America was assembled for its annual meeting in Fargo, North Dakota. Attendance amounted to several thousand, and the buildings of the city were decked with the uncluttered red, white, and blue cross of the Norwegian flag. Editor Johannes B. Wist of *Decorah-Posten* would interpret the significance of this event in an article in *Kvartalskrift*: It "strengthened our faith in ourselves, built confidence in our own capacities as a nationality, and enriched our intellectual life."[17]

One of the progressive causes that Ager chose to sponsor in this heady period was votes for women, which would be adopted in Norway in 1913, as it already had been in some American states. In reply to criticism from a subscriber who accused him of working to "break down the position of the home," Ager denied that there was any biblical authority for or against making woman the master of the house. "The question is only whether she can be regarded as a human being, as men are. If so, it will be just to give her human rights." Another critic sent him a tirade citing the authority of the Bible. To this Ager replied, "If we fail in a single issue of *Reform* to write something that can offend or anger some of our readers, we hope for the sake of the cause that we will be kicked out of our office." "We do not intend to pay any attention to what some people think is taught in the word of God. We have our conscience and our own Bible to which we are answerable. 'These people' are

51

Ager as a young man

responsible for themselves and their own muddled thinking. There are still some Christians whose consciences will not let them participate in the temperance movement until they can learn about the percentage of alcohol in the wine that Jesus served at the wedding in Cana."[18] Ager's stand on this question was clear: women should have the vote regardless of what the apostle Paul may have said!

Another discussion of the problem of Norwegian-American creativity occupied Ager in a 1904 editorial. "What has been accomplished among us has not been brought about either by the Americanized Norwegians or by the Norwegian Norwegians who just go around and criticize everything, but by Norwegian Americans who maintain their Norwegian language and build in this country on the basis of the best in both nations and are fully conscious of their ancestry and their present position. We may as well add here that our spiritual love for our kinsmen across the sea is an unrequited love that leads only to disappointment. It is of no use for us to go around sighing despairingly for the appearance of Ibsens, Bjørnsons, and Garborgs among us, no matter how much we admire many of their books. . . . It is our opinion that we our-

52

selves must create our own literature and art. We will build a bridge—when we have something to build for and to build with."[19]

Ager had a further chance to develop this idea in an article in *Kvartalskrift* in 1905, titled "Our Cultural Possibilities." Here he contended that "we must have faith in our own potentialities." He argued that it was hopeless to expect Norwegian Americans to appreciate the literature of Norway: "It is not so much a question of artistic content as it is of what we, at our present stage, can digest." He compared the Norwegian Americans to the people of Swedish language in Finland or the Norwegians in relation to Denmark, "It can readily be admitted that it is difficult to 'live' in two languages and have two 'fatherlands.' . . . But, properly utilized, this difficulty can even be an advantage." Norwegians have now been in America long enough to take care of their material needs and their basic institutions. "In order to create a book market, we must have faith in it. . . . Our first Norwegian-American author will have to be very tolerant, but he will come—and perhaps we won't know him when he does come." "Should it be impossible to obtain authors, painters, musicians, sculptors if it really becomes clear to us that we have need of them? Not if our Norwegian schools, for instance, would show more interest—and also the newspapers."[20]

Ager would vary this message in infinite ways during the next few years. But his own production is the best evidence of how seriously he took his task. Single-handed he created a whole body of what would be the best evidence of a Norwegian-American literature that had yet been created. His example was crucial for a number of writers who appeared in the early part of the new century. While still pursuing the goals of his temperance agitation, he succeeded in making himself the leader of a whole generation of writers. Though this development came late in the history of Norwegian immigration to America, it did come.

In the year 1905 that saw Norway a free country, Ager not only started the first important critical journal among Norwegian Americans, *Kvartalskrift*, but also published his first secular collection of short stories: *Fortællinger for Eyvind* (Stories for Eyvind). For the next few years he would devote himself to the writing of short stories.

7

Short Stories: 1905–1910

AS THE RECENTLY installed editor of *Reform*, Ager had new opportunities and new challenges. Not only was he free to write editorials, but he could also publish two successive collections of short stories. While the first still deals overwhelmingly with the evils of drink, the second moves out into a less propagandistic world.

In November, 1905, he appealed on behalf of his publisher, the Fremad Publishing Company, asking his readers to help pay for a linotype machine by buying new ten-dollar shares. The type was by now so worn that in any case it had to be replaced. He enumerated some of the books that had been printed at the press and promised an increased production when they could pass over from typesetting by hand to machine. In this connection he could proudly announce that he had printed and sold over 4,000 copies of *Paa drikkeondets konto*, 2,000 of *I strømmen*, 900 of *Afholdssmuler fra boghylden*, and even 1,700 of the recently published *Fortællinger for Eyvind*. He lists a number of other works also, and points out that "this is a colossal production, when we recall that the newspaper has always battled with poverty and has never had any capital to speak of."[1]

Two years later he was able to present the new machine and write an amusing sketch about "the new and the old." He writes of himself as one who has difficulty finding words for the change: "His heart clung to the old, while he yet saw the need of the new." He imagines that the old, discarded type sadly speaks up: "So this is the end; we've been worn out in the work and now we're being scrapped. . . . We aren't good enough any more. That's the thanks we get." In the person of the printer's "shooting stick," a bar to hold a frame of type together, the editor replies, "You are the ones who have secured the new machine. . . . When you were young and bright you stood faithfully in your ranks, and you did not fall out when you got old. Even though you were worn, you proclaimed the truth and served loyally, until you had opened the path for the new." He takes this as an allegory about the temperance movement, initiated by the poor and simple but now supported by a growing multitude. "What does it matter if we old rejects have become worn, when we can rise from the dead in this way?"[2]

The first collection of short stories is in many ways a continuation of his work in *Paa drikkeondets konto*. He does his best to make the problems of drinking vivid to his readers by embodying his moral lessons in story form. He must have been writing those stories as early as 1901, when one of them, "Hvorfor? Fordi—" appeared in *Reform* on March 26. The 1905 collection bore the title *Fortællinger for Eyvind* (Stories for Eyvind) and was dedicated with an introductory verse to his oldest son, Eyvind, born in 1900.[3] When evening comes, and Eyvind is tired of playing, the father takes him on his lap and tells him stories. "By choosing this form," wrote a reviewer, S. O. Møst, "he was enabled to adopt that personal, reflective language in which he most easily moves."[4] There are sixteen stories, each with a tone of its own.

The first story is directed at his sleepy son, "to whom I will tell strange fairy tales and stories." The title is "Tidlig Vaar og sen Høst" (Early Spring and Late Autumn), in reference to the boy as a tender shoot of spring and as an old gardener who rakes leaves in his master's garden. He adjures the boy to play while he can, "while the apple trees are blooming and your feet tread the earth lightly." "Dream that you are a king or a prince—you will soon enough discover that you are only a poor wanderer among thieves; dream about angels whose heads are hidden behind the drifting banks of cloud—you will soon enough discover the devil, whose hoof cannot always be concealed down here on earth." "But one thing you must believe, and that is that in spite of all, you are living in God's world." This story serves as an introductory sermon about the sadness of life, relieved only by an assurance of God's presence.

"To Brødre" (Two Brothers) is a retelling of the story of Cain and Abel, the "dark" and the "light" brothers. The dark brother was only of the earth. He killed his brother and became an important man: "His descendants were gifted at forging weapons. They reshaped the wooden club into an axe and the axe into a sword and the sword into a spear. They invented the bow and the art of poisoning their arrows. They made a system out of murder and called it discipline and the art of war, and they laid underwater mines in the harbors and invented guns which kill without sound at a distance and called it modern civilization. The mastery of the earth was at stake. The earth has been fertilized with the blood of brothers; and woe to him who stands in their way." But God has placed a mark on these men of the sword: They can never accept the responsibility to be "my brother's keeper."

55

"Skjødehunden" (The Lapdog) describes a good Christian family into which the devil craftily insinuates himself in the shape of a delightful little puppy. It becomes quite indispensable to the family until one day it bites a boy in the neighboring house. The boy dies and the family is unhappy, but the dog wags its tail and they excuse it, for "it is really strange how one can come to love such a little animal." Its depredations grow steadily worse until it becomes a terror in the neighborhood. The family only give the dog gentle slaps, "for it had such a soft tongue and its fur was like silk." "But the devil laughed." The allusion here is clearly to the vice of drinking.

"En hjemsøgt Stad" (A Stricken City) is the story of a calamity that visits a city which "only a few days ago was a happy city, where people gave in marriage and took in marriage, bought and sold, discussed politics and religious eccentricities, cheated and were cheated, spoke well and ill of one another, performed many quite good deeds, and sinned in moderation." "The bitter north wind created icicles in the beards of good men as well as evil ones, and the saloons sold beer for five cents and hard liquor for ten to both the just and the unjust." Then the city is visited by a case of smallpox, which grows into an epidemic. The smallpox devil is accused before the high court, along with an earlier devil, the saloon devil. A famous lawyer, Mr. Factum, addresses the jury and accuses the two devils in almost exactly the same terms. But the smallpox devil is immediately convicted, for "it was a poor, infamous devil, who had no defenders." But the saloon devil had a very eloquent defender, Mr. License, with thirty shekels of silver in his hands. He spoke of personal freedom and its blessings, and the jury acquitted the saloon devil on condition that it pay its thirty shekels to the city treasury. "And there was once more peace in the town. They could sleep well at night, both the bad and the good."

"En Fiskehistorie" (A Fish Story) is an allegory in which a convention of fish is going on under the water while a man sits fishing. Ager, himself an avid fisherman, sees the cork as a telegraph by means of which a simple fish can communicate with a simple soul to explain why the fish are not biting. The fish are holding a mass meeting to discuss what fish can do about the destruction that constantly threatens them at the hands of human beings. The story reminds one of tales by Hans Christian Andersen, with which Ager was of course familiar. Each fish represents a different point of view. The perch, for example, regards the danger as exaggerated: all one needed was to exercise moderation, "as a fishly virtue"; "it had bitten off many a bait without suffering any damage to its body." The eel "declared that it agreed with the last honored speaker." The bass on the other hand warns that temptations are many and proposes that all fish should be prohibited from approaching the bait. Again the eel agrees with the last speaker. Fish after fish makes its contribution, representing all sorts of views, clearly aimed at caricaturing the participants in discussions for

56

and against prohibition. The sheephead, a character no doubt suggesting the clergy, "wished to know what the will of providence was. It would not approve a change in anything that providence undoubtedly had arranged in the best possible way." The fish which represents Ager's own view is, characteristically, the bullhead, which argues in favor of "the most radical law." But the suckers vote for an amendment to a law proposed by the eel that some fish should be forbidden to partake. Ager has here clearly lampooned some of his opponents in an amusing way.

"Korsets Tegn" (The Sign of the Cross) is "the saddest of fairy tales," told to the boy while he is asleep. It tells of a mother who fondles her child and thinks of how innocent he still is, while hearing the ravings of a drunk outside. She dreams of seeing an assembly of hundreds of thousands of such children, only to have a white-aproned man sprinkle drops of wine on them, followed by drops of beer, and ending with drops of brandy. After each "baptism" the children's playing stops, sweet words turn into oaths, and laughter is replaced by screams. The mother pleads for her child, but the man is uninterested; he has the flag and the sign of the cross behind him.

"Et Spørgsmaalstegn" (A Question Mark) continues the mother's dream. She seeks salvation for her child and goes first to the saloonkeeper, who assures her that his business is legal. He advises her to go to the legislator, who advises her to go to the pastor; but the pastor can do nothing, and advises her to turn to the press. She seeks out the editor, only to hear that his income is dependent on advertising by the saloon interests. He tells her to go to the people and make her appeal; but the people reply that she is a fanatic and stop up their ears, for they have more important things to do. "And they continued to buy and sell and quarrel and fight about those things that were so much more important."

"Hvorfor? Fordi—" (Why? Because—) is a parable about a dove which appears one day among the hens in the writer's barnyard. Ager contrasts the dove "who sails on broad, shining wings up in the sunlight" with the hens who are "birds of the earth." The dove is fine and light, the hens busy and heavy; the dove is misplaced among the hens: "Here it is a matter of the struggle for existence." The dove is "a little dream—a beautiful poem." The hens are fat and their wings are useless: "Their purpose is to be butchered, their pride to lay eggs at fifteen cents a dozen." The dove stays for four days, and then it dies; the writer reveals that it had a deep, open wound in its breast. One can find people like this, who suffer from maladjustments "that may possibly be traced back to a wound in the breast—one of these deep, hidden wounds that heal only with difficulty." One feels that Ager may be picturing himself here as a poet misplaced among people who fail to understand. Is he himself so sorely wounded?

Immigrant Idealist

"Præmiefrøet" (The Prize Seed) tells of a man who has received packets of seed in the mail and finds among them one with flower seeds, which he discards in a corner of the post office. A pale, barefoot farm boy picks it up and hurries home to plant the seed—he "had seen so many beautiful flowers in the gardens of city people." The author describes them as the boy sees them in his imagination. His mother notices that he looks happy and asks him why. But Eddie is ashamed, for it "wasn't customary to be happy in their house, and he got the feeling that he had done something that wasn't right." He is glad that his father has not noticed, for the father is a very unhappy man, depressed and miserable; his misfortunes have even led him to drink. The boy plants his seed surreptitiously. But one day, when the plants have begun to sprout, his father comes home drunk and scolds the boy, while he tramps down his flowers. He kicks the boy so that he faints, and only then does the father realize what he has done. In repentance he spends the time while the boy is ill tending his flowers; one day the boy is able to enjoy their fragrance, and he gets well. "Little Eddie had had complications, as the doctor called it; the father didn't understand what that meant, for he was a simple man. . . . But on the day when he lay on his knees in the sunny garden, he got an indefinite feeling that he, too, had his complications, besides the drunkenness which was his obvious vice." From that day peace, love, and happiness made their entry into the home.

"Den stygge Jerven" (The Nasty Wolverine) is another animal fable. It begins: "There are many strange animals in the world, and the strangest are the tame ones—the civilized animals." The story is about the war that the tame animals decide to wage against the depredations of the wolverine, which was a very bad animal. The tame animals have a meeting at which they discuss what they can do. The ox advises that the wolverine can best be handled by making a big noise to scare it away, a real bellow. The dog points out that he is only supposed to guard the yard; anything else is beyond his jurisdiction. The rabbit recommends hiding their heads in a hole in the ground, while the rooster advises a loud crow, chiefly "to maintain an individual's right to utter battle cries in the hour of danger." The geese are concerned to know if the wolverine is red: they could not for their conscience's sake fight against anything red. The cat, which has just borne four kittens, takes the point of view that it would kill the wolverine if it posed a threat to the kittens. The parable appears to be directed against the liquor traffic, but also has reference to other human relations.

"Bror min" (My Brother) is about a boy of sixteen who was planning to fight another boy, whom he considers to be bad. "The essence of all corruption and evil in this world walked around with a tall white collar, a red tie, and a stiff hat." One night he dreamt that he had him in his power, but as he raised his arm to strike, he discovered that the boy was his brother, and his arm was restrained. "He was not only my brother; he was small and helpless. Someone had been mean to him; for he wept and was dejected." "He was not in fact my brother. Yet we were undoubtedly related." They had many similarities; for example, "he cried out if anyone stepped on his toes and he had an inborn tendency to strike back when he was attacked." "And when I now think of him, it is with joy, as when one thinks of a brother that one has lost and forgotten, but found again." Nowhere has Ager more poignantly expressed his sense of humanity than in this little sketch.

"En Enfoldig spurgte i al sin Enfoldighed" (A Simpleton Asked in All Simplicity) is a sort of reverse catechism in which a pastor is faced with the consequences of his assertion that "there are many honorable people who use beer, wine, and brandy in moderation without thereby harming either themselves or others." In scene after scene he is presented with instances of people who lose fortune, happiness, even life because of alcohol. But the masses thank the Lord that they are not like the fanatics who oppose the moderate use of liquor.

"Et Eventyr om 'Reform' " (A Fairy Tale about *Reform*) is a story told by the newspaper. It is an amusing account of how a newspaper gets made from a clean sheet of paper. *Reform* complains that it does not do very well, since it will not take as many patent medicines as other newspapers. The son of a farmer wonders about the snake on the front cover which entwines a church, a school, and a home: no doubt the demon rum. "I went through the presses, for one must go through something if one is to become anything." He sees editor Ole Br. Olson and the author, who is "chewing his pencil while he arranges some papers." There are many puns and little asides, ending with his awakening from his dream when the brakeman calls out, "Chippewa Falls, change for Eau Claire."

"Den gamle Kone og det graa Sjal" (The Old Woman and the Gray Shawl) tells of a young man who has worked in the Dakota harvest. When he comes home, he expects his mother to meet him, but she has given up waiting. He stops at the saloon and loses his way, but he is sober when he reaches home at dawn. The thought of his mother and her old shawl, which she had used to cover him when he was ill, leads him to surprise her by going with her to church that morning, to sit next to the old gray shawl.

"Saloon Interiør" (A Saloon Interior) portrays a scene in which the bartender, because of a mother's plea, refuses the saloonkeeper's request to serve a drunkard another drink. The saloonkeeper is annoyed, since such occurrences are bad for business: "It has always been my intention to run a saloon in such a way that people can get respect and love for it."

"Et Stykke af et vindfældt Træ" (A Piece of a Windfelled Tree) refers to a folk belief that a sharp cracking noise in a wooden wall is due to a crack the

59

tree received when it fell. Ager applies this idea to the experience of a boy of six who has been sent to fetch his father home from the saloon. He is ejected by the saloonkeeper, who holds him by his left ear; ever since, his left ear has burned when he has to face a saloonkeeper. People can't understand why he will not recognize that there are many good and kind saloonkeepers: he has become a fanatic. He tells about another little boy who witnesses his father in a drunken fit bloodying his mother's nose. Could these be reminiscences of Ager's own childhood?

The total impression of *Stories for Eyvind* is that Ager has developed into a successful narrator, while not moving very far out of his concern with the temperance issue. Nearly all the stories have the influence of alcohol as a main focus; they take the form of parables or fairy tales more than of realistic short stories. But they are well told, with vivid details and convincing descriptions. Two satirical tales mock human foibles in animal form, but Ager also has a sentimental feeling for children and mothers. In "Two Brothers" he shows a humanitarian concern and there is a definite religious tone in some of the early tales drawn from the Bible.

Ager was not delighted with the reviews he got. To Buslett he wrote that it is "darn near impossible to get a book properly reviewed among us." He quotes snatches from various reviews to show how little reviewers understood of "some short stories that I thought would describe various kinds of people, each with its own point." One reviewer wrote, "It makes the most serious person burst out laughing" (*Folkebladet*); another that "the book is quite instructive" (*Fremad*); a third that it was "touching, with a little dash of merriment" (*Folkevennen*); a fourth that it "is gloomy and sad" (*Den Norske Amerikaneren*); a fifth finds in one story an attack on religion (*Revyen*); a sixth says that the stories "are well written and morally pure" (*Kirketidende*); while a seventh (*Budbæreren*) saw them as "light tales that one can read with benefit and enjoyment."[5]

While Ager may not have found the full "understanding" that he hoped for from reviewers, he did have reason to appreciate a somewhat over-generous review by S. O. Møst, printed in his own newspaper. Møst expressed regret that Norwegians, who had successfully tamed the prairie, had contributed so little to literature. A change had now set in, and the chief contributor to the new trend was Ager. "He is a very entertaining narrator: his style is lively, his language simple, attractive, and challenging. His thoughts are concentrated in short, pregnant sentences." The reviewer goes a bit overboard when he calls the stories "poetry in prose form, that can be compared with the best that is written in Norwegian." He notes that while Ager is "a poet, an artist, he does not cultivate art for art's sake. He uses it as a means, a weapon directed against the most malignant evil of our time." "Even if this book is a plea in the struggle for temperance and prohibition, it satisfies the most discriminating literary demands. Therefore it will be read with profit by anyone who loves real literature, even if he is antagonistic to the temperance movement."[6]

The real fulfillment of Ager's promise as a short story writer came with his next collection, in 1908, which he titled *Hverdagsfolk* (Everyday People) and dedicated with a verse to Gudrun, his second child, born in 1904, "papa's girl."[7] There are nine stories, some of them among his best.

The first one, "Hvorledes Magnus blev beskjæmmet" (How Magnus was Put to Shame), reflects what might have been an experience of his own in the editor's office. Olaf Winge is a typographer who is temporarily in charge while the editor is absent. A shabby old man brings him a neatly written manuscript which he wants the editor to publish. Winge quickly discovers that it is all copied from other writers, but he is moved by the old man's assurance that his friend Magnus, for whom he works as a cook, is mistaken in calling him crazy. He pretends to accept the manuscript and gives the old man a minimal sum of money, which leads him to exclaim happily that "this will put Magnus to shame." The typographer puts the manuscript away on a shelf and forgets it, only to find it after many years when he has really become the editor. He realizes that just like the old man he has slaved for another, and what was it all worth? He is about to sell out to new owners, but at the last moment he telegraphs that "the deal is off": "Now Magnus will really be put to shame."

"Det slukkede Blik" (The Light that Went Out) is the reminiscence of an old dying farmer who recalls his young wife's bright eyes, which are now dull from a long life of faithful service. "En Teddy-Bjørn" (A Teddy Bear) is the story of a pastor who is thought stern by his parishioners, but has a soft spot for his little daughter. Coming home from a trip to Minneapolis, he remembers not only to visit his sister-in-law, but also to buy his little girl a teddy bear, then a novelty. But on the train he impulsively gives the teddy bear away to a crying, feverish girl in a nearby seat. When he gets home, he desperately sits up half the night to make a teddy bear for his own child, only to fall asleep. The next morning he is greeted happily by the little girl, who has gotten a teddy bear from the sister-in-law. Both the pastor and his daughter are fine portrayals of character.

"Løst fra alt" (Freed from Everything) is the account of a grandmother who gets her bright little granddaughter Olga to accompany her to the poorhouse as an interpreter. The grandmother has decided to free herself of all obligations so she will no longer be a burden to her children; she has even drowned her beloved cat, Sina. But she still has some pride and she tells Olga to make it clear to the supervisor that she comes of *kondisjonerte* people, that is, the Norwegian upper class. Olga does not understand the word and she translates it by telling him that her grandmother "is a fine lady" and that they are not poor.

61

The supervisor therefore can not admit her to the poorhouse and they trot back home. She proves not to be "freed from everything;" even the cat Sina returns. This pearl of a story brings out all possible humor in the conflict between Norwegian and American concepts.

"Et Stjerneskud" (A Shooting Star) is the least successful of the stories, being a throwback to the genre of temperance tales. A man who breaks his vow of abstinence on Christmas Eve and a saloonkeeper who fails to bring gifts to his children are compared. The drinker renews his vow under the image of a shooting star, which is supposed to bring luck.

"Naar Græker møder Græker" (When Greek Meets Greek) is a hilarious fishing tale about two Norwegians who are trying to steal a march on the fishing season on a Sunday. "When you looked at them from behind, it was impossible to see any difference except that one was a little bowlegged and the other a little knock-kneed. But in Andreas' opinion Johannes was a religious fanatic, while in Johannes' confirmed opinion Andreas was a worldly person." They keep close watch on each other's illegal activity, and when Johannes gets a fine bass, Andreas is bitterly envious. On the streetcar home Johannes has an attack of conscience and drops the bass overboard; but Andreas seizes the chance to get off the car and, presumably, pick up the fish. It is a fine study in hypocrisy and the ethics of fishing.

"Norskie" is the rather sentimental story of an illegitimate child who is adopted by an Irish couple; one day she falls into an open well and drowns. The adoptive father tells the story to the author, who ponders on the contrast between the Irishman's love for "Norskie" and the indifference of her real mother and father.

"Han saa liden og uanselig ud" (He Looked Small and Insignificant) is virtually an illustration of Ager's thesis about the break between the older and the younger generations. He visits one of the finest farms in the settlement where the young people are having a lively party. He wanders out to the kitchen to find a match for his cigar, only to meet the elderly parents, alone and neglected. He treats the old man to a cigar and gets into conversation with the couple. The loud noise of the young folks, singing popular songs, is heard alternately with the quiet voice of the old man telling about the life they have lived. They have worked hard, struggled with grasshoppers and drought, built a farm and brought up children. The writer thinks about the honor that should have been paid to them. But when he leaves, he sees the old man standing in the yard: "His back was bowed, and he looked small and insignificant."

"En Skjæbne" (A Fate) is a brief sketch of the deathbed of an old inventor, who had spent his whole life trying to build a steamboat. But when it was finally built it proved to be a total failure. The author concludes: "Who knows?

Perhaps any one of us might die if we saw our dearest dreams transformed into reality."

These stories about "everyday people" were composed between 1904 and 1908, when Ager was in his late thirties. They reflect both his humor and his sense of tragedy: amusement at the quirks of character of his fellow Norwegians and a sentimental attachment to the old traditions. An anonymous reviewer in *Kvartalskrift* seems misguided when he writes that "Ager does not have a robust or a fertile imagination."[8]

Beside editing *Reform* and publishing stories, Ager was busy during these years editing *Kvartalskrift* as the organ of the Norwegian Society to promote the literary scene among Norwegian Americans. The magazine got some unexpected competition when two editors of *Decorah-Posten*, Johannes B. Wist and Kristian Prestgard, started a literary periodical in Decorah, Iowa, in 1905 with a much more pretentious format; they called it *Symra, en Aarbog for Norske paa begge Sider af Havet* (Symra, a Yearbook for Norwegians on both Sides of the Ocean). They persisted only to 1914, while Ager kept his *Kvartalskrift* going until 1922.

Ager wrote most of the major contributions to his journal himself. In the course of the first five years he managed to write lengthy essays on several of the leading writers of Norway—Henrik Wergeland, herald of the Norwegian movement for democracy; Henrik Ibsen, renowned dramatist; Bjørnstjerne Bjørnson, nationalistic poet; Alexander Kielland, novelist from Stavanger; Jonas Lie, storyteller from northern Norway—as well as a survey of "Modern Norwegian Literature." He also wrote somewhat outspoken notices of Norwegian-American writers—Simon Johnson, O. A. Buslett, Jon Norstog, a survey of Norwegian-American literature.

Possibly his most important contributions to *Kvartalskrift* are two essays on the maintenance of the Norwegian language. The first is "Om at bevare vort Morsmaal" (Preserving Our Mother Tongue).[9] It was also issued as a pamphlet, which was reviewed in *Reform* by Professor J. N. Kildahl. Kildahl notes that "Ager always writes well, both in form and in content." He would wish that all Norwegian Americans who have children could read the essay. As a professor at the theological school of the Church, he saw many students who objected to learning Norwegian. "Children of Norwegians do not become Yankees just by learning English. Each people has its special peculiarities and one does not get away from them just by not learning one's people's language."[10]

Ager's second essay is titled "Det viktigste" (The Most Important Thing). He argues against those who believe that an interest in the Norwegian heritage can survive the loss of language. He points to the poor response among the Norwegian Americans to American services in the Lutheran churches and to

English-language journals. In a bold suggestion, he writes, "We ought to make it fashionable to know Norwegian." He recommends that declamatory contests in Norwegian be arranged, which he actually succeeded in doing, beginning in 1911. He concludes his essay: "I fully and completely believe that if we permit the language to be lost, then anything else that we have in our hands will surely die."[11]

Ager also wrote essays in *Reform* during these years, for example, a review of a Minneapolis performance of Ibsen's *Peer Gynt* with Richard Mansfield. He admits that in spite of necessary cuts in the text and the translation into English, "this was really Peer himself that we saw." It was a moving performance, and he concludes, "What a triumph for a small and poor country to produce an Ibsen and a Grieg."[12] Ager also printed a series of articles on "the natural solution of the problems of society."[13] In 1908 he became a member of the Eau Claire Public Library Board, on which he continued to serve for the rest of his life.

In sum these early years were successful and profitable years for Ager's advancement as editor and author. He was giving the notion of Norwegian-American literature real substance. Peer Strømme, once his chief as editor of *Norden*, now a freelance journalist, summed up Ager's progress in an article on Norwegian-American authors: "He has with great diligence and learning read Shakespeare and Goethe and Ibsen, but only to find new weapons in the battle against the evil of drink. . . . We are tempted to wish that Ager for once would drink himself halfway tipsy so that he could let himself go." Strømme found the story "He Looked Small and Insignificant" to be Ager's best: "he is fond of the step-children of society."[14]

Ager was not likely to become tipsy, but he did try to meet Strømme's challenge in his second novel.

8

Christ Before Pilate: 1910

AGER HAD ALREADY written a novel, *I strømmen*, reflecting his child-hood in Norway; but in 1910, at the age of forty-one, after twenty-five years in America, he ventured a novel about life in the New World. He titled it *Kristus for Pilatus* (Christ before Pilate), with the bold subtitle: *En norsk-amerikansk fortælling* (A Norwegian-American Story).[1] It was Ager's bid to be considered a novelist on a par with such great Norwegian storytellers as Bjørnson and Jonas Lie. It was also his first major step out of the temperance genre into the secular world of letters. It fulfilled his own program for the crea-tion of a Norwegian-American literature and immediately won him a position as the leading figure in that literature.

The setting is identified in the first chapter: "There were two Norwegian churches in town. One was large and elegant and was located in the best dis-trict. The other was a modest little wooden structure with a tiny tower that rose scarcely higher than the surrounding chimney tops." The pastor of the first is Conrad Walther Welde, whose patrician name identifies him as the scion of a succession of state church pastors in Norway.[2] His upper-class origins have made him a man of good taste, but they have left him with some weaknesses of character. His antagonist is the Reverend Mosevig, pastor of the smaller church, a one-time sailor and carpenter, whose humble origin in a West Nor-wegian fjord community is emphasized. His name, meaning "Moss Bay," is evidently that of a farmstead. He has made his way into the ministry via ex-perience as a lay preacher, one who has been "called," and converted "from an early life in sin," and he is suspicious of the high-church air of Welde's church.

The scene is realistic enough, reflecting the many cleavages of both social and doctrinal nature among Norwegian-American congregations. There were indeed two Norwegian Lutheran churches in Ager's Eau Claire, but they did not correspond in any detail with those in Ager's novel.[3]

The theme around which Ager spun his tale and his title was Pastor Welde's profound involvement in ideas suggested by Mihály Munkáczy's 1881 painting of Christ before Pilate, which Ager had first studied in the art gallery in Liverpool in 1900. In the novel the painting has been left in the parsonage by Welde's predecessor; Ager himself had a copy in his office and put a reproduction on the cover of his book. Christ stands there while Pilate ponders what to do with Him. The angry mob demands that He be crucified, and Welde detects something in their distorted faces that reminds him of Mosevig. Christ and Pilate represent the highest attainments of spiritual and worldly culture respectively: love and grace versus power and justice. "They should have stuck together — against the mob," thinks Welde. But then the crux of the problem occurs to him: it was to save the mob that Christ died on the cross! Welde is torn within, and it seems likely that he may himself have to face a Calvary.

Mosevig's personality weighs upon Welde's tender conscience, giving him the feeling that his rival "had something to demand of him that he could not pay." He thinks back on the privileges of his boyhood on a pioneer Wisconsin farm. As a boy he had the advantage and the responsibilities of a powerful physique. As a pastor he became the tool of his subordinates: on the one hand are the people who want him to recommend them for jobs, on the other are the leading members of the congregation who wish to dictate the affairs of the congregation. Cliques are formed, some worldly, some puritanical, some liberal but business-minded.

In the Norwegian neighborhood there is rivalry among the residents on such matters as fixing up their lots and houses. Garfield Avenue becomes a hotbed of gossip. Everyone condemned the gossip, but meanwhile "it improved sidewalks, repaired stairways, washed windows, and got children baptized and sent to school." A special rivalry arose between a Mrs. Thompson and the newly-arrived Mrs. Berven, who both conceive the newfangled idea of organizing a church supper where the well-known Norwegian dish of *lutefisk* will be served. Mrs. Berven succeeds in shifting responsibility for preparing the fish to Mrs. Thompson, who in her ignorance lets it spoil. Mrs. Thompson is so angry that she leaves the congregation to join Mosevig's church.

Welde starts out well, being so effective in his sickbed visits that Doctor Spohr jokes about sharing his fee with him. He successfully organizes a young people's society to meet in the church basement. But the congregation takes offense when their program "dialogues" develop into theater. He is popular with young people and even arranges language courses in Norwegian and English for them. It is hard for him to be stern, and when he sets out to rebuke members for drinking or the like, he is so well received that he forgets his

66

reprimand. He gets into an argument with the doctor, who makes fun of his devotion to Munkáczy's picture, while Welde accuses the doctor of being a materialist. Doctor Spohr terms Welde a dreamer, but both are in reality kind-hearted and self-sacrificing. Welde is shown at the funeral of a drunkard not preaching against drunkenness, but confessing his regret that he had not done what he could for him.

Welde, who is a bachelor, often dreams of a girl he once knew named Maggie, who refused to marry him because she was more interested in pursuing her career as a painter. He now gets a letter from her, written from Paris, in which she reports that she has done well and offers him a life of leisure and travel if he will come to her. But his pastoral cares have now become so important to him that he fails even to answer her letter, feeling that her offer must be rejected as Christ rejected the devil's temptations. He shoulders his daily work, even taking part in election campaigns to vote out the saloon. Some members of his congregation are unhappy about Welde's growing engagement in such peripheral affairs.

Welde's thoughts often revolve around his rival Mosevig, for whom he somehow feels responsible: he even dreams about him. Mosevig's daughter Ellen begins coming to the young people's society in Welde's church, presumably to spy. She seems pale and dispirited, but not unattractive. One day he is out walking and meets her by the river and goes for a walk with her. He amuses her and breaks down her reserve by using his strength to help a farmer lift his wagon out of the mud. He begins to pay attention to her: "He had the feeling that in some mysterious way he was in debt to her, that he owed her something."

So far Welde's life has been fortunate, but here he reaches a turning point in his career and makes a series of false moves. He completely misunderstands the girl, who ridicules him behind his back. He comes across her by the river, when she is actually on the way to a meeting with her lover. He sketches her, having taken up painting in memory of Maggie, and jokes about "taking her home with him." He goes walking with her in full view of members of his congregation after he has found her crying. He even rescues her from committing suicide by drowning; but when he takes her home, his old servant Jørgine hints at what is actually the matter with her. He is surprised and practically ejects a friend who warns him. Welde is increasingly taken with her: "He suddenly felt an almost uncontrollable desire to embrace her and hold her tight, as if he thereby could protect both her and himself."

He goes so far as to ask pastor Mosevig for his daughter's hand, but is rejected. Welde then writes to Ellen's lover and persuades him to return and marry her. His baseless feeling of guilt makes him anonymously pay the mortgage on Mosevig's church, thus staving off a foreclosure. As Doctor Spohr says, "Whom the gods would destroy, they strike with blindness." Welde manages to alienate his supporters among the unions when he preaches to them about their responsibilities to their employers. Each of these decisions is taken with the best of intentions, but people agree that he has made his position impossible. He is doing his utmost to keep from standing in Pilate's position; inevitably he maneuvers himself into that of Christ.

The end comes on Christmas Eve: instead of going home to his parents, Welde, troubled and confused, goes out into town to buy Christmas presents for all his friends and gets lost in the fog. Friends find him dying of a heart attack and bring him home, where he dies on his knees before the figure of Christ in the painting. The man who is to give his funeral oration has trouble finding any particular trait that he can use for a theme. With this ironic conclusion Ager brings Welde's sad story to an end.

While the novel reads well, one is troubled by the choice of a figure like Welde as the hero of a Norwegian-American novel. Idealists who come to a bad end are well known in Norwegian literature, the prime example being Brand in Ibsen's drama by that name. But Welde is cheerful, not stern like Brand. He is more like Bjørnson's pastor Adolph Sang in his 1883 drama *Over Ævne* (Beyond Human Power). Bjørnson depicts a cheerful man who causes harm to ordinary people by his excess of idealism. But Ager is rather trying to show that a Christlike figure must fail when he faces the realities of daily life. Actually his hero is most akin to the protagonists in Arne Garborg's novel *Fred* (Peace, 1892) and his drama *Læraren* (The Teacher, 1896). Both of these men see in Christian idealism a solution to life's problems, but are rebuffed by the antagonism and hateful neglect of the people. Ager confirmed the kinship in a letter he sent to Garborg with a copy of his book: "I have had great pleasure from your books . . . and more benefit than from any others I can think of at the moment."[4]

While Ager was writing a standard Norwegian language, which nowadays has become a bit old-fashioned because of the numerous Norwegian spelling reforms, he did not hesitate to pepper the language with an abundance of Americanisms. They were drawn from Norwegian-American speech and were no doubt calculated both to bring verisimilitude and to appeal to readers. He writes of "store græsklædte Bluffer" (great grass-clad *bluffs*); a mother supports her family "ved Vadsketubben" (at the wash *tub*); a wife is said to be "spirituelt anlagt" (*spiritually* inclined); he speaks of "Sagarbeidernes Union" (the *union* of the sawmill workers); a man is said to have "stak op for disse kaffekjærringerne" (*stuck* up for these coffee-drinking women); another has "hans Suitcase pakket" (his *suitcase* packed); common sense is said to regard someone as "en aabenbar Failure" (an obvious *failure*). Some of these locutions are italicized or placed between quotation marks, but most of them appear without markers.

The novel is unquestionably a landmark not only in Ager's production but also in Norwegian-American literature. Ager portrays his Norwegian-American small town in a sharp but good-natured fashion, with numerous excellent vignettes of rivalries, gossip, and very human reactions. The conclusion seems improbably dramatic, given what has preceded. One would rather expect that Welde, instead of dying, would simply lose his job and move elsewhere, as so many pastors did in an uncertain and volatile job market. Ministers did not, as in Norway, enjoy job security for life: in America the congregation was sovereign. What is evident is that Ager had in mind the Norwegian tradition of the idealist's inevitable tragedy in the clash between his ideals and the facts of everyday life. He uses as his motto the lines by Welhaven:

> Hvo som gaar foran i en Alvorsdyst,
> han seirer ei men falder.
> (He who takes the lead in battle
> Will not conquer but perish.)

In Ager's own struggle with the twin forces of the liquor trade and assimilation he exhibited much of the same inclination: fight whatever the outcome! But as he confessed to Buslett, he could not write unless he either loved or hated, whatever blindness might result.

Within the year the book was reprinted by the prestigious firm of Aschehoug Publishers in Norway with a new title: *Presten Conrad Walther Welde*. It was the first Norwegian-American novel to be so honored. The new title was apparently chosen to avoid the assumption that it was a religious tract.

As a matter of fact, a Norwegian-American lay preacher made just that mistake. In *Folkebladet* (Minneapolis) one P. Overlid, writing from Benson, Minnesota, warned readers against it. He cautioned them that the book "consists of some invented popular tales written in a language that at many points oversteps the limits of decency. It is perhaps to be expected that W. Ager would publish a book of made-up lies and comical sketches, with side thrusts and scornful witticisms about pastoral and congregational work." Ager reprinted the attack and found it worth replying to. When Overlid told him that he "had not found the explanation of why Christ stood before Pilate," Ager answered that he had not intended to "find an answer that is among the first elements in one's childhood instruction." But he was interested "in the raging desire of a good many people to crucify anything that surpasses their own little understanding and perception."[5]

Most contemporary reviewers were enthusiastic in their judgments. Buslett declared that the book was an event in the Norwegian-American world. He felt that some reviewers had missed the main point: that Welde is a Christ figure. The author depicts how a Christian congregation would treat Christ Himself if He came among us. He only regretted that Ager had not pursued the theme and shown how the triumphant Mosevig would have acted in that event. He also suggested that Dr. Spohr might be the author's portrait of the Norwegian radical Marcus Thrane, who spent the last years of his exile in Eau Claire. "Let people read the book: there is more in it than any reviewer has discovered."[6]

E. E. Løbeck, Ager's fellow temperance man and a Minnesota state legislator, held that "the characterizations are sharp, the narrative masterly, and the observations overwhelming." He insisted that the book "is superior in verbal copiousness, imagination, syntax, and narrative movement to anything that has appeared either here or in Norway in recent years." Strangely enough, the reviewer was unable to find in the book "a well-integrated personality embodying a great idea." "I have never read a book where so many people get their hides tanned." "The author seems to be demonstrating the withering effect on our time of electricity and automobiles." These comments, enthusiastic as they are, seem to confirm the comment of an anonymous reviewer that it is difficult to write for a Norwegian-American public, in part because readers lack literary training, and in part because literature is remote from their daily economic struggle. He avers: "I have never read a sadder book." Yet he is grateful to Ager "for the love he shows towards his people and their church and for the faithfulness with which he makes use of the talent with which he has been entrusted."[7]

These comments may stand as representative of the whole Norwegian-American press, whether religious or secular, who were overwhelmed and impressed by Ager's accomplishment. Privately he got some incisive comments, for example from poet and professor Agnes M. Wergeland in Wyoming: "If I should describe it, I would say it is a book about blindness. . . . You have been fortunate in making the shabby look absurd, but oh what a vote of non-confidence in Norwegian America; it makes me shudder."[8] A medical man, Dr. Christian Johnson, writes that he has never found a Welde in real life; the pastors he knows are all petrified theologians. He sees the heart of the novel in the episode of the drunkard's funeral, one of the finest things he has read: "This is the great and hopeful lesson of your book."[9] Professor J. L. Nydahl, a fellow editor, writes that "there ought to have been room for a man or a woman with the spirit of Christ, who also had sufficient sense to gain general respect and confidence."[10] Most important was a new voice, that of Ole Edvart Rølvaag, since 1906 a member of the faculty at St. Olaf College, who would eventually outstrip Ager in fame and importance, but who was still unknown as an author. He had written a review that he hoped "would contribute to getting the book sold." But he says outright that he disagrees with Ager's portrayal of Welde: "He is far from being an ideal Lutheran minister . . . nor is his congregation a typical Norwegian-American congregation. The depiction is too dark." Yet he encourages Ager to continue writing: "You have precisely the qualifications for describing Norwegian-American cultural life."[11]

Ager was no doubt even more concerned about the reviews from Norway. He need not have feared: he won unanimous praise from a wide spectrum of newspapers throughout the country. Oslo's *Aftenposten* found that "the picture of pioneer life in a small American city is shown with such vividness and the struggle inside a congregation is so exquisitely drawn that it will make a lasting impression on the mind of the reader." *Verdens Gang*, another leading Oslo newspaper, was deeply impressed: "As portraiture of human nature it is brilliant, and as a picture of cultural life among the Norwegian Americans it may well be said to be without a peer." The Oslo *Social-Demokraten* warns against taking the book simply as a depiction of Norwegian Americans: "True and striking as it may be, the book is a work of art of universal validity."[12]

The most important Norwegian review was by the man who had followed Ager's career for some time, being himself a temperance man and author, Idar Handagard. He wrote that "Ager is an agitator, and there has long been a conflict within him and in his books between the agitator, the tendentious author, on the one hand and the artist on the other. The struggle has now ended in a striking harmony and a uniquely artistic breakthrough in his great novel." "I don't know what to admire most in this work—the author's original vision, his now droll humor, now caustic satire, or his intimate and detailed familiarity with the men and women of the Norwegian-American pioneer society, especially the women, whom he seems to esteem more highly than the men."[13]

A slightly more reserved note is struck in *Morgenbladet*, a conservative Oslo newspaper: "Of course it has its weaknesses, but it is the work of a poet and it contains a goodly portion of ideas, in addition to which it is the first good book that has been offered us from the society of Norwegian emigrants, to which half of Norway is bound with such strong bonds."[14] Danish reviewers also had reservations. *Nationaltidende* in Copenhagen agrees that the book is worth reading, but finds Welde's relationship to the two young women to whom he is drawn "quite incomprehensible. . . . The hero goes to pieces for Ager, so that in reality there is no other recourse except to let him suddenly die. . . . His heart failed, but one doubts if his head was much stronger." *Extrabladet* (Copenhagen), however, speaks of its "delicate, intimate and keenly made observations," and asks with interest: "Who is Waldemar Ager?"[15]

For all its objective weaknesses, it is safe to say that the book not only launched Ager on a career of literary importance, but also confirmed him in his dream of a Norwegian-American literature, to which he himself had offered the best and most effective testimony.

On November 20, 1912, Ager was given a fifty-dollar prize by O. M. Olesen of Fort Dodge, Iowa, for the year's best Norwegian-American book. Olesen wrote to Ager that he was proud to learn of a Norwegian American who had written such a book.[16]

In the same year he was included in *Who's Who in America* for the first time; for many years he was the only Eau Claire man so honored.

9

From Peace to War: 1911–1917

THE YEARS that followed Ager's success with *Kristus for Pilatus* also marked the end of a long era of world peace. The European war that broke out in 1914 cast a pall over the western world, including the United States, where Wilson campaigned on a promise to keep America out of war. America's entry was nevertheless assured, and soon the whole world was at war.

In the years preceding the war the pace of life was quickening with the advent of electricity and the automobile. English was slowly but surely making its way into the Norwegian and other immigrant communities of the Midwest. Ager continued to advocate prohibition in election after election without success. His interests broadened as he became involved in travel—though none of it yet by automobile—and a variety of speaking engagements throughout the Norwegian settlements. He worked tirelessly, spending nights in railroad stations or shabby hotels, always on the go.

In 1911 he began a series of travel accounts in *Reform* under the heading "Ude med Skræppen," meaning something like "on the road with a satchel." A *skræppe* is actually a bag or pouch such as a traveler might carry slung over his shoulder. Ager was in fact coming not only to bring his message of prohibition and Norwegianness to his audiences but also to promote his newspaper by gaining new subscribers. He was quite literally on a selling mission. He gave his audiences good value, mixing humor with exhortation and quickly becoming the most popular Norwegian on the circuit. His travel letters could also be quite entertaining, though they tended to become repetitious, often consisting of little more than lists of people he met on the road. He was no longer confined to temperance lodges, but could include Sons of Norway meetings

Ager in the editor's office

and especially local festivals to celebrate the Norwegian holiday of May 17th, which commemorated the signing of the Constitution of 1814.

One can follow him from place to place around the Norwegian centers in the Midwest. In 1911 he was in the Westby area of Wisconsin; he tells of meeting a boy who was "more Norwegian than I," for when they went fishing together the boy called the trout "aure" in his dialect, while Ager confessed to using the English "trout." He was in Black River Falls, Wisconsin, for the Working Men's Society, in Spring Grove, Minnesota, for the Norwegian Soci-

Masthead of Reform, *1917*

ety, and in Minneapolis for the local temperance group. He makes frequent reference to the abundance of food served and to his own enjoyment of an extra cup of coffee.

Late in October he set off for the West Coast, going by way of Minneapolis, Underwood, and Fergus Falls in Minnesota to Devil's Lake, North Dakota, then on to such places in Montana as Conrad and Kalispell. From there he traveled to Oregon and Washington, where he managed to find Norwegians, many of whom had had to clear forests under exhausting conditions. In Silvana, Washington, he finally met face to face a friend with whom he had long corresponded, the poet and temperance man O. S. Sneve, after whom he would name his son Roald Sneve, born in 1913. Sneve's songs had enlivened and strengthened the abstinence movement, and Ager called him "one of the most remarkable men that Norwegian America has produced." Sneve was born in Oppdal, Norway, in 1846 and emigrated to America in 1871, working as a farmer and a postman before he found his outlet in poetry. Ager emphasized his dreamy and impractical nature. In an article in *Symra* Ager produced a sketch of his life and cited some of his best verse, thus providing a deeply felt tribute to the old "farmer poet."[1] Ager had not been back home very long when he had to report both the appearance of Sneve's collected verse in 1912 and his death on June 4, 1913.[2]

In Everett, Washington, Ager had his first chance to observe women in the process of voting. "Some are of the opinion that it is a sin to let women vote. But at least it did not look very sinful." And he compared the polls there to the all-male voting places in Eau Claire, which were "full of tobacco smoke, oaths, and beer fumes."[3] A visit to a farm near Stanwood caused him to note the indifference most farmers showed toward beautifying their farms. "They regard such things as gardens, flowers, and pavilions as wasted capital and energy"; they think only of profit and overlook the fact that farms are also homes. In nearby Canada Ager was pleased at a certain "foreign" air; he noticed a group of turbaned Hindus and made the ironic comment: "I knew that they were heathen, people on a much lower level than the whites, but I looked in vain for an equally intelligent face among the whites." They were generally discriminated against, but had found employment in the sawmills, "because

75

they are sober and can be depended on even on Monday," as by implication the Norwegians could not.

Back in Washington Ager spoke to Norwegian audiences in Poulsbo and Ballard. He commented that Norwegians seemed to seek each other's company much less there than in the Middle West and were much more "on the move."[4] The rest of his tour was upset by floods caused by chinook winds, and he made his way slowly back east to what he gaily called the "towers and minarets" of Fargo. In Seattle he had visited *Washington Posten*, a Norwegian-language newspaper edited then by Gunnar Lund; but he had the impression that people appreciated their newspapers less than in the Middle West.[5]

In these happy years Ager had no problem placing his writings in a variety of journals. In addition to his own *Kvartalskrift* there was *Symra*, the literary magazine published by the editors of *Decorah-Posten*, and *Vesterheimen*, the handsome Christmas annual edited by A. M. Sundheim and put out by Augsburg Publishing House in Minneapolis. Ager became a contributor in 1911 and wrote frequently for its later issues, where his stories appeared from time to time and constituted a popular feature of the annual.

In *Symra* he published an important article on modern Norwegian literature, much of it reprinted from *Kvartalskrift*.[6] Earlier, Ager had come to the defense of a generation of writers against R. B. Anderson's charge of "swinishness." But now that he was himself getting older, he made virtually the same charge against his younger contemporaries in Norway. He began by positing that literatures like people go through phases of youth, adulthood, and old age. Youth was represented by the romanticism of Wergeland and Welhaven and adulthood by Bjørnson's and Ibsen's realism, while the modern writers represented old age. But they falsely pretended to be youthful. "Nearly all the love stories in this literature head into the bedroom. The authors may be young, but this is not youth. The shy, hesitant approach of youth, usually finding its climax in a blush or an understanding glance, has become the lustful groping of the old man." He noted this trend in the last works of Bjørnson and Ibsen, but he was mostly concerned with such new writers as Knut Hamsun, Sigrid Undset, and Arne Garborg. He accused them of rejecting religion and of tossing in sexual scenes without motivation in a desperate attempt to overcome the head start of the earlier generation of writers, whose fame had gone out beyond Norway.

In so disparaging the literature of the day he was denigrating his contemporaries. His own concept of life and love was clearly anchored in a more traditional view. The only writer who won his enthusiastic recognition was the short-story writer Hans Aanrud, mentioned earlier as a possible model for Ager's own writing. He grudgingly granted that nearly all of these writers "write well; the art of narrative is so highly developed in Norway that a badly written book is a rarity indeed." Interesting enough in view of his lifelong aversion to the *landsmål* alternative rural language of Norway is his opinion that "in spite of its endless harping on rural life and the worship of the countryside," literature in this medium is "more universally human" and "has a broader vision through its narrow windows than the *riksmål* literature." "Even if the room is stuffy, it is not nauseating."[7]

By way of contrast he followed up his blast against recent Norwegian literature by giving accounts of two Norwegian-American writers, O. S. Sneve and O. A. Buslett. His treatment of Sneve has already been mentioned. His vignette of Buslett was something of a masterpiece. He emphasized Buslett's pugnacity: "He wields his sledge hammer against the philistines; but he has adorned it most lovingly with flowers and ribbons, so that no one but he realizes that it is a sledge hammer. . . . This disparity between what he feels himself to be and what the philistines think him to be finds its obvious expression in his fantastic adornments and is the great tragedy of his talent." Born in Gausdal in 1855, Buslett immigrated in 1868. He was encouraged to write by R. B. Anderson in 1882. Over the years he published novels, narrative poems, and plays, all of them highly dependent on the great Norwegians. Ager found that his work represented "the intelligent Norwegian farm boy's unclear fumbling towards the great and powerful cultural life of Norway." His protagonist falls between stools in "a helpless unclarity about where he really belongs. Buslett writes philosophy that seems to be profound but is incomprehensible." Ager explained his failure as due to "not having any real audience; so he wrote for himself, contrary to the temperance authors who at least had something to say and someone to listen." One can read a bit of Ager's own problem in this account of his older countryman, whom he portrays with paradoxical humor and deep sympathy.[8]

In the pages of *Symra* for 1913 the position of the Church with regard to the Norwegian language was debated pro and con by pastors of the Norwegian Synod, I. B. Torrison for English and Kristen Kvamme for Norwegian. Ager entered the fray only in reply to his fellow editor in Minneapolis, Luth. Jæger, when Jæger maintained that American children of Norwegian parents were and felt themselves to be Americans. Ager disagreed, since he insisted that "to be an American is not a question of language." He himself evidently felt that he was as good an American as anyone, even though he continued to use Norwegian.[9] In 1913-1914 Ager was invited by the Sons of Norway to give a series of lectures that brought him to small towns in North Dakota, Minnesota, and Wisconsin. In each place he reported on the programs and on people he met; one can gather much local historical information from these accounts.[10]

But the most important literary event of this period was the appearance in 1913 of a new collection of short stories, which he titled *Fortællinger og skisser* (Stories and Sketches).[11] He dedicated the stories, some of which had appeared as early as 1909, to his third child, Trygve, born in 1906, whom he called "min lille flinke Gut" (my clever little boy). This group of stories includes some of Ager's best. There are no sermons on drinking; in fact, drinking is mentioned only in passing and is treated humorously. Each story has its focus on some human problem and the characters are treated with respect.

In "Borte! — Hjemme!" (Gone! — Home!) Oline, a pious woman in a northern Wisconsin hamlet, is upset by the visit of her sister Josephine, known as Joe, who comes from Chicago. Joe is not interested in the sister's prayer meetings or her attempts to discuss spiritual topics. In short, although a faithful church member, she is in Oline's eyes a frivolous and worldly person. Oline is especially concerned when she hears loud laughter from the room where Joe is entertaining Oline's children, a baby daughter and a son Timotheus. From the kitchen Oline breaks out into a hymn, but in their exuberance Joe and the children do not even hear her. Joe has taught the baby to do a clapping game called "Gone!" and "Home!", which she enters into with delight. It is more than Oline can endure. "When Timotheus had gotten his spanking and Joe her reprimand, the house settled back into its usual solemnity." But when the baby falls ill and is about to die, her last effort is to move her hands for the game Joe has taught her. The mother, who has wrestled with God for the child's life, has to say, "Little sister is gone." But Timotheus counters, "No, mother! She said she was 'home'; didn't you hear how happy she was?" The story successfully opposes a puritanical view of life to one that is human.

"Lars" is about a recently arrived sawmill worker who shyly presents himself to the pastor to be married. He and his wife establish a home and produce a family, but soon he is threatened with economic ruin. Neither he nor his pastor is in favor of taking out insurance. They believe that everything the lodges do is sinful, for "the best insurance is Almighty God and his word"; the lodges even require that you take sinful oaths that endanger your soul. But when a fellow worker dies without insurance and Lars sees the consequences for the widow and the children, he changes his mind and takes out insurance. He has a bad conscience about it and on his death bed he asks the pastor to destroy the policy. When the pastor sees the widow, "all his arguments collapse" and he advises her to keep the policy. Life triumphs over dogma.

"Nu kommer jeg, mor" (Now I'm Coming, Mother) is the story of a successful businessman who had "come to town as a poor farm boy, but with an inherited and long dammed-up desire to get rich." He has married the daughter of his American employer and succeeded to his business. He thinks "with a certain sense of triumph" about his brother Andrew, who had been his mother's favorite, and who always responded to her call by saying, "Now I'm coming, mother." It occurs to him to visit her so that he can show off his present wealth and give Andrew a check of two thousand dollars. He reaches the little farm town in Wisconsin on Christmas Eve, but is unable to get a cab, so he gets a ride with his brother, who does not recognize him. In the snowstorm that arises they are run down by a train and the brother Andrew is injured. The rich man wraps him in his coat and starts off to look for help but is lost and freezes to death. Before he dies, he cries out, "Now I'm coming, mother."

"Et gammelt Koncert-program" (An Old Concert Program) is about a writer who is trying to compose something for a Christmas annual. He is out of humor, and when his little daughter comes to him, he chases her away. But she returns and hides under his desk. In his annoyance he knocks down and breaks a doll that is standing there, a doll in the shape of a clown perched on a hemisphere. The wife informs him that this was his daughter's birthday present to him and puts it back on his desk. In a search for some papers in the desk he finds an old concert program that reminds him of the time twenty years before when he was courting his wife. His thoughts circle around the fact that he can lose the little girl, either through illness or through her growing up and away from him. Then the doll will gain a value for him, and he begins considering what has real value in life. The day will come when values will not be in the dollars he has accumulated: "You are a rootless race in a foreign country, which doesn't even care about its own heart." When the little girl asks her father for the program, he tells her he will save it for her: "Your father will buy himself warmth with it when he gets old and sits freezing in the corner."

In "Den gamle Prest" (The Old Pastor) a minister receives a letter brought him by Helga, the daughter of a parishioner, warning that the congregation is considering a call to a new minister. This is in the spring and Ager describes the vernal season, which contrasts bitterly with the feelings of the aging pastor. Even though he cannot afford it, he generously gives the girl a quarter for bringing the letter. He muses that when he came the parishioners were poor and he was satisfied with little; he made no great demands. But now that they are well off, they still pay him badly. The pastor cheers up at the thought that he and his wife will soon celebrate their golden wedding, and he hopes the congregation will "surprise" them. He is in fine humor and when he reads his letter of resignation the congregation decides to postpone accepting it. But before they can vote, he falls forward and dies. In this story the author sums up a lifetime of devoted and insufficiently appreciated service.

"Hvad Skolemesteren fortalte" (What the Schoolmaster Said) is an allegorical tale about a schoolmaster's garden. In spring it lies neglected and overgrown, but he spades it up and watches the plants struggling for life: "They fought for mastery, just like people; they choked each other, shaded each other, robbed each other, and buried each other just like people." "One day I brought a lily . . . and I said I would clear a space for it in my overgrown garden." "But in my heart I said, 'There is always time.' " The lily grows and dies and he never enjoys it, for it was planted too late. "To neglect what one loves; isn't that to murder one's soul?"

"Et Drømmebillede. Humoresk" (A Dream Picture: Humoresque) is a fantasy about a drunkard who recites poetry by Henrik Wergeland until he is thrown out of a saloon in Moorhead and lands in front of the Wergeland statue in neighboring Fargo. In his befuddlement he thinks he hears a conversation between some American statues raised for famous Norwegians, Ole Bull, violinist, Leif Ericson, discoverer, and Wergeland, poet. The conversation is full of local allusions, mostly about Norwegian issues, but with a dig at Norwegian-American parochialism: "If you are a musical genius, you will never be a genius outside the church synod you belong to; if you are a poet, you will not be read elsewhere; if you are a speaker, you won't be heard elsewhere." Some readers may have been amused by this rather unsuccessful sketch.

"Johan Arndt og Mor hans" (Johan Arndt and his Mother) is a well-told story about Mother Larsen in Norway whose son Johan Arndt is in America. He has failed to write to her for so long that she is troubled, but does not like to admit it to the other women. So she starts telling them that she expects him home by Christmas. When she hears that a visitor to her community is returning to America, she knits a pair of stockings for him to take to Johan Arndt, and includes a hymn book. "This package the American should give to Johan Arndt as soon as he got to a little station called Chicago, for she was sure he'd see him right away, she said." "In 1891 there were over 4,000 saloons in Chicago. In one of these there stood a man one day who had been to Norway on a Christmas visit." He tells his companions about the funny old woman who gave him a hymn book and a pair of socks to give to Johan Arndt. To his surprise one of the men listening is Johan Arndt, who demands what his mother had intended for him. Overcome with remorse, he goes on a spree, gets into a fight, and ends in the hospital. Here a minister helps him, and he resolves to go home to his mother in Norway. "Then the proudest hen in the coop was Mother Larsen."

"To tomme Hænder" (Two Empty Hands) is the most moving of the stories. It follows a boy who left for America amid the tears of his family and friends. "But in this grief he was still glad. 'I'll be coming back,' his heart sang inside him. Just a few years. He would show them over there that he could work; he would save and come home as others had come home, in a fine suit and with a fat wallet." But step by step his resolve fades. Although he is determined never to forget his homeland, as so many others have done, there is always something that keeps him from returning. "My soul is left among these mountains, — and how can a man be separated from his soul?" He learns that his fa-

80

ther has died, then that his mother has died. The years pass and he establishes a home of his own; but he finds that he cannot communicate with his children. His wife dies and a new generation grows up. A letter from his brother, the only survivor, lies unread because his eyes are befogged. But as he dies, he cries out: "I'm coming home, for I am Norwegian. I've been so busy, but now I'm not busy; now I'll come home." "But at his bedside stand several young ladies in their best dresses, and they look at each other with questioning glances: 'What does he say?' " Thus graphically Ager depicts what he sees as the tragedy of the immigrant.

The stories in this volume are a blend of humor and tragedy taken right out of the lives of Ager's contemporaries. They distill his own view of emigration and its consequences, both in religious rigidity and in human pathos.

Apparently no one considered this collection of enough consequence to review it. But Ager included three of the stories—"Nu kommer jeg, Mor," "Johan Arndt og Mor hans," and "To tomme Hænder"—in his *Udvalgte Fortællinger* (Selected Stories) in 1918.

In these years Ager was much concerned with an organization newly founded in Norway for cultivating relations with Norwegians abroad, Nordmanns Forbundet (The Norsemen's Federation). Started in 1907, the organization was warmly supported by leading Norwegian personalities who had been abroad and perceived the need of maintaining relations with emigrants, not least those in America. Ager's reminiscent article about his 1900 return to Norway appeared in its periodical in 1934 and bore the title "Før og nu" (Then and Now).[12] The reference is to the difference in attitude in Norway since the founding of Nordmanns Forbundet in contrast with the general contempt for emigrants before. Ager's articles as well as items about him and his work appeared from time to time in this periodical.

In 1913 he received a request from one of the organization's leaders, N. B. Tvedt, to assist in the publication of a volume of Norwegian-American writings as part of a series to be entitled *Boken om Norge* (The Book about Norway), edited by a well-known author of school readers, Nordahl Rolfsen. The Norwegian-American volume appeared in 1915 as the fifth in the set. It was in fact the first anthology of Norwegian-American writings to appear in Norway and it bears the mark of Ager's participation. Not only does it contain several essays by him on historical aspects of Norwegian-American life, but also several of Ager's short stories, such as "To tomme Hænder" and "Han saa liden og uanselig ud."[13]

Norway in 1914 was still in a state of innocence. Her prime minister, Gunnar Knudsen, had proclaimed the year a hopeful one, in which "European skies are clear." The country was still enjoying the fruits of its full independence, obtained from Sweden in 1905. The summer of 1914 was also one of extraordinary sunshine, which was of great benefit to the centennial exhibition arranged in Frogner Park to celebrate the signing of Norway's constitution in 1814.

Among the exhibits displayed were some from the Norwegian settlements in America. Ager was invited to manage a special exhibit for the state of Wisconsin and even had an official appointment from the governor, Francis McGovern. Ager's well-filled scrapbook from his trip teems with memorabilia, including postcards, snapshots, tickets, postage stamps, official invitations, even a display of Norwegian cigar wrappers. The Wisconsin exhibit won attention with its display of mementos of the Fifteenth Wisconsin Regiment in the Civil War, including its battle-scarred banner. On July 4 a bust of Abraham Lincoln was unveiled in Frogner Park, a gift from the people of the state of North Dakota.

Ager reported fully on the journey in both *Reform* and *Kvartalskrift*.[14] For the first time he could sail on a steamer of the newly founded Norwegian America Line, the *Bergensfjord*, which left New York on May 26 and arrived in Bergen on June 4. Ager lists fellow passengers and emphasizes how restful such an ocean voyage could be. He contrasts the food and accommodations favorably with those of the White Star Line that he sailed with on his first return in 1900. Captain Irgens made friends with the passengers, and there were constant programs, including speeches by Ager. In one of these he told the story of the Wisconsin regiment whose standard he had brought with him for the exhibit. He was delighted to meet a veteran of the war, who was hailed by the audience.

Ager was naturally moved by the dramatic approach to Bergen in a bright summer night through the gray cliffs of the long, narrow fjord. "There were not many who slept that night." He described the fish market in Bergen with some enthusiasm, but he was especially charmed by the Bergen railroad line to Oslo, which joined east and west Norway by land for the first time. Clean, well-clad children, with their arms full of flowers, awaited them at the stations, and Ager involuntarily compared them with the ragged population he had seen in the mountain regions of Kentucky and Tennessee. He admired the impressive engineering of the railroad, with its many tunnels and mountain vistas. At its high point at Finse there was full winter and the passengers got out and threw snowballs. The mountain air was light and stimulating. Coming down from the mountains into Hallingdal one saw many small farms with stone fences and steep hillsides. "All this is Norway and all is beautiful and well-ordered. We have heard that Norway is a poor country, but this is not the impression we get from looking at it." At the station in Oslo Ager was met by friends and relatives, and before long "I was well anchored and the railroad trip was over."[15]

In Oslo Ager was impressed by its growth since he had left there as a boy in 1882. He described the new buildings and the streetcars, as well as workers' wages, which had mounted noticeably. But costs of travel and housing were modest for the traveler, even though store prices were about as high as in the United States. He commented amusingly on the typical difference in journalistic practice from what America had accustomed him to: Norwegians had not learned reportorial techniques. "If a journalist here is talented enough to write a news story or tell an episode interestingly, he doesn't wish to remain a journalist, but wants to become an author and write a book."

As a guest of the exhibition Ager was invited to various banquets, one of which was graced by the presence of the prime minister. Ager also made an excursion to Eidsvoll to inspect the hall where the Norwegian constitution had been signed. He was obviously seeing it for the first time and reported quite fully on it. "One inevitably speaks in a low voice in this modest hall where the future of Norway was sealed. You can't help thinking of how things might have been if the Assembly had not met or had made a different decision."[16]

In commemoration of the occasion a Norwegian-American volume was published by the Symra Company, titled *Norsk-amerikanernes festskrift 1914* (Festival Volume of the Norwegian Americans 1914). Under the editorship of Johannes B. Wist this volume featured some of the best pens of Norwegian America, writing surveys of the press, the church, schools, societies, politicians, teachers, and writers. The chapter on Norwegian-American writers was a delightful essay by Ager, though entirely omitting his own contribution. He begins with some general remarks about Norwegian immigration and proceeds to say that "it is the great tragedy over here that most literary attempts have been choked. People have no use for anything besides the church and politics." "Our Norwegian-American literary efforts can best be characterized as in part incomprehensible and half-choked eruptions. There is often something inarticulate, something that struggles to find expression and has never learned to speak clearly." He has dug out thirty-four collections of poetry: "Common to them all is a sense of forces that struggle to get air and that wheeze and gasp instead of breathing." He begins with Buslett, the pioneer, and works his way through the list of writers, with brief, often witty, remarks to characterize each. He is not without hope: "When we some day recognize that we are a people, and the ground has been plowed by poets and fertilized by historians, we may expect that some seeds will find their way so that a Norwegian-American literature will and must grow."[17]

The fact that Ager modestly omitted his own work in the article meant that it was obviously incomplete, since he was by far the most interesting writer in the Norwegian-American world. In 1915 his Norwegian friend Idar Handagard gave a thorough and favorable account of Ager in a volume he published in Trondheim. He described Ager's career in Norway and America and declared that he had made a breakthrough for Norwegian-American literature. "In American literature in Norwegian his novel [*Kristus for Pilatus*] stands as the most significant and original one, perhaps as the only one that is significant and original."[18]

The outbreak of the European war that would come to be called World War I did not at first affect Norwegian or Norwegian-American interests, since Norway managed to stay neutral. But things were changing in Norwegian America. A striking evidence of the interests of a new generation was the Fourth Biennial Convention of the Young People's League of the Norwegian Lutheran Church in October 20–23, 1914, held in Eau Claire. For the first time the program was printed in English. While there were speeches and sermons in both English and Norwegian, English was already dominant. The congregation to which Ager's family belonged gradually changed over from Norwegian to English, and over Ager's determined opposition the church itself dropped "Norwegian" from its name in the middle thirties, though the change was not made formally until 1947.

These events as well as the evident American trend toward participation in the war created a dilemma for Ager. As long as America was neutral, he could look on the war as primarily an English concern. He was appalled at President Wilson's obvious pro-English bias, which belied his 1916 campaign slogan to "keep us out of the war." In Wisconsin and generally in the Midwest there was strong neutral and even pro-German sentiment. Wisconsin had a heavy concentration of German-American citizens, and its senator Robert LaFollette was one of a handful who voted against American entry into the war.

Ager was also aware of the growth of anti-foreign feeling, which while primarily directed at the German Americans also threatened the Norwegians. After all, weren't they both Lutherans? Ager pleaded for tolerance and an understanding of the difficult position in which America's German population was placed. In 1915 he wrote that "the president's message included an enormous increase in armaments and a violent attack on foreign-born citizens which makes it difficult for our country to preserve its neutrality." He was disturbed by the president's appeal for a "vigorous countrywide de-hyphenization campaign." He regretted the call for a universal "denationalization" of foreigners, insisting that this would not make Americans of them, but "would only cast them adrift." "The hyphen is in the end the bond of blood that ties us to the motherland Europe, from which even Wilson's and [Theodore] Roosevelt's ancestors have come. It should form a bridge to peace and understanding, for we all have our family over there. It is the roots from which we whites have sprung, whether we think things are as they ought to be or not."[19]

The war did provide Ager with a welcome opportunity to collect and publish

Print shop of the Fremad Publishing Company, publishers of Reform, *photograph taken around 1907-1908. Ager on the left. Courtesy Eyvind Ager.*

his material on the Fifteenth Wisconsin Regiment, largely composed of Norwegians and led by a Norwegian, Colonel Hans Christian Heg. Ager had already lectured on the honorable record of this regiment in the Civil War. When he visited Norway in the summer of 1914 to supervise the Wisconsin exhibit at the Centennial Exhibition, a prominent place was assigned to the banner that had been given the regiment by the Nora Society in Chicago when it was on its way to the battlefield.

In 1916 Ager's book appeared, titled *Oberst Heg og hans gutter* (Colonel Heg and his Boys). He wrote that he had not intended a history of the regiment—as he noted, that had already been done by O. A. Buslett in 1894. He merely "wished to collect between two covers some pictures and memoirs that might otherwise get lost." But in his preface he also confessed to a subtler and more remote goal: to let the world know that "the regiment provided the most tangible proof that the most Norwegian-minded Norwegians over here are also the best Americans, that is, the most willing to sacrifice, the first to report when the war trumpet calls and their new land is placed in jeopardy."[20] In the uneasy atmosphere of threatening war, this kind of information could be used as a shield for the Norwegians.

Actually, the book contains much useful information, such as pictures of the participants and maps of the battlefields. Ager wrote various essays to give a somewhat fictionalized account of the battles. As a whole, the book is not well organized, which Ager pleads was due to the piecemeal nature of his sources.

Statue of Civil War hero Colonel Hans C. Heg, raised at Capitol in Madison, Wisconsin, in 1925 through efforts of Waldemar Ager. Courtesy State Historical Society of Wisconsin.

The book became a link in Ager's campaign to collect funds for a statue of Colonel Heg, which was raised in 1926 on the grounds of the state capitol in Madison. Much of the material collected here would eventually find its way into his 1926 novel, *Gamlelandets sønner* (Sons of the Old Country).

Sales were not encouraging during these years. He complained to Buslett as early as 1911: "I had never imagined that it would be as difficult to sell books as it really is." Concerning *Kristus for Pilatus* he reported that "in spite of all the hullabaloo we sold only about six hundred copies, and if I had been paid wages for my work, the book would not have appeared."[21] In 1915 he wrote that the newspaper also had done badly. "It was intended as an organ for agitation and now the prohibition people seem to think agitation is superfluous."[22] Nevertheless he kept pouring out book reviews, both in *Kvartalskrift* and in *Reform*, too many to report here.

Worse things were to come: America entered the war in 1917 and in the same year Ager vented his anger in what would be his bitterest book, *Paa veien til smeltepotten* (On the Way to the Melting Pot).

10

The Melting Pot: 1917

IN 1920 the American writer Sinclair Lewis wrote a controversial and widely-read novel, *Main Street*, called by one critic "a textbook on American provincialism." But three years earlier Waldemar Ager had written a Norwegian-American novel that could be called a "Main Street" of immigrant life. With much the same savagery as Lewis would use about the characters in his Minnesota setting, Ager lambasted and lampooned his Norwegian Americans for their worship of the dollar and their readiness to throw away their Norwegian heritage.

While the book has never been published in translation, it would amply deserve it, if only for the amusing dialogue and the contrasts he depicts between Lars, his average immigrant working man, and Karoline, the Norwegian girl to whom he has been engaged.[1] Like Lewis's Carol, a New Englander, she represents the solid values of the old-world heritage which are discarded in the heady atmosphere of American enterprise. In September, 1916, Ager told Buslett that he was "working on a novel—a sketchy drawing perhaps, which I am afraid is going to cause pain [*svi stygt*]. I have felt ill over Anglo-American snobbishness and pretended elegance until it is impossible to keep my mouth shut any longer."[2]

This became his novel *Paa veien til smeltepotten* (On the Way to the Melting Pot), which ran first as a serial in *Reform* from January 9 to July 24, 1917.[3] When the book appeared, it was dedicated to Ager's fourth child, Valborg, born in 1907, who even rated a three-stanza poem. The title was obviously borrowed from *The Melting Pot*, the much-discussed 1908 play by the English-Jewish playwright and Zionist leader Israel Zangwill (1864–1926). Zangwill created an idealistic image of America "as a crucible wherein the European nationalities would be transformed into a new race."[4] Ager showed his

88

Ager home in Eau Claire, side view

Ager home, front view

distaste for this image by twisting the Norwegian term for "melting pot," *smeltedigel*, into the Norwegian-American and mildly derisive *smeltepotte*.

The setting of the novel is an unspecified American city with a Norwegian population of fairly recent immigrants, no doubt drawn from Ager's experiences in Eau Claire. From beginning to end it is a satirical depiction of a population in full flight from their Norwegian past to their American future. The book is a striking product of Ager the agitator, this time not against the demon rum but against the demon of assimilation. To say that the book is one-sided is only to state the obvious. In fact, however, the picture is so distorted as to become entertaining. The specific details are so down to earth and truly delineated that the reader is curious concerning the outcome. These people are indeed real, but their characteristics are heavily loaded in the direction of Ager's convictions and prejudices.

There is a whole gallery of characters, sharply drawn, with the Omley family as the focus. The story opens with Mrs. Omley struggling to prepare for guests, including the pastor, who are coming to dinner after the baptism of her fourth child: "For she was busy making an American meal and this was not easy." She has learned about a "boiled dinner" and in the sweat of her brow she is struggling with unfamiliar dishes and mysterious recipes. Her daughter Sophy is languidly helping her mother and when she is about to leave to greet the guests, the mother tells her "Jeg vi'kke vetta ta no'n Monkeybisnis a dig, Sophy. Hurry up kvik nu med en Gang." (I don't want any monkey business out of you, Sophy. Hurry up quickly at once.) This sentence with its heavy mixture of Norwegian dialect and twisted English loans (Monkeybisnis, hurry up kvik) sufficiently characterizes the atmosphere. It is a Norwegian-American household, with the mother a rural or small-town immigrant and the daughter an English-speaking child. The mother is unduly impressed by her daughter: "Naar Sophy blev sint og snakket Engelsk, saa var det ligesom noget saa fint og ladylike ved hende, at hun ofte bluedes ved Tanken paa sin egen Tarvelighed." (When Sophy got angry and spoke English, there was something so fine and ladylike about her that she often felt ashamed at the thought of her own shabbiness.) The mother's principle is ironically summed up as "One really had nothing else to live for but the children and one couldn't do too much for them."

The pastor plays a dominant role in the conversation, and he forcefully expresses the second-generation point of view. "His childhood had been darkened by the Norwegian religious school. In his home they spoke only English; but his father, who was a very serious Lutheran of the old type, had demanded that he go to this school and learn the catechism and the explanation in Norwegian. So he had memorized it in the shadow of the rod. First it was the ten commandments or a whipping. Then it was the articles or a whipping

90

and the Lord's prayer or the threat of a whipping. He had chewed on words like 'nidkjærhed' (zealousness), 'miskundelse' (mercifulness), 'vederkvægelse' (rejuvenation), 'retfærdiggjørelse' (justification), and 'vederstyggelighed' (abomination), and the like until his stomach turned so that he was almost ill." Even though he eventually learned them, he now wanted the church to turn to English as soon as possible — though not before adequate funds had been collected for the church's needs. To this a cynical plumber comments that the church is just like the fine houses Norwegians build for Americans: on the day the house is finished, the Norwegians are kicked out.

At this party a newcomer to America, Lars Olson, is introduced; at first he is somewhat confused, but he learns quickly. In fact, he becomes a kind of unifying or thematic figure, who illustrates the pernicious effects of assimilation as Ager sees them. He writes a boastful letter to his parents in Norway, telling of the fine wages he is earning as an apprentice in Omley's paintshop, and the elegant company at the party, "where nearly all speak English." He does not tell them that he is entranced with Omley's daughter Sophy, who almost drives the memory of his Norwegian sweetheart, Karoline Huseby, out of his mind. His workmate is an Irishman who "had the advantage that he drank and therefore had to work for less." Lars struggles hard to keep up and only gradually learns to be less scrupulous about doing good work. He rooms with Mrs. Nelson, whose son Henry is large and handsome and the apple of his mother's eye. While going to high school he earns nothing for his keep. But he is the best player on the football team, and his mother is proud: "There was something great in the thought that she who was so common could have so elegant a son." One day Sophy invites Lars to go to the zoo with her and her best friend Mabel Overhus; Lars is thrilled and even treats them to a boat ride. But the girls talk in English to each other, so Lars does not understand much of it; and only when they are away from others, in the boat, are the girls willing to speak Norwegian.

The best thing in the novel is the conversations, in which the various characters reveal their ideas and prejudices. At the Omleys' everyone except the plumber regards English as the most elegant language, and the women tend to use it, though the men do not. Lars wonders why "the women were more elegant than the men." There are times when he is overcome by homesickness, which leads him to join a friend in playing billiards and seeking company of other Norwegians at the saloon, "where no one was ashamed of being Norwegian." But Lars stays away from drink; this is not a temperance tract, though his being there gives the author a chance to describe some of the human wrecks that frequent the saloon. Lars saves the money he earns and regrets the extra expense of having to treat the others. He prefers to go with the young people who attend church: "The nicest thing was that feeling of being with the upper

91

class, among people who did not need to do any work and who went to advanced schools or took lessons." "Plush rocking chairs were good to sit in and Lars adopted many elegant postures that were suitable for an expensive chair. They should see him back home." Lars decides to make and save money: "One of his dearest occupations was to figure out how much he would have in the bank in a year, in two years, in five years."

Lars's housemate Henry Nelson continues to be idle even after his high-school graduation, while his mother washes clothes to support him. The cynical plumber tells Lars that this is a Norwegian-American problem: the parents regard their own language and traditions as too vulgar to teach them to the children. "They take pride in learning about Columbus and Patrick Henry and Alfred the Great, but learn nothing about their own parents and their family." While there are said to be animals that eat their own young, the "Norwegians in America are even more foolish, for they let themselves be eaten by their young." Lars still dreams of going back to Norway, and Sophy is included in his dreams: "he delighted in her name and could hardly understand how a fellow like Omley could have figured out such a beautiful name." Lars studies the streams of people out walking and is impressed by everyone's elegance. "Children were so elegant and cultivated that their Norwegian parents were ashamed to be seen with them; they feared they would cause offense by their own crudeness and lack of breeding."

Henry has begun to show interest in Edith Perkins, daughter of a rich merchant; but the Perkinses reject him after scolding him for his idleness. This leads him to take a job ditchdigging, which upsets his mother but rather impresses Mr. Perkins. Mrs. Nelson having injured her leg, Lars has to move, now to the Skare family; here the daughters are only interested in clothes and of course they speak only English, though the mother remains Norwegian. "Mother became a household utensil, the most useful in the whole house, indispensable and incomprehensible, something that existed as a fact and neither needed nor demanded any explanation." Back at the Nelsons', Lars discovers that Henry has become more human, and even enjoys speaking Norwegian; Lars is not quite as proud of him as he was. He is invited to the Overhus home for Christmas; by now Mrs. Overhus has learned from "Americans" "to lift the arm up very high when she shook your hand; this was a trump card she played. One after the other entered the parlor with a conceited upper-class feeling in their arm." The men discuss the problem of building a new church, and to attract the young people some want a basement where the young people can have some fun. The cynical plumber, who seems to represent Ager's views, suggests that a saloon and a billiard hall would be better. The men complain that young people are not interested in the same simple pleasures as they were when they were young. Sophy allows Lars to take her home and before she leaves, she gives him a kiss. "Lars did not sleep much that night. . . . He built house after house. . . . Nothing was fine enough for such an elegant lady as Sophy."

We follow Henry's gradual advances toward Edith Perkins and Lars's to Sophy Omley. Mr. Omley is annoyed. If he had imagined that there was a possibility of anything coming of the relationship with Lars, he would not have spent as much money on Sophy as he had. "For she would have been elegant enough as she was for a common, simple Norwegian, without any extra expense." Lars feels rejected by the Omleys and his thoughts revert to his sweetheart in Norway, Karoline Huseby. After some hesitation she promises to come to America. When she arrives, Lars is surprised to discover that she is no simple country girl; she has even learned some English. They agree to postpone their wedding while she gets a job as a maid to learn the ways of America. She gets Lars to organize a Good Templar lodge and they come to know some young people who are interested in speaking Norwegian.

Karoline starts working for a district judge who stems from New England and whose family is genuinely cultivated. She is well treated and enjoys life; on May 17th, the Norwegian national holiday, she wears a tricolored ribbon to mark the day. When Judge Highbee asks her why and she tells him, he orders his stable boy to run up two American flags to honor the day. Karoline and Lars still postpone their wedding and they gradually drift apart. Sophy marries the son of a local American banker and her father decides to build a large, fancy house. The new son-in-law involves him in a ruinous financial speculation, and Omley dies. Henry Nelson wins fame on the victorious university football team, so Perkins is persuaded to let his daughter marry him. Henry's mother is so impressed that she comes and offers a hundred dollars in hard-earned savings to the Perkinses for having had expenses on his behalf. This moving scene causes Edith to decide that Henry's mother shall live with her and Henry when they are married.

Lars becomes more and more important in Overhus's store, as Overhus ages. To Karoline he speaks only of the business and he no longer has any interest in anything but making money. Karoline feels that the man he was has vanished, the man she loved. She freezes, right through her winter coat: Lars has become a stranger. When Lars decides to leave Overhus and demands his back pay, Overhus in desperation commits suicide. Lars takes over the store as "Louis Olson," Karoline returns to Norway, and Lars marries Mabel Overhus, at the same time that Henry Nelson marries Edith. Neither couple is especially happy, since they have little in common.

Karoline returns to Norway and gets satisfactory work as a nurse, but she is dismayed by the attitude of Norwegians toward Americans. She has become accustomed to the American politeness and sense of personal equality, so that she is even annoyed by her own patients, some of whom treat her as a servant. Only the doctor at her clinic understands her problem. He tells her she is not likely to find any Norwegians who are like the New England Highbees. She gradually gets used to conditions in Norway, and it is only by chance that she goes back to America, to accompany a patient. She visits her former town and finds it disappointing and depressing. After visiting her friends there, she returns to Norway to marry the doctor at her clinic.

Before returning to Norway she attends Mrs. Nelson's funeral and sees Lars again. She ponders on how he has become the tycoon he now is. Ager concludes his novel with a summing up of her thoughts: "There were many who became like that. Then they were ready for the great melting pot. First they tore away their love for their parents; then they sacrificed their love for the one they were fond of, then the language they had learned from their mother, then their love for religion, for God and man, then the songs they had learned as children, then their memories and their youthful ideals. . . . And when one had thrown out of one's heart and soul all that one had loved before, there was plenty of space to be filled with love for one's self, egotism, money madness, and all that. The Lord had not created them for harboring such things, and now they went around with a secret fear of being discovered, so they tried to hide by changing their names and their exteriors." Ager describes how different people reacted to the process of being melted down: "Lars was one of those who parted with their best qualities first. And this was natural, for the melting pot was precisely made for the spiritually blunted, for those who no longer had any character by which one could see what they were or what they had been."

Lars in the end becomes the theme of a sermon on the Americanization of the immigrant. Ager discriminates clearly between the genuine, old-line Americans and the new, half-baked immigrants and their assimilated descendants. The latter are interested only in making money; what he plays down is of course the fact that immigrants had to make money before they could emulate the "old" Americans. The Norwegian Americans whom he castigates so vehemently in this book are almost to a man concerned with class status. Ager himself had undoubtedly felt the discrimination directed against immigrants who in their striving for upward mobility were not at once able to reach pinnacles of culture, who see the outward trappings that money can bring and look down on what American society despises: the raw immigrant. The strength of this novel lies in its many amusing details. But as a whole the novel is diffuse, attempting to follow too many characters and losing its focus in the varied episodes.

Two reviews will indicate how Ager's contemporaries reacted to his depiction of their absurdities.

His old friend J. J. Skørdalsvold wrote that "it is taken right out of life when these ordinary persons struggle so hard to Americanize themselves that they become zeroes, or if they have better luck, make monkeys out of themselves. The description of these people seems to me to be art that one cannot mistake." In contrast to Peer Gynt's rejection of the melting ladle, "Waldemar Ager's melting pot candidates long for and rush to vanish in the pot." "We owe Ager great thanks for making us remember what fools we often are in this very important respect: our position and our contribution to the great American republic." "There are many of us who in reality are not on our way to the melting pot. So we do not belong in this book. We feel ourselves fully the equals of other citizens of this country. We need to get some of our pettiness rubbed off; but we Norwegians must also bring with us a heritage from old Norway."[5]

The other review appeared anonymously in a Seattle newspaper: "This is the great book of the year, and it will win a place among the very best of Norwegian book production in America." "Ager gets a chance to pass judgment on the Norwegian-American cotter spirit." "With a master's skill he swings the whip of satire and every other kind of whip that he has in hand over meanness and soul-sickness. No one has ever made such fun of veneration for all that is foreign [English] and contempt for native values." "The story is interesting and as entertainment in an idle hour the book is excellent, even aside from its significance as a source book for Norwegian-American psychology."[6]

A largely favorable review by editor Carl G. O. Hansen in his newspaper *Minneapolis Tidende* drew an interesting reply from Ager. To Hansen's expressed wish that Ager had treated his characters more evenhandedly, Ager replied that this objection had been raised to his earlier books as well. "This is because my books are not constructed that way. In a romance one could set up these opposing elements effectively, as a conflict between persons. In a book of the type of *Smeltepotten*, the effect would be that of a blossoming cherry tree in a winter scene. It would, at least under my pencil, destroy the 'atmosphere,' to use a learned expression. As you noticed, I have got along with a spokesman in the figure of the plumber. But even he should have been omitted, if I had allowed literary considerations to govern me." But he admits that the ending is weak: "I wrote the last part as the book was being printed in the newspaper. When the foreman of our printshop died last year in March, all the make-up, advertising, and the like fell on me, so that I have been working night and day ever since. I had to *make* a conclusion to get rid of the book."[7]

The reply is interesting because it clearly reveals that Ager understood that his strength lay in his polemic talent. The fact that he does not write what he calls "romances" (for which he misuses the Norwegian word *roman*) simply means that he could or would not construct a novel that saw "life and saw it

95

whole." To write he had to love or hate, as he had written earlier to Buslett. His further plea that he had to tack on an ending "to get rid of the book" and that he finished it while it was being printed merely reflects his mode of work. He wrote much and he wrote fast, with little or no time to reflect on a book or to rewrite it. He speaks early of his ready memory: he could simply sit down and write a story, an editorial, a news article, and a dozen letters, all in one sitting, and feed them to the press.

His point of view was that his work mattered because he had a mission that literature would help to realize. He was only too aware of the impulse to assimilation that not only possessed young Norwegian Americans, especially in the second generation, but was also actively and persuasively being promoted by Americans from the presidency on down. The period of World War I had traumatic social effects. It was a period of great social changes in American life: a new economy of cheap manufactured goods, of automobiles and railroads, of opulence that was available to the fortunate. All this involved an attitude that could only be destructive of the old domestic values that had prevailed both in Norway and in America. It was not just Norwegian values that were being lost.

But Ager had a special stake in the changes that were occurring. He wrote to Buslett: "We are living in strange times. 'God be merciful to us,' say you, as you well may. I see that foreign language newspapers are going to be forbidden to have an opinion about the war. . . . It is being or will be forbidden for parents to ask questions about why their boys are going to be sent thousands of miles away to be killed."[8]

He had just received his first inkling of the new campaign of hate that would soon break out.

11

From War to Peace: 1917–1921

IN SEPTEMBER of 1917 Ager received a letter from a distinguished Norwegian American, Magnus Swenson of Madison, Wisconsin, chemist and manufacturer. But it was not a fan letter or a missive calculated to make him happy. It was a letter questioning Ager's loyalty to the war effort, written by Swenson as chairman of the Wisconsin State Council of Defense. As a retiree the wealthy Swenson had built a home in the vicinity of the state capital and was playing a role as a leading citizen. To Ager he wrote: "I can hardly believe it is true that you and your paper are so unpatriotic as to assume a critical and unfriendly attitude to our government in the present crisis, but I have received so many complaints with reference to the attitudes of your paper that I cannot but take notice and write you to find out the truth."[1]

Such inquiries were not to be taken lightly in those parlous days, and Ager replied with dignity, saying among other things that "our newspaper has advocated anti-war sentiments since it was started more than thirty years ago. . . . Consequently we have taken the stand that this war is a misfortune. . . . We have also held that it is everyone's duty to lighten this misfortune . . . and to stand by and support to the utmost the war measures taken by the government." Ager mentions some who have attacked his newspaper publicly and suggests that these people have their reasons for doing so. He has supported the draft law and the Liberty Loan. "But we do not rejoice over the war and are neither proud nor glad that we were mixed into it – we even think that it might have been avoided. We are and have been opposed to mixing into foreign alliances or tying up with 'foreign princes, potentates, states or sovereignties,' which some of us under oath consented to abjure and renounce when we became citizens."[2]

Swenson was a major stockholder in the Norwegian America Line and would be president of the Norwegian-American Historical Association from 1930 to 1933.[3] He surely did not write his letter out of ill will to Ager, and as far as is known, Ager heard from him no more.

Whatever distress America's entry into the war may have caused Ager, as one can find by studying his editorials during these years, his immediate problems did not last long. An armistice was declared in 1918, and America entered into a prolonged period of postwar reevaluation.

Ager could take some comfort from the success of his agitation for a prohibition amendment. In 1917 the resolution for submission of an amendment to the states received the needed two-thirds vote in Congress, and on January 16, 1919, the Eighteenth Amendment was ratified. Norwegian support had contributed to the victory, if only as a small part of a national effort. The Prohibition Act of October 28, 1919, bore the name of a Norwegian-American congressman from Minnesota, Andrew Volstead; his name would shortly become a household word, bandied about by both friend and foe. By 1920 Ager gave *Reform* "a new hat," as he put it. The entwining serpent no longer seemed apt, and the symbols of home and church stand free in the sunshine.

With the slackening of attention to the temperance issue, Ager was free to devote himself more intently to literature. In 1918 a Minneapolis concern brought out a collection of fifteen stories selected from his previous production. This volume, *Udvalgte fortællinger* (Selected Stories), became the classic corpus of Ager's stories, and was illustrated with pen-and-ink drawings.[4] The stories came from *Fortællinger for Eyvind* ("Bror min," "Hvorfor? Fordi — ," "Præmiefrøet," "Den gamle Kone og det graa Sjal," "Tidlig Vaar og sen Høst"), *Hverdagsfolk* ("Løst fra alt," "En Teddy-bjørn," "Det slukkede Blik," "Naar Græker møder Græker," "Han saa liden og uanselig ud," "Et Stjerneskud," "Norskie"), and *Fortællinger og skisser* ("Johan Arndt og Mor hans," "To tomme Hænder," "Nu kommer jeg, Mor!").

After the war Ager published a series of articles in *Kvartalskrift* under the title "Den store Udjævning" (The Great Leveling).[5] Two of them were published in the 1977 volume of Ager's essays edited by Odd Lovoll. In the first, "The Great Leveling," he argued vigorously against assimilation by the leveling out of national cultures in America. He compared the sequence of events in America with that in Europe: the former has become uniform while the latter remains diverse. He contrasted the cultural wealth of European countries with the trend toward oneness in America. "Culturally, the leveling could be compared to the killing of the creativity of whole nations." "Italian music is born out of the Italian folk life, not out of correspondence courses in harmonics and composition." "It is as important for nations as it is for individuals to have a distinctive character. We may even take a step further and say that it is imperative to have a soul of one's own — for oneself first, but also for the sake of others." As he saw it, American culture is an outcropping of British impulses as adapted to America. He commented especially on American humor as a brand of "moral wit," reflecting a long tradition of English humor; the comic writers, mostly of English descent, succeeded in preserving their ancestral heritage. His conclusion was that "if we are to contribute anything, it must be on the basis of our Norwegian heritage. We do not say that it is greater, for that it is not, nor do we say that it is better. But we must say that it is ours, and we must make our cultural contribution on the basis of it."[6]

The other essay, "The Citizen and the State," is a frontal attack on current doctrines of "100-percent Americanism," exemplified by the North Dakota judge who declared that a defendant had failed "to build up an American soul within himself." Ager took as his point of departure the words of Jesus that one should "render to Caesar what is Caesar's and to God what is God's." He takes this to mean that one should not idolize the state: "You shall not permit a political rule to mold your soul." He outlines some of the historical examples of governments that have tried to mold souls and feels that this is contrary to American political principles. "It is only recently and under the special situation created by the World War that our government has begun to emerge as guardian of the people's thought and conscience." He calls this a kind of secular evangelism, requiring successively self-abasement, conversion, and sanctification. "The government should allow us to seek nourishment for our soul through our mother tongue, the instrument the Lord gave us."[7]

He had more than one occasion to comment on the same theme in reviewing the books that poured out from Norwegian-American writers after the war. He summed up a new book by Simon Johnson, *Fire fortællinger* (Four Stories), in 1918, as dealing with the question of whether Norwegian Americans "have done well in America." "As a North Dakota prairie dweller, Johnson has constantly at hand the evidence of material prosperity, but also of the spiritual poverty behind the prosperity." He identifies cultural achievement with those who have not done well materially, but stupidity and brutality with those who have. Ager praised Johnson's language conditionally: "He is a bit of an artist with language; at times one has the impression that the way a thing is said is more important than the thing itself," a point of view that Ager no doubt found foreign. He is grateful to Augsburg Publishing House for giving the book "a solid and handsome appearance and the opportunity for sales."[8]

Soon afterward he had occasion to review a new book by Jon Norstog, a biblical drama called *Josef*. He granted that Norstog had "a quite remarkable capacity for playing with images from the Old Testament." But he shook his head over the North Dakota *nynorsk* poet's tendency "to take paths of his own." In fact, Ager found Norstog's work difficult, though he was pleased that Norstog did not wish anyone to "erase his racial stamp."[9]

In March, 1919, he was again faced with a hostile writer, the Norwegian-born pastor Andreas Bersagel, who wrote an article on "Norskdom i Amerika" (Norwegianness in America), which Ager reprinted. Ager replied to it by putting his finger on a statement by the pastor to the effect that "language is a substitute for thought." He made this his theme, noting that this was no doubt true of the pastor, for "the language is there, but not the thought." Bersagel had maintained that there are "among us a group of poets who have conceived of a little Norway in America, only more isolated, unadulterated, and naive, a Norway with a nimbus of romantic memories." He then went on to name some of these writers, among them Ager, who indignantly replied that the struggle for the Norwegian language in America was in the best interests of Americans. "Norwegianness here is American and its purpose is not just to give a sunny side to a life among strangers that is strenuous and often sad, important as that is, but also to contribute the best we can toward building this country."[10]

In those years of rampant anglomania there were plenty of occasions for Ager's polemics. An article in the Eau Claire *Leader* by one P. J. Slettedahl called for a movement by Americans against speakers of foreign languages: one should walk up to them and cry "Shame! Shame! Speak English!" In a long and reasoned reply Ager asked just who this was directed against: obviously not the college-bred American, but the common laborer, farmer, or craftsman. He concluded that Slettedahl did not think like an American, but like a Prussian: "Perhaps we need a 'Shame! Shame! Think American' movement . . . with more stress upon an American way of thinking than the English way of speaking." His article was followed by a burlesque written by O. E. Rølvaag, in which he addressed Mr. Slettedahl as "Mr. Levelvalley," translating his name, and signed himself "Aulay Edward Rolfsbay."[11] The letters provoked a southerner from Virginia who called the Norwegians "Lapps" to write a tirade against both the North and all non-English immigrants: "To admit you Lapps, Micks, and Huns was the greatest mistake this country ever made. There is no longer room here for any of you, nor for Lutherans or Popists. Get a move on, Judge Lynch is still on deck. This country was English, has remained so in spirit, and God speed the day when she will 'queen' it again."[12]

Relief was on the way. On March 23, 1919, Ager's fiftieth birthday, he was given a surprise party in honor of the day, organized jointly by two committees, one from Minneapolis and one from Eau Claire. Old friends lauded him for his work, but they had also gathered a substantial gift of $1,000, which proved to be sufficient to buy him a cottage on Lake Chetek, some forty miles north of Eau Claire, in Rusk county, his favorite retreat from this time on. The Agers and all their nine children were guests of honor; in his response, according to the Eau Claire *Leader*, Ager modestly "denied the good things that had been said about him. He had, he thought, done the best he could, but what he

Cabin on Lake Chetek, bought by Ager in 1925. Named "Huldrestua" after "Hulder," the Norwegian folklore siren.

had done did not merit the honor and attention accorded him."[13] However, his modesty did not prevent him from enjoying the tributes of two hundred guests. In the words of one speaker, "If you were to ask how much Ager was worth in money, the answer would be 'nothing!' " But "if you asked what he had done for his fellow citizens, the answer would be 'a great deal.' "[14] The *Leader* ran a photograph of Ager at his desk in the *Reform* office, and such good friends as Julius Baumann and Jon Norstog wrote verses in his honor.[15] The *Leader* even made a point of the fact that the honoring guests included several of Eau Claire's saloonkeepers![16]

On his next birthday Ager was differently occupied: he spent most of the day in court defending himself against the only lawsuit known to have been directed at him. The suit was initiated by his Norwegian-American colleague Lars Siljan, the editor of *Normanden* in Grand Forks, North Dakota, because Ager had printed an article by a subscriber accusing *Normanden* of being a "kept paper" of the opponents of the Nonpartisan League in that state. The plaintiff sued the Fremad Publishing Company for $100,000 in damages. In a letter to his sister Camilla, Ager wrote that "it is no fun to sit for hours in a witness chair and especially to sit reading Norwegian articles in English." "But things went even worse for our opponent, who was handled in a way that would have taken my life, I think, for it was proved that all the farmer's charges were true." The jury was on Ager's side and voted in his favor, but

101

Ager fishing on Lake Chetek with son Trygve

the judge, who was "an old, reactionary fellow," awarded damages of $1.00 to the plaintiff, so that Ager could not force the other newspaper to pay the costs of litigation.[17]

In spite of opposition and controversy, the postwar years were in general a period of intense literary activity among the immigrants. It was as if the writers of Ager's and later generations were trying to repair the damage of the war.

One writer, Sigurd Folkestad, had been a pastor in America and had returned to Norway. Ager reviewed a book of poems by him, entitled *Fra udflytterkampen* (From the Emigrant's Struggle, 1919). He comments on the delicate expression the author gives to his love of home. Two very different sentiments are combined in his writing, the religious and the ethical. The prophets of Israel and the Church in their wake agreed in joining religion to a feeling for race and nationality. Lutheranism had a particularly national basis. Ager develops the theme: the God that an emigrant needs is his father's and mother's God.[18]

Another volume he reviewed was by the editor of *Decorah-Posten*, Johannes B. Wist, using the pseudonym "Arnljot." The book, *Nykommer-billeder* (Newcomer's Pictures, 1920), is the story of Jonas Olsen, just arrived from Norway. It is a lively, humorous tale of a Norwegian who quickly makes good in an urban environment. Ager enjoyed the book and pointed out that under its humorous guise it was a serious work, satirizing the too-adaptable newcomer. "The language is amusing — sadly ridiculous, that is. One shouldn't really laugh at it; but one laughs anyway with a kind of self-reproach, for one should rather weep at seeing two maltreated languages wed in the chains of Hymen. . . . But what other language would do? The language is exactly like the life they live."[19]

He is less happy reviewing a book by his old friend O. A. Buslett titled *Benedictus og Jacobus* (1920). It tells of the conflict between Benedictus, a dreamer, and Jacobus, a selfish businessman. "It is obvious that the author has a personal account to settle with Jacobus and his adherents. The story kicks over the traces like an unruly horse and is now on this and now on that side of the road; yet when one has read it, one understands the author's purpose. . . . It is in many ways a significant book."[20]

Ager is less reserved in treating a new book by Rølvaag, *To tullinger* (Two Fools, 1920). "This is an important book. . . . It is a comedy that is not amusing, a tragedy with a conclusion that inspires loathing, hardly sympathy." He sees the author's purpose as that of portraying Norwegian Americans "who have been torn loose from an ancient culture and cannot entirely acquire a new one, except for a solid point of gravity in gold." He finds that Rølvaag has produced a book that is interesting and entertaining and makes a strong and enduring impression. "This he has achieved in a greater degree than anyone over here whom we can recall at the moment; and that is saying a great deal."[21]

Before long he had a new book by Rølvaag to review, *Længselens baat* (Boat of Longing, 1921). This is the story of a newcomer from northern Norway whose fate brings him to Minneapolis. Ager declared that "Rølvaag was close to producing a masterpiece." "We can't understand why he couldn't have let these creatures of the sea stay where they were. . . . Just as we have become fond of these people . . . we are plopped down outside a grocery store on the corner of Cedar Avenue and Fourth Street in Minneapolis." " . . . if anyone should have been sent back 'where they came from,' it's the author." But he concedes that Rølvaag's new book will be read with greater interest than any other of the year's Norwegian-American books.[22]

One author in Norway of whom Ager disapproved but whom he could not overlook was Knut Hamsun. His 1917 *Markens grøde* (Growth of the Soil) led to his winning the Nobel prize for literature in 1920. To an admirer of Hamsun Ager admitted that "it is brilliant storytelling art. . . . His descriptions of nature are unexcelled; but this does not change the fact that some of his books are anything but commendable."[23] He asserted that Hamsun describes his characters as "creatures of nature," without religion or morality. Real pioneers would hardly find any point of contact with Hamsun's Isak, but "the upper intelligentsia, which can afford to buy a novel for six dollars, will think that the type is absolutely right. It is about the same impression of Scandinavian and other pioneers that floats about in the brains of high-born, aristocratic Americans."[24]

By 1921 Ager had collected a new group of ten stories, some of them written as far back as 1917. The title was *Ny samling: Fortællinger og skisser* (New Collection: Stories and Sketches). The book was dedicated to the fifth of his children, daughter Solveig Camilla, born in 1909: "Of all the miscellany that her dad had written, he just barely managed to scrape together these pages for his little girl." Nevertheless, this collection contains some of Ager's best stories, written in his full maturity.

"Hvorledes Ægteparret fik Nattero" (How the Couple got their Night's Sleep) tells of a married couple, whom Ager depicts as talking Trønder dialect, who hated children. Halvor and his wife agree that little children should be done away with, particularly the youngsters who annoy them by making noise around their house. "They did not, like so many other farm folk, have a rascal of a son to keep in school or start in business once a year or any grown daughters to throw away a lot of money on, only to have them go and get married to a German or a Catholic." They are well off and have rented their farm out so that they can move to town and enjoy themselves. But in fact they are not happy, for they are bored: "The Norwegian wives always talked about their children and the American wives about their operations, so Mrs. Tromvold, who had had neither, counted for nothing." But the local pastor has the opposite trouble: he keeps taking home children to his overburdened wife, and when he comes with the child of a girl who has died, she lays down the law. He cannot place it, until he gets to the Tromvolds' house; he tries in desperation to get them to take it overnight. They agree, and once they see the infant, they fall in love with it, and shamefacedly admit to wanting to keep it.

"En Fortælling om tre Trold" (A Story about Three Trolls) is the story of Lester Stubbevik, farmer and real estate man, who has lodged for years at the house of Gertie Larson, whom he has known since confirmation. Everyone tells him he ought to marry her, but he has reached the age of thirty without proposing. One day he is confronted by a child from the nearby children's home, who jumps out at him. "Her hair was mussed and she held a hair ribbon in her hand, her dark eyes flashed angrily, and tears hung like pearls from her long eyelashes—she was furious and perturbed. 'Say, you's my dad, ain't you?' she hissed at him." The other children, who have obviously teased her, are watching and Lester is so taken by surprise that he answers, "Course I am; who says I ain't?" He sees the girl again and takes her home with him at Christmas; the result is that she also adopts Gertie as her mother, Lester and Gertie are married, and the "three trolls" become one happy family.

"Da Graagaasen trak mod Syd" (When the Grey Goose Trekked to the South) is an animal fable with clear reference to the war just ended. The queen goose has lost her mate to hunters, and she is unable to understand why. But on her way to a summer haven by the Caspian Sea, she witnesses the effects of the war and in fact makes her way all along the allies' front lines. She witnesses the carnage and is equally unable to understand what it is all about. "Its head was small and it had room only for the facts in a certain order." "It tried to ask the swallows, but they only winked at each other and said, as was true, that a goose could ask more than ten wise swallows could answer."

"John McEstees Vuggesang" (John McEstee's Lullaby) tells of Johan Maakestad's life. From being a poor immigrant boy he becomes an American saloonkeeper, then a well-to-do real estate agent in northern Wisconsin. He is now John McEstee, a member of the board of directors of the local symphony orchestra. He has arranged a concert which includes a string quartet from Minneapolis, with a famous cellist named Carlo Fischer. John has two daughters among the sopranos and a son in the orchestra and "a silk-clad better half in the first row." But when the cellist is urged to play a solo at the end of the concert, he chooses a Norwegian lullaby, which takes John back to his childhood in Norway. He forgets the present and remembers his sister and the doll she sang this lullaby to; he decides to go back to visit Norway and take his family with him.

"Ungdom" (Youth) is an ironic story about two bridges over a town's river: an old and a new. The new bridge is fancy and well-lighted; the old one is closed to traffic but handy for poor people who live in the district. Young people also like it for its seclusion; a couple of lovers make it their rendezvous and they jokingly throw banana peels at each other. A washerwoman goes to town to buy food for supper; she falls and injures her leg, all because of the banana peels left by the thoughtless young people.

"Et Minde fra Forbudskampen" (A Reminiscence from the Struggle for Prohibition) concerns John Bent, who was thought to be of very limited intelligence but was a faithful helper to every temperance speaker who came to the community. One can no doubt perceive an experience of Ager's behind this episode. John had a background of excessive drinking before he quit for religious reasons. Aging, he writes at length to tell the temperance society that he has found two young men to take his place. He dies before he can receive the secretary's letter of thanks; the next speaker is delighted to find that the young men are not only devoted to the cause but are proud to help and will actually bring out the crowd.

"Det fandtes ikke Ondt i ham" (There was no Evil in Him) is the amusing tale of a farm girl who marries a boy with money because he is sickly and probably won't live very long. However, he lives on and on, and her real lover gives up and marries someone else. She and her husband emigrate to America and get a farm, and he still goes on living, until he even outlives her. The constant refrain at every turn is that "there was no evil in him." But the moral is clear: Don't marry anyone in the hope that he will die.

"Hans Hustru" (His Wife) tells another tale of work with a Good Templar lodge. An ex-sailor joins the lodge because as a former drinker he still needs their support; he originally met his wife there, but she has lost interest and now suspects that he goes there because he is looking for other women. In the end her influence drives him out of the lodge, and some years later the author finds him in Chicago, a drunken wreck.

"En Kveldstund paa 'Driven' " (An Evening on the 'Drive') is an amusing rehash of Paul Bunyan stories, as told by one who is working as a cook's helper on the lumber "drive" in northern Wisconsin.

"Ellefson og Ingvold" is about two avid fishermen, Ellefson, who is a minister, and Ingvold, who was his classmate at Augsburg Seminary in Minneapolis. They live in a small town in Wisconsin, near a lake that is full of fish. They both smoke, but the pastor's wife opposes smoking. One day they decide to throw away their smoking gear; the result is that both of them are unhappy, until they finally get together again and restore harmony over a good pipe.

While two of the stories deal with alcohol and temperance, they are not so

106

much propaganda as they are history. The Paul Bunyan story is not original. The rest are well constructed and bring out a humorous point, aside from the story of the goose: this was clearly inspired by the horrors of the World War and reflects Ager's pacifist stance.

Ager's old friend Skørdalsvold called the book "characteristically Ager-ian all through." He criticized the dialect, however, being a Trønder himself: if Ager must use dialect, he should stick to Fredrikstad. He commented on the miracle by which Ager could tear off his little stories in the midst of an active career as factotum on the newspaper, with friends to meet and correspond with in great number. "When he starts off to make a picture for us, he reaches down into the storehouse of his memory and uses whatever fits. This is what makes his descriptions so striking and unfailingly faithful to nature. . . . His imagination is so bold that sometimes he only needs to let it go, and before you realize it, you don't know if you have feet under you or not. As a sample of his art I would mention 'When the Grey Goose Treks to the South'—a glorious poem that does not look like a poem."[26] J. B. Wist, in *Decorah-Posten*, commented on Ager's good taste and his literary judgment. "He possesses that altogether too rare skill among literary persons of producing a particular effect on the reader with the fewest possible words and apparently simple means. . . . It is as close to fine writing as anything I have read for a long time." He characterized Ager as a master of the sketch, and he mentioned three or four of the stories as outstanding: " 'The couple who got their night's sleep,' 'The story of the three trolls,' 'John McEstee's Lullaby,' and the story about the goose—world problems in a nutshell."[27]

12

Looking Back on the War: 1922–1923

IN 1922 AGER received a tribute from Sigurd Folkestad, writing from Norway. "My first collection of poetry was printed by Fremad Publishing Company. In Waldemar Ager's literary country store there was a meeting place for the 'spirits,' where they could freely strike out at the bad part of the world, beat its rugs so the dust flew, and get time to light their pipes while Ager let his witticisms crackle. . . . Ager is like the cat with seven lives; you can't kill him off." "I will always remember Ager's town . . . where great, titanic, and beautiful thoughts were born and brought to fruition without being appreciated for as much as a gold filling in one of Ager's teeth."[1]

In the same year Ager edited a volume for the society of emigrants from the province of Smaalenene (now Østfold), where he was born. It was one of the *bygdelag* organizations that flourished in the 20s. Ager noted that no settlement in America was dominated by people from Smaalenene, which he called "Norway's most cosmopolitan area."[2] The society had been organized in 1915; in 1922 Ager inserted a notice in *Reform* calling for an annual meeting in Minneapolis.[3] Another Norwegian-minded organization, For Fædrearven (For the Ancestral Heritage), was created at a meeting in Eau Claire on October 19, 1919, in which Ager took part, but the chief spirit of the organization was Rølvaag.[4]

The year 1922 was evidently a banner year for Norwegian-American books. Ager reviewed a new volume by "Arnljot" (Wist) in the Jonas Olsen saga, *Jonasville*. This is the story of the battle between Jonas and the American boss Elihu Ward over the placing of the county seat. Ager compared it to a battle of Vikings, without a trace of Christianity. "We miss the milieu, the descriptions of nature, at least enough to give the picture colors instead of just contours." "While the book is not sympathetic, it seems to have no other purpose than to describe life as it is."[5] Wist also had another book, *Reisen til Rochester* (The Journey to Rochester), the hilarious tale of Bonifacius Bonifaciussen, who drives a Ford from Decorah, Iowa, to Rochester, Minnesota. "This wonderful trip . . . is extremely amusing reading. . . . Its language is in Arnljot's well-known style, which is such that even one who has not learned Norwegian can read it."[6] Ager is obviously being facetious here. "Arnljot's" style is marked by the use of many American words Norwegianized in typical immigrant fashion. Before the end of 1923 he would sadly have to chronicle Wist's death.[7] He also reviewed two collections of poems by pastors, Wilhelm Pettersen's *Naar juleklokkerne ringer* (When the Christmas Bells Ring) and D. G. Ristad's *Fra det nye Normandie* (From the New Normandy), both of them appreciatively. "Many of these poems are suitable for reading aloud."

Then there was a new novel by Simon Johnson, *Falliten paa Braastad* (Bankruptcy at Braastad). Ager declared that the most interesting personality in the book was the author: "He speaks through half a dozen different persons." "It is Simon who thirsts for beauty and purity amid the monotony and uniformity of the prairie." One can criticize the stilted language of his characters' dialogues, "but the book gives a strong impression," though it is far from his best. "In the end Johnson is the one we become fond of: he has delivered his sermon against our godless and beauty-bereft materialism, and that is a sermon we all can benefit from."[8]

Ager also reviewed a volume of essays by O. E. Rølvaag in 1922 titled *Omkring fædrearven* (About the Ancestral Heritage), a collection of newspaper articles written for the organization For Fædrearven. Ager naturally sympathized deeply with Rølvaag's thesis: "Rølvaag has faith in his heritage—we could almost call it a religious faith." He emphasized its value for America: "It is us and our greater or lesser usefulness in our own country that is at stake. Here is where our heritage is to be translated into character, ambition, and genius."[9]

In 1922 a writer named Bjarne Blehr launched a blanket attack on Norwegian-American writers in a Duluth newspaper. He wrote what Ager called a "jeremiad" about these authors as being unwilling to starve for their art. This rather absurd attack was taken jovially by Ager: "There is no doubt that a man like Professor Rølvaag could well have starved a little more. It is almost a scandal how well he looks." After mentioning a few others whose girth was noticeable, he points out that there are exceptions: "As for Baumann, Rønning, Dorthea Dahl, Simon Johnson, and one more whose name we can not mention for modesty's sake, they are all so skinny that it is a joy, and anyone can see with half an eye that they take their authorship seriously." "As for the Norwegian authors in Norway, the ones who starve cannot compare with those who thirst."[10]

109

Blehr went on to attack the Norwegian-American authors as picturing the immigrants too darkly. "If their books represent our people in America, there are not two decent persons among us."[11] Ager replied that "fully honorable and normal persons" are difficult to write about. "It is not possible to create tension in a story unless you surround them with scoundrels, and that is still worse." He then took up the characters Blehr had attacked and showed for each one how and why Blehr was mistaken. As for Ager's works, Blehr found that in his writings "the world has become a vale of tears with foul weather and very few glimpses of the sun." On the contrary, Ager pointed out that he had often been described as a humorist, the "funny man" of the temperance movement. He went through the critic's quotations to show that Blehr had picked passages out of context. "Of all that has been written, Bjarne Blehr's article easily takes the prize as the most idiotic."[12]

During the year 1923 Ager was constantly on the road and from time to time reported on his travels in *Reform*. In February he visited Blair and Whitehall in Wisconsin, where he spoke in the local churches.[13] In March he visited Minneapolis to participate in a Good Templar festival; on the way he visited old friends.[14] A visit to Duluth involved a speech on Colonel Heg and an appeal on behalf of the monument in his honor. Trips to Minneapolis and Chicago for the same purpose followed. At the latter the amount of $1,000 was secured and Ager thought that this would be adequate to assure that the statue would be erected.[15] Ager reminisced amusingly about his early years in Chicago, describing the streets where Norwegians used to live; now they were mostly occupied by Italians and Poles. Much was changed, but he found some landmarks untouched, for example the newspaper *Skandinaven*, which he visited. He remembered the editor John Benson from a collection of poems called *Ved gry og kveld* (At Dawn and Eve, 1889), which he enjoyed because they were easy to remember.[16]

In April Ager gave a talk in Norwegian to the assembled students of St. Olaf College, where he was met by Rølvaag and others. "My first impression of Rølvaag was quaint. It was as if someone had given him a great blow on the head with a steam hammer to crush him, but had only succeeded in making him a little shorter and more concentrated." "He has succeeded in awakening an interest in Norwegian language and the Norwegian heritage to an extent that will please many of their parents."[17] In May Rølvaag came to Eau Claire to give a speech and he and Ager spent some time fishing; Ager gives an amusing account of the occasion, with emphasis on the fisherman's exaggerations. Also in May Ager attended a temperance picnic in Chetek, Wisconsin.[18] In June he attended a convention of For Fædrearven in Northfield, Wisconsin, and reported Rølvaag's speech there on the Norwegians as bearers of the democratic idea down through the ages.[19]

110

In September Ager was in Northwood, Iowa, for a Sons of Norway picnic. There he reported on a speech by Congressman Gilbert Haugen, who spoke out about the burden laid on the American people by armaments and preparations for war. Immediately afterwards he was due in Iola, Wisconsin, another Norwegian center, which Ager recognized as the domain of Thor Helgeson and O. A. Buslett.[20] In November Ager was invited to North Dakota, where he stopped in Grand Forks on the way to Minot. There he called on Simon Johnson, who was editing *Normanden*. In Minot he got his first chance to see his fellow author H. A. Foss, with whom he had had various battles in the past. "Then he was radical; now he is conservative." But whatever he was, Ager believed he was primarily "a man of heart and feeling." "His heart usually runs away with his judgment, and he has suffered for it." However, Ager found he had a large and handsome home—"much too large and nice for one who has devoted himself to Norwegian-American literature. It looks almost indecent."[21]

In 1923 Ager had his final say about the war in a book that represents a new note in his production: *Det vældige navn* (The Mighty Name).[22] He calls it "a dream picture from the World War." Dedicated to his son Magne, his sixth child, born in 1910, he presents it as a narrative about a Russian Jew named Samuel P. Morrison, who in 1916 has through his financial dealings somehow attained power to control the actions of the warring nations. Endowed with a fantastic brain and wide knowledge, but totally unaffected by patriotism, religion, or sentimentality of any kind, he simply has no heart. Gold is his God, and the fates of individuals do not affect him. Morrison has a conference with a representative of the Russian czar, who pleads with him for a loan to sustain the Russian army. Morrison will give him the loan only on condition that Russia mount a large-scale offensive, which the Russian nobleman admits is impossible.

Morrison happily sets off into the English countryside for a spin in his chauffeured car. But they encounter fog and on the way they run over some gray figures. Morrison's conscience is undisturbed. The car has to be repaired and they stop near a store that is operated by an old Jew, with whom Morrison converses. The old Jew tells Morrison that Russia is doomed because the Russians have shed Jewish blood. The Jews will have their revenge. When Morrison asks him how this is to be, the old Jew tells him that it will be due to the Name, the name of the Almighty, the one with the three consonants to which no one knows the vowels: J-H-V. This name is the greatest power in the universe. Anyone who possesses it has the world in his hands.

Morrison is intrigued by the problem of how to find the name. He puzzles over the riddle until he suddenly finds that his newspaper has caught fire: it burns to ashes, but leaves a sign in his hand. He has stumbled upon the mighty

111

name and his hand has acquired magic power. In raving terror he runs into the street. He is amazed at the power his hand has given him, for he feels that nothing can harm him, and that he is as if alone in the world, which has ceased to have any meaning for him. He sees a blind beggar in the street and for the first time he feels compassion for another being. He gives the beggar some money and as he touches him with his hand, the beggar is suddenly able to see again. Then he meets a crippled soldier who had been shell-shocked in the first battle at Ypres. Morrison takes him by the arm, for the first time in his life, only to find that the man is immediately cured.

Morrison proceeds across the Channel to Paris and on to the battlefields where the great war is raging. He passes the smoking ruins, the ashes that had been homes, and the piles of corpses that mark the front. He finds a machine gun that has been left in the field; when he touches it, the gun is transformed into a plow. He seems to fill up space, with his feet on the earth and his forehead among the stars.

Then he seems to stumble on something; it proves to be a doll made of rags, trampled and made shapeless by the warring armies. He picks it up and clasps it to his bosom, knowing that some child has fondled it, and suddenly he feels that it is alive, "born of the same power that casts worlds into the abyss." He recalls stories from the history of Israel, where the Lord appeared in storm, fire, or earthquake. A question he can no longer ignore fills him: what is he doing here?

In trying to solve this riddle he sees as in a vision the destruction that the war has wrought: "Wasn't many a heaven on earth transformed into hell on earth?" He sees a connection between the power that grapples with solar systems and the rags that breathe in the dirt. "Far out [in the universe] his own soul is fastened to this little rag's breath as if by an endlessly fine, fragile thread that can break." He decides to go in search of the child who lost the doll. He sets out to find her and has many strange adventures along the way. People laugh at his search as an idle dream, but he persists. "He sees starving children and desperate women; hate and hopelessness wander together, suffering and licentiousness embrace and will in due course bring forth revolution and anarchism." "Mighty men have always struggled for power; one ruler after another has tried to unite the whole world's power and get all the threads in his hand." The doll grows into a woman who is at the same time his beloved and his mother and his sister. The phantasmagoria goes on until Morrison loses his arm in a sudden smash, which proves to be when his car is struck by a bus. The chauffeur has been gone for only twenty minutes.

Morrison's dream is a strange and somewhat incoherent account by Ager of the horrors of war and the financier's repentance of his hardhearted view of the world. It is a plea for the simple values of the child and the power of love. Unconnected with Ager's previous concerns about temperance or the Norwegian language, it reflects his accumulated abhorrence at the events of the war. It almost gives the effect of having been written or composed during the war, perhaps in the year 1916 which he gives as the time of Morrison's dream. One wonders what his Norwegian-American readers made of it. A present-day reader is all too aware of the element of anti-Semitism, which is only partly moderated by the figure of the old Jew who advises Morrison. The talk about Jewish revenge to be visited on the world for sins against their race seems ironic in relation to what has happened since, but can be understood in terms of 1923, when the book was published.

Ager got more discriminating reviewers for this book than for most of his others. His old friend and reviewer J. J. Skørdalsvold is understandably confused by the book. He has to read and reread it to get the picture: that it is a dream from beginning to end. "I knew as well as anyone that Ager was a cunning fellow, and he would not have produced so elaborate a work without a great idea." He agrees with Ager that "more than any other cause, it is crucial for the world that war be quite abolished." In the end he concludes that the book is an "unalloyed masterpiece."[23] Poet O. A. Buslett, writing in *Skandinaven*, also finds the book strange, but only because Ager "steps forth as a creative author." Buslett mistakenly regards his other stories as mere "reflections of life" and clearly not as literature or poetry. He calls attention to a poem by Ager that had appeared in *Kvartalskrift* in 1916, the year *Det vældige navn* takes place, with much the same idea. After summarizing the story, Buslett expresses his pleasure at Ager's use of symbols, in this case the doll as a symbol of the lost child in Morrison. He concludes by declaring that this is Ager's best book; one feels that Buslett senses a kinship to his own writings of a philosophical and idealistic tenor.[24]

Olav Lie, editor of the church organ *Lutheraneren*, also gave the book an appreciative review. He advises the reader to peruse it as he would Bunyan's *Pilgrim's Progress*, as an allegory. He speaks well of Ager's short stories, "which are unexcelled in our literature; he is our storyteller as Aanrud is Norway's." But here he shows even greater mastery: "In no writing known to me has the frightening horror of war been better revealed in a few strokes of the pen. The book should be translated and published by a major firm. Only by becoming generally known will the book help 'to make the world safe for humanity.' "[25] Rølvaag is subtler and even more positive in his judgment. He recognizes that Ager is a master of the short story and the sketch. Here he has concentrated what could have been a multi-volume work into the form of a long sketch. Ager wishes to preach, and his sermon has as its topic "Life is sacred." It is sacred because it has come into being at the word of the Almighty, which was in the beginning. "When one considers how horribly the world has

Ager with Norwegian decoration, Order of St. Olaf

sinned against life in these years, it will be good for anyone to read this book."[26]

The most amusing review is signed "Jens K. Hansen," but sounds suspiciously like O. E. Rølvaag. While it is called "Et Par Ord om en Bog" (A Couple of Words about a Book), it is much longer than a couple of words. He discusses the publisher Edward Bok's prize of $100,000 offered for the best and most practical plan to ensure lasting peace. He takes it that Ager's book was intended to compete for the prize, but its solution to the burning problem was much too simple. It consists only in the idea that men should start living according to the commandment that says "Thou shalt not kill." The entire message of the book can be reduced to a doctrine of love: "Thou shalt love thy neighbor as thyself." The reviewer feels that if all Norwegians understood this, they would buy and read Ager's book by the thousands.[27]

The postwar years were full of literary activity among Norwegians in America, but Ager was only too aware of what was happening to the language in everyday life. He wrote despondently to Buslett as early as 1921: "It really burns me up when I see how they are nicely and quietly choking the Norwegian language and the Norwegian religious school and the Norwegian services.

114

Right here in our town I can see an enormous change. No one speaks against Norwegian or writes against it; it is just being gently and quietly undermined. The old Norwegians don't see it and they plod on, carrying nine-tenths of the burden of the society that is being hollowed out under them. There will be a reversal, but it will come too late."[28]

His pessimistic view was confirmed in 1922 by a woman who signed herself "En gammel Lærerinde" (An old teacher). She had spent a lifetime teaching in the Norwegian religious schools, usually held during the summer vacations. She had noted a marked change in the attitude of the children since the war. "A few years ago the children in the country often spoke Norwegian to each other when they were out on the playgrounds. But now since the war there is a noticeable change among the children—and I may add—among the parents, too. To show that they are 100-percent Americans they are speaking more and more English in the homes. . . . When they come to the Norwegian schools, one soon notices that English is the language of their hearts and that they are even proud not to know Norwegian."[29]

The Americanist propaganda had had its effect, along with the ever-increasing rural exodus. Rural isolation was disappearing. Ager's hope for a reversal did not seem realistic.

Perhaps it was a feeling that his work was done that led to a growing recognition of the value of that work. In October, 1923, King Haakon of Norway conferred on Ager a knighthood of the Order of St. Olaf, in recognition of his long and faithful service on behalf of Norwegian interests in the United States.

13

Sons of the Old Country: 1924–1929

WITH THE COMING of national prohibition it would seem that *Reform* had no further function. But, as Ager noted in an editorial, "That the newspaper has been able to continue is due to the fact that it added other causes to its program." "It is not easy to be small in our age: the small stores are swallowed up by the big ones." He appealed to the Norwegian Americans to support their press—"in their own interest."[1]

He was constantly on the road to promote his newspaper. Writing of a visit to Madison, Wisconsin, he gave a lively vignette of Julius E. Olson, the professor of Scandinavian languages in the University of Wisconsin. "He is akin to cyclones and whirlwinds—he absorbs people and flings them hither and yon as he wishes and does tricks with them and makes them weak-willed and tractable so he can manage them as he wishes." Olson, with R. N. Qualley of the Sons of Norway, was his guide in the Wisconsin capitol building, where he had occasion to admire the Norwegian granite used in its construction.[2] In a later speech he would use the composite materials of the Wisconsin capitol as a metaphor for the composition of the United States: Built of Norwegian granite, Italian, Greek, and German marble, and Egyptian porphyry, and furnished with Persian rugs, the capitol was "one of the most beautiful, strongest, and most American structures in the whole land."[3]

Later in the same year he attended an occasion in Minneapolis where he received a copy of Skørdalsvold's translation of his old novel *Christ before Pilate*. His thoughts were led back to the controversies that had been spun around his pastoral hero. He proudly noted that other writers had followed in his footsteps, making it possible really to speak of a Norwegian-American literature. He hoped that three or four hundred persons would spend some dollars buying

116

their books, since they "are a more enduring and more adequate monument over our lives and struggles than anything else we could invent."[4]

In 1924 also he had the sad duty of writing an obituary for O. A. Buslett, the pioneer in the field, where he had been "a lone warrior" for many years. "He was the strangest mixture of child, sage, and savage." He had an unshakeable faith in goodness, an "almost childlike innocence and helplessness in relation to all the complicated, entangled, ramified, ossified, or damnable things that are comprised in the term 'the world.'" Ager in his moving account praised him for having been a true Norwegian American "who believed in the possibilities of Norwegian-American literature when no one else did."[5]

To offset this loss to literature Ager could take comfort in the appearance of several new Norwegian-American books.

Simon Johnson published *Frihetens hjem* (Home of Freedom, 1925) and Ager called it an "event". This prairie tale portrays the second generation and their sense of disappointment, not so much over their financial problems as over the emptiness of their lives. The farm movement plays a role, and North Dakota politics, as well as the suspicion of the foreign-born aroused by the war. Ager's criticism was that the author "philosophizes too much; one constantly runs across the author's own opinions, which is not good art nowadays. The hero and heroine say such exquisitely beautiful things and choose their words as if they knew that Simon Johnson would reproduce them word for word and that he was a man with a discriminating taste." A book by Dorthea Dahl, *Byen paa berget* (The City on the Mountain, 1925), Ager acclaimed as a "real Norwegian-American novel . . . one of the most significant literary products that has come to light among us." "It gives a trustworthy picture of life among children on a Norwegian-American farm in the eighties and in a small town."[6]

Ager was less pleased with *Genier* (Geniuses, 1925) by Palma Pedersen. "It is much easier to review the author than the book." "She manages to give color to the worst improbabilities"; "she treats the language badly and uses a multitude of superfluous adjectives."[7] Nor was he happy about a *History of the Norwegian People in America* by O. M. Norlie. He criticized severely this essentially statistical compendium covering the gamut of Norwegian-American life, with great emphasis on the Church and endless enumerations, some of them inaccurate.[8]

Best of all was the contribution of his younger colleague, Ole Edvart Rølvaag of St. Olaf College. Although Ager may not have recognized it at first, Rølvaag was the man who would fulfill Ager's hopes for a breakthrough in Norwegian-American literature. The books that together would become *Giants in the Earth* appeared in 1923 and 1924 as *I de dage* (In Those Days) and

117

Riket grundlægges (The Founding of the Kingdom), published by Aschehoug Forlag in Oslo.

About the first volume Ager wrote: "It is without doubt Rølvaag's best and a pioneer novel that is in every respect a literary work of art." He commented that Rølvaag's "latest book is always his best." He particularly enjoyed the good humor of his pioneers as they plod across the South Dakota prairie looking for a place to settle. He commended the characterization and though he mentioned the lack of plot complications he still found it fascinating reading. He also noted that the humor was offset by Beret's mysterious dissatisfaction; she suffers from the feeling that there is nothing to conceal her or protect her out there on the prairie. This is a cloud that bodes ill. Ager here put his finger on the book's central theme, which the author would develop in the second half.[9]

He commended the sequel as being even better than *I de dage*; "The author lets himself go, is more self-assured, and has given us an image of an early Norwegian settlement as vigorous and lively as it can be, snatched right out of life." Only the ending displeased Ager; he was distressed, as most readers have been, by the idea of Per Hansa being left to die by a strawstack on the prairie. The conclusion "is not made to please or amuse the reader. But life did not always end well out there. Presumably that is what the author has wanted to emphasize." "The author presents a receipt for part of the price that has been paid for the 'kingdom' we are so proud of."[10]

He was also pleased with a novel by Johan Bojer, a well-known Norwegian author, about Norwegian emigrants, *Vor egen stamme* (Our Own Tribe, 1925), translated as *The Emigrants*. He compares this book with Rølvaag's *I de dage*. Rølvaag's book is literature on a Norwegian scale, "while Bojer has a sermon to deliver." The sermon directed at Norway maintains that young people are taught only about the past and do not learn to understand the present, so they become dissatisfied and emigrate. To the Norwegian Americans he says that the danger is to forget spiritual things in favor of the material. Even though the book was written by a Norwegian and was therefore not a Norwegian-American book, Ager welcomed it as an honest portrayal of the question of emigration.[11]

The burst of novels and historical publications in 1925 had a special explanation: this was the year when Norwegians commemorated the first shipload of Norwegian emigrants, the one that arrived in New York from Stavanger in 1825. There was a major celebration on the Minnesota Fairgrounds in St. Paul, with exhibits, speeches, and musical programs. All the leading Norwegian Americans were involved, and important representatives were invited from Norway. President Calvin Coolidge was the ace card in the celebration and a special series of stamps was issued by the United States Post Office.

Ager was represented by a prize essay, titled "Hvorfor feirer vi Hundred-

118

aarsfesten i 1925" (Why we celebrate the Centennial in 1925). One reason he mentions is its significance for Americans of Norwegian ancestry, to "make them feel more at home, more entitled to participate on an equal footing with the Anglo-Saxon immigrants." He contended that Norwegian-American children would not feel that the founders of America were their ancestors and would remain outside the tabernacle, in its outer court, unless the exploits of their own ancestors were made a part of American history. He emphasized that the story of the Norwegians was no different in kind from that of the first English settlers: a dangerous crossing, wild nature, physical obstacles, red Indians. It is important to make immigrant groups understand that they have participated in building this land. If they are to be a part of the American nation, it must be in terms of their own culture. "No people has been given more than one soul." "As they respect their parents, they will themselves be respected, and because they understand the struggles of their own families, they will also learn to understand those of others, and thereby gain the great mutual and common respect which all immigrated races owe to each other and which in the end is the only reliable foundation of the nation."[12]

Ager did not entirely escape criticism for his essay. A church organ called *Familiens Magasin* denied that the children of Norwegian immigrants felt themselves excluded from the "tabernacle". The writer's experience was that children read the history of America as their own and do not feel in any way excluded. Ager's reply to this was significant, but basically mystical. In religion, art, music, or natural beauty, he believed, the most important thing is personal engagement, the "tabernacle" that one carries within. It is the sense that this is mine and only mine. "It is the difference between father's and mother's old home and all other houses in the world."[13]

Rølvaag's speech on the same occasion was also printed in *Reform*. His emphasis was on the heritage; his analogies were more biological than social. He pointed to the various species of trees and plants, wild animals and tame, and insisted that none of them favored hybrids. He spelled out some of the traits that Norwegians have inherited: a yearning to leave home coupled with a love of home; individualistic independence coupled with respect for the law; love of literature as well as Christian values. He reminded his people of the split in Israel between the ten tribes which disappeared and the two which remained faithful and were given the task of rebuilding the temples of Zion. Norwegians in America, he said, have this choice.[14]

An important initiative was taken on the occasion of the Norwegian-American centennial. A group of leading cultural personalities gathered and founded a society that was called the Norwegian-American Historical Association. This proved to be of the highest importance for the continuation of a Norwegian tradition in America. Although Ager had been in the forefront in creating organizations to support Norwegian interests, he looked at this organization with some skepticism and accepted it only reluctantly. A major reason for his attitude was certainly its decision to publish in English. Its editorship was placed in the hands of Theodore C. Blegen, a brilliant young historian at the University of Minnesota and the Minnesota Historical Society. But Ager saw in the organization a nail in the coffin of the Norwegian language. "And so we get busy writing our history, which is the same as arranging our estate in advance." "It seems to us that we should be more concerned about making history than about writing it." "Our race is not old enough here, nor has it accomplished enough to make ourselves an interesting rarity in Uncle Sam's historical museum." *Decorah-Posten*, through its editor Kristian Prestgard, protested that writing history is hardly the last thing a people does; he cited the example of the writing of history in Norway and other European nations. Ager replied that he hoped his critic was right, but he was firmly convinced that "when the Norwegian language dies out among our people, the academic interest and the *bygdelag* and the newspapers and the societies will also die." Norwegian America was at a critical point: "The Norwegian language is beginning to disappear from homes where it has been maintained for generations, from churches, congregational schools, and societies. Preservation of the language is the sector where we now need to gather our best forces."[15]

It is not necessary to linger over Ager's controversy with Torkel Oftelie about the Norwegian language movement; Oftelie was a user and lover of *nynorsk*, while Ager now as always was a determined opponent of it. He compared it with American 100-percentism: "Among Norway's language reformers it is not a question of whether a word is good, only whether it is Norwegian." Ager's particular *bête noir* was the writer Jon Norstog, whom he found worth reviewing, but with exasperation.[16]

In addition to attending the centennial festivities in St. Paul, Ager spent some time "on the road" in 1925 and 1926. He wrote about spending weekends in Chetek now that the gifts given him at his fiftieth birthday celebration had enabled him to buy a cottage by the lake. A trip to the old settlements in Muskego and Koshkonong in Wisconsin convinced him that even there Norwegian was still understood.[17] A trip to Coon Valley and Westby included a visit with Dr. Adolph Gunderson of LaCrosse, from whom Ager borrowed a book by Sigrid Undset which comforted him on a tiresome bus trip back to Eau Claire, since she fortunately was "somewhat long-winded."[18]

No doubt stimulated by Rølvaag's example, Ager produced his own story of Norwegian pioneers, *Gamlelandets sønner* (Sons of the Old Country). It was printed in Oslo by the same publisher and in much the same format as Rølvaag's books.[19] But while Rølvaag placed his pioneers in South Dakota in the 1870s, Ager placed his in the Eau Claire area of Wisconsin in the 1850s.

The reason was not merely that he knew this region best, but also that this period was one in which Ager could demonstrate the values of hard work and thrift. He could even romanticize the saloon, against which he had so successfully fought throughout his life. He could also fit in his newly acquired knowledge of the Civil War and Colonel Heg's Fifteenth Wisconsin Regiment. While Rølvaag's immigrants came from the land and went to the land, Ager's had a more urban background and sought urban environments in America.

The attractive title he gave it, "Sons of the Old Country," combined the Norwegian background with the American future. The book was well translated by his journalist son Trygve, but unlike Rølvaag's book was not accepted by Harper's and languished in manuscript until 1983, long after Ager's, and his son's, death.

The story begins and ends in Norway, and its central figure is Frederik, the youngest son of Consul Kristian Berg. In the opening scene Frederik is being thrown out of his home by the father, who tells him to go to hell. Frederik has angered his father by accusing him of mistreating his late wife, and by disapproving of his plans for remarriage. Consul Berg has himself worked hard to build up his estate after it had been owned for a generation by his neighbor and rival, Consul Christian Lundested. He had counted on Frederik to take over after him, but the young man preferred to putter with small tasks around the estate. So Frederik joins the relatively small contingent of Norwegian immigrants from upper-class homes.

The scene shifts rapidly to the woods of northern Wisconsin and begins with a description of logging operations. Skilled loggers hook the logs and swear at them as the need arises. There is a vivid description of nature along the Chippewa River, as a passenger steamboat makes its way slowly up against the current. On board are Frederik and a group of common immigrants on their way to the woods. The immigrants are presented one after the other: Isak Isaksrud, a humorous and self-important youngster; Karine, the only woman, with her husband Andreas and her son by her first husband, Karinius, a thirteen-year old, for whom this is his life's greatest adventure. Another is Evan Evanson. While their conversation is sprightly and amusing, they grow serious as they approach their goal, which obviously is Eau Claire. "Before them lay the future, like a fog. They had only hazy conceptions of what awaited them. . . . The only thing these immigrants knew for sure was that they would get jobs." "Silently they wished that was all there was to it. . . . Consider the rest of it: the strange language, strange people, strange customs, strange food, strange surroundings. They shook their heads: God alone could know how it would all turn out. But there was no way back."

Each of them has thoughts of his own: Evan thinks of his wife and the twins he has left behind—and of the mittens she has knitted for him, working in a

121

strand of her hair. Isak is here to find his brother, only now realizing that it is like seeking a needle in a haystack. Ole Brekke is an officer aspirant who seeks out Frederik because he is obviously of the upper classes. Frederik has escaped from the watchful eye of Hans, a young man whom his father has sent over to keep track of him. Frederik now realizes that he is alone and that he will have to make all his own decisions: "The feeling that he was free began to oppress him."

The immigrants have a passing contact with the "better class" of Americans when the boat hits a sandbar and lists to one side, throwing a girl and the boy Karinius into the water. Karinius gets credit for saving the girl and is well rewarded by her father, to which he replies with his only English sentence: "I'll be damned!"

Meanwhile Hans has made his way by road to the town and meets Frederik on the street; they make friends. Hans winds up in Olson's saloon, where he sees a man who had insulted him on the road and goes after him; he makes him recite the Lord's prayer and shows him up as a paltry fellow. There is a lively picture of life in the saloon, with only slight hints of Ager's temperance stance.

Before long the men get their work assignments on the river and Frederik joins the rest, over Hans's protests. The various saws and their functions are described; Frederik is assigned to an edging saw, "an infernal machine to work by." Here he meets Greger Gregersen, who loses two fingers but continues to work. "Slowly and imperceptibly the spirit of the mill crept into Frederik's blood; he became a part of the great mechanism." Gregersen had been involved in the Thrane labor movement in Norway, and it is later revealed that he recognized Frederik, since he had worked for his father.

Frederik stays at a place called Scandia House, run by one Nils Myhra, an asthmatic. Myhra's daughter Annie is one of three waitresses at table, only seventeen and almost supernaturally beautiful. Frederik feels a little out of place: "His language was not theirs and his manners were different." He ponders the conflict within himself between his father's stubbornness and his mother's idealism. But he finds himself in the heavy work, which he gradually masters.

This is a collective novel, and the fate of each individual is not important enough to retell here. Suffice it to say that there is an attempted seduction of Annie by a wicked "Yankee," that a church is built in which Gregersen surprisingly becomes *klokker* (precentor), and that when the Civil War breaks out several of the men enlist in the Norwegian regiment headed by Colonel Hans C. Heg. In the end Frederik, wounded in battle, is nursed back to health by Gunda, Gregersen's daughter. The main point of the novel is that Frederik has learned the value of hard work and has been purged of his antagonism to his father. So the story ends with his return to Norway, accompanied by his new bride, Gunda, to be welcomed back into the fold.

So ends this predominantly happy story of Norwegians building their share of America in the woods of Wisconsin. There is a world of difference between this book and Ager's previous novels. In *I strømmen* a problem of alcoholism results in tragedy; in *Kristus for Pilatus* an idealist fights in vain; and *Paa veien til smeltepotten* is a satirical portrayal of assimilation. In the last-named book every step forward and upward is seen in terms of upstart vanity, while in *Gamlelandets sønner* it is seen as a positive force contributing to the growth of America.

The story is told with great skill. Little touches of humor are strewn throughout, as in his short stories. The dialogue is vivid and credible. He weaves in the story of lumbering so that it becomes exciting, from the saloon brawls between Norwegians and Irishmen to the log jams and the simple pleasures of the camps and the chatter of the floating logs. A typical boarding house is delineated as well as a hard winter and a spring flood. The time is well chosen for Ager's purposes, since it was a period of growing Norwegian migration, but long before the Norwegian language began to decline in home, school, and church.

Structurally the novel suffers from the amount of historical information that must be conveyed. One is startled by the death of Annie, who one assumes early on will be united with Frederik. But she does play an important role in his life by releasing his humanity and penetrating the hard shell that had made him resist his father. That the Norwegian capitalist's son should marry Gunda, the daughter of the labor leader whom the capitalist had driven out of Norway, is a valuable ironic touch. The detailed account of the Civil War and the role of the Fifteenth Wisconsin seems tacked on at the end. It fits Ager's purpose well but is an anti-climax in the development of the story.

Critics have generally given this book good marks. It is well written and makes for easy, exciting reading. It is unfortunate that it did not reach the great American public at the same time as Rølvaag's masterpiece.

Commentary on the book included an interesting testimonial to its accuracy: a former cook in the lumber camps in 1881–1882 wrote that "it is a faithful picture of real conditions."[20]

D. G. Ristad declared that "reading *Gamlelandets sønner* is like hearing Ager speak. His supple Norwegian, his love of his theme, his sharp insight into our peculiarities, and his half-weeping, half-laughing humor keeps us awake and interested." "The book is in reality a long chain of pearls consisting of short stories, portraits, episodes, personalities. It is not a book that discusses problems. The persons do not go through any psychological development." "Ager has had the courage to let these people be themselves in drinking and dancing, as well as in work to build homes and found congregations and churches."[21] Hans Olav in *Nordisk Tidende* praised it as a book of "broad humor, spiced with amusing happenings and strong men and enterprising women."[22]

Idar Handagard in Norway commented that Ager "has observed his countrymen and noted their virtues and faults." "He has humor, a sense of what is ridiculous in the midst of sorrow." "He has realized that you can't let Norwegian countryfolk talk Danish any longer, and he tries to make them talk dialect."[23]

The most important review was Rølvaag's. He praised Ager as an understanding father to his characters. "Now and then he is overcome by a kind of dry irony over their stupidities; the smile threatens to become a derisive sneer, but it immediately clears up into goodwill—Lord, these are only human beings—they are far from being angels." "Hitherto we have seen the pioneer period as something almost supernaturally good and beautiful. And Ager makes his characters good in spite of all they do; such magic power does he possess that he makes us fond of them all. That is great art!" He found a bit of old-fashioned melodrama in the episode about Annie and young Adams, her would-be seducer. He was particularly happy that "Ager can enter a saloon, take a glass or two, strike out at the Irish, and enjoy it. . . . The temperance man has retired for a moment, so that the artist could stand forth."

Rølvaag would have liked a more detailed character analysis in some parts, but he recognized that the novel was not intended to be analytic: "It is a book full of priceless depictions from the 1850s and 1860s." He found the Civil War section to be a burden to the book; it would have been better integrated without it. "But the book is Ager himself in his very best moments, sparkling in his humor, brilliant in his dialogue."[24]

A modern analysis has been given the book by Øyvind Gulliksen, a Norwegian scholar; it is a valuable perspective. He makes the point that Ager drew as much on American humor as on the Norwegian background and characterizes it as a collective novel, in which "the group as a whole is certainly more important . . . than any individual character." He targets Greger Gregersen and Frederik as vehicles for Ager's thesis: that America could change a man for the better, Greger from a doctrinaire socialist to a hardworking, church-building family man, and Frederik from a self-willed and rebellious son of wealth into a valuable asset to Norway's future.[25]

Ager and Rølvaag had known or known of each other for many years, reviewing each other's books with growing admiration. Their cooperation became especially close in the 1920s, when they both participated in the work of the Norwegian Society. Ager recognized in Rølvaag a fellow Norwegian activist; in 1927–1928 they arranged declamatory evenings for one of the latter's students, Palma Helgeson. In 1928 Ager praised the Norwegian govern-

Ager and Rølvaag enjoying a smoke in Rølvaag's yard in Northfield, Minnesota. Courtesy Eyvind Ager.

ment for inviting Rølvaag to the Ibsen centennial in Oslo. "We like to interpret this honor as intended for him not only as the famous author, but also as the distinguished representative of 'Norwegian America.' "[26]

Privately he could grumble to Rølvaag in a joshing way: "It's annoying to see how well that new good-for-nothing book of yours is doing in Norway. It shows how much they understand about literature. Now I suppose you are going around in Northfield with a stuck-up nose to the annoyance of others who don't have a book to brag about."[27] He might actually have been annoyed when Rølvaag's recommendation of *Sons of the Old Country* to Harper's was accepted only with the proviso that Rølvaag do the translation. Rølvaag replied that this was impossible: "I have more than I can do with getting my own books into readable English." Ager thanked Rølvaag for the effort: "You are the only one who has done anything for me in this direction." He was convinced that "the damnable fellow down there insists on making money on your name." He felt that the New York publisher could not have understood what the book was about: a period that interested historians and that would never return. "It was a goal of the immigrants to earn enough money to get land; they were here in the green years."[28]

In 1929 Ager was granted an honorary degree of Doctor of Letters from St.

125

1929 Commencement at St. Olaf College: Ager receiving doctor's hood from Rølvaag, with son Trygve in foreground.

1929 Commencement: W. Ager, Litt. D., and son Trygve, B. A.

Olaf College at the same commencement where his son Trygve received a bachelor's degree. Before the ceremony Ager wrote to Rølvaag; "Who gets named as honorary doctors at St. Olaf? Are you in on it, or anyone you know? Does it cost anything? Does a man have to bring a pastor's gown? Is he permitted (in case of great need) to say 'shucks' or 'gosh darn it' or 'the dickens'? Does it hurt to go through the ceremony? Would a person lose friends if he played hooky? I ask you all this with tears in my eyes."[29] Rølvaag was no doubt behind it, but the president, Lars Boe, was a close friend of the Norwegian faculty and had himself grown up in a Norwegian community.

A book that awakened Ager's concern in this period was the autobiography of Judge Andreas Ueland in Minneapolis: *Recollections of an Immigrant* (1929). In reviewing it Ager was succinct and insightful. While Ueland might wish his book to be a contribution to the study of immigration, one soon realizes that "the obvious purpose of the book is to let people know what a remarkable fellow the author is—and with some justice, for his life is indeed one that is worth noticing." "After a while one becomes tired of seeing how very satisfied the author is with himself, his family, and his ancestors." Ueland was the son of a famous Norwegian peasant leader, Ole Gabriel Ueland, but his attitude to Ager's precious Norwegian heritage was if anything negative. Ueland spent a great deal of space denigrating what he conceived to be that heritage, including above all an orthodox belief in Satan, which Ueland did not share. After meeting Ueland's arguments point by point, Ager admitted that

127

they made interesting reading, but noted also that in fact Ueland was extremely proud of his Norwegian ancestry and that he had played an important role as a lawyer for many Norwegian clients. But the heritage was none of the things Ueland enumerated: "It is that indescribable force that in a few years drew Andreas Ueland back to Norway four times and made him take his family with him. For he himself is totally Norwegian (*kav norsk*), as his book shows—if merely inside out."[30]

In these years Ager also took the opportunity to gaze backward on his own history: first, in 1928, at the twenty-fifth anniversary of his Norwegian Society, whose founding and many accomplishments he enumerated: fifteen volumes of *Kvartalskrift*, nearly 2000 pages of reading matter; a history of Norwegian settlements by H. R. Holand; monuments to Henrik Wergeland and Rollo of Normandy in Fargo; stimulation of Norwegian-American literature; a monument to Colonel Heg in Madison; the Sigvald Quale competitions in Norwegian declamation, which had awarded 291 silver medals and 22 gold medals. But the present membership consisted of only fifty persons.

The other occasion for reminiscence was the fortieth anniversary of *Reform*, which was started under that name by Ole Br. Olson in 1888 in Eau Claire. Ager commented that it was now the only Norwegian newspaper in Wisconsin, and he believed it was significant for the community that such a newspaper existed: it would be missed if it ceased to appear. He hoped that the occasion would cause someone to "surprise" him with a new subscriber![31]

With his usual self-effacing modesty Ager found occasion during this period to pay tribute to none other than his one-time adversary, Rasmus B. Anderson. In a few strokes he portrayed Anderson's democratic folksiness, his remarkable life, as glimpsed in his 1915 autobiography, and his unfailing sensitivity to criticism. He emphasized Anderson's contribution to raising the self-respect of American Norwegians, above all by his championship of Leif Ericson as the true discoverer of America. "Anderson has been a fighting man. Not always wisely, but to his honor be it said: always openly." "We owe him much, perhaps more than any other Norwegian American, dead or alive."[33]

On his sixtieth birthday in 1929 Ager received a tribute to his work from his old friend Sigurd Folkestad, the poet-pastor who had returned to Norway for good. Folkestad called him "an invaluable pioneer," not only because of his journal *Reform*, but also as "an apostle of Norwegianness in his stirring popular talks, a literary critic and godfather of poets, and an author with a typically Norwegian-American content and outlook." He nominated him "chieftain of the emigrants" and noted that "his life work could not be contained in any single book: one would also have to include his many thousands of articles." "One cannot write any authoritative Norwegian-American cultural history without familiarizing oneself with his versatile and brilliant work."[34]

14

I Sit Alone: 1929–1931

AGER'S LAST NOVEL, *Hundeøine*, is written in the first person, a feature that makes it sound more like Ager's own story than any of his other books. The hero-narrator furnishes the Norwegian title when he looks at himself in a mirror and sees that his eyes "resemble a dog's eyes, a dog that begs." In English someone, either Charles Wharton Stork, the translator, or Harper Brothers, the publishers, decided that "Dog's Eyes" was not a suitable title. They selected instead the opening words of the text: "I Sit Alone." The Norwegian original, like *Gamlelandets sønner*, was published by Aschehoug in Oslo.[1]

Some parts of the novel, the narrator's early life, do follow the known course of Ager's childhood. But most of it is a retrospective reckoning with a life that has deviated markedly from Ager's. The hero is introduced at a late point in his career, in his early forties, when he has fled his home in Chicago and settled in a cabin on the prairie, apparently in western North Dakota. It opens: "I sit alone out here on the prairie in a little cabin, and time rests heavy. . . . I am only a fugitive who is trying to dig myself down, while the others around here are trying to dig themselves up." Clarence Kilde has perceptively suggested that this may reflect Ager's musings while sitting in his lake cabin in Wisconsin.[2]

The name Ager gave his alter ego is also significant: Christian Pedersen. "Christian" because Ager for all his skeptical and rationalistic view of Lutheranism considered himself, and no doubt was, a good Christian, "Pedersen" probably because Knut Hamsun's original family name was "Pedersen." This requires a bit of explanation. The first-person narrative stance, so useful for books of a semi-autobiographical type, had been popularized in Norwegian literature by Hamsun, particularly in his first famous books, *Sult* (Hunger,

Cover of Ager's last novel, in English translation, 1931

1890) and *Pan* (1894). While Ager remained a severe critic of some aspects of Hamsun's work, particularly his treatment of sexual matters, he could not help being captivated by Hamsun's smooth-flowing style, so full of caprices and witty turns of phrase. In both books Hamsun's hero is an outsider, who finds in nature a wildness that corresponds to his own inner turmoil. In *Hundeøine* Ager undertakes a flight of fancy into the wildness of the prairie that permits him to ponder ideas that involve him deeply in both sexual and religious themes. While *Gamlelandets sønner* called on Ager the historian, *Hundeøine* calls on Ager the philosopher.

The narrative alternates back and forth between the present on the prairie and in a small frontier town and the past in the city of Chicago. In the present Christian is busy writing his memoirs and chatting with people he meets in the frontier town, above all a self-styled pastor, with whom he has long, penetrating conversations. The man who functions as a pastor on the frontier tells a story of his own career, which is not unlike the story of Ager's pastor in *Christ before Pilate*. But for the most part he interprets the Bible for Christian in an undogmatic, human way, which the narrator finds deeply satisfying and quite surprising. He draws a clear line between two worlds, the world of the flesh and the world of the spirit that Christ brought into existence. The world of the spirit is one in which all the values of ordinary life are turned topsy-turvy: "The least becomes the greatest, perfection is to be everyone's servant, one gains by losing." The usual world is dominated by materialism, Christ's new world by the spirit: "They are as opposite as darkness and light, night and day, winter and summer, cold and hot, high and low, distant and near." In the usual world hours have sixty minutes, but in that world of spirit there are both "long" and "sad" hours, which cannot be measured on any scale.

All this philosophizing has a distinctly transcendental cast which may be assumed to represent what Ager, with his background of Lutheranism, Methodism, and cosmopolitan reading believed in deeply. This book may therefore serve as a testament in which he embodied his basic beliefs.

Christian Pedersen is known among other prairie residents as Inslie, which is obviously the Norwegian word "enslig," meaning "lonely." His childhood in Norway is sketched in, corresponding very closely to what is known of Ager's own. He describes a gloriously happy infancy, with his mother as the central figure: besides Christian there is an older brother named Alfred, an eleven-year-old sister named Anette, and an eight-year-younger sister Jossa (known as Tulla). The father has left the family for America and seems to have disappeared there, since they never hear from him and when they follow him to Chicago he fails to meet them. The physical surroundings of Ager's childhood in Gressvik are replicated, with the main part of the city on the "other" side of the river. On their side "the little houses looked as if they had fled from

131

the city with its city hall and taxes and all that was evil. Now they sat crouched together and on their haunches each in its corner, as if they were afraid that someone would see them, and peeked as if frightened over at the city through their small, shiny panes."

Scenes of both joy and sorrow are pictured; but the greatest sorrow was the death of Christian's older brother Alfred. He already had a bad conscience because he had been unkind to Alfred over a broken toy: "That left a mark on me for life. I became afraid to offend my conscience. I developed a sickly fear of avenging myself and was too afraid of wounding somebody, even in self-defense." But there were many joys as well: Sundays in the woods picking flowers, boat rides on the fjord, earning small sums at children's work.

By the time an older sister has a job in Oslo, and a small brother has been added to the family, they finally decide to leave for America. On this expedition the boy Christian considers himself a leader since he is the only man in the company. He describes their stay in Christiania, the voyage to America via England from Liverpool, Castle Garden in New York, and the train trip that brings them to the Canal Street station in Chicago. Earlier immigrants are helpful to the abandoned family, especially when they have to cope with the death of Jossa. From here on the story deviates markedly from Ager's own; Christian remains in Chicago and the children find work, he as a "cash boy" in Marshall Field's department store and Anette as a maid in an American family. While the mother gets work sewing, she also takes in a boarder named Karsten, a newcomer from Norway who turns out to have remarkable talents. He is nineteen when Christian is sixteen, and they soon become inseparable friends. Girl problems concern them, especially after they have been to their first parties. A friend of Anette's brings a Norwegian-American girl named Rachel into the family; Rachel is clearly enamoured of Karsten. Christian's interest in girls awakens his interest in eyes, those of people as well as animals. He decides that there is something "solid, reliable and motherly" about Rachel, for she has "a pair of large, softly radiant eyes with something rather velvety in them."

It gradually becomes evident that Karsten is not interested in Rachel and she turns more and more to Christian. One evening they become engaged, though with some reluctance on his side. They are married and build their own home on Chicago's northwest side and at first are very happy. Christian starts a clothing store with a Danish companion named Nielsen and they do well. Nielsen introduces him to other Danes and they appreciate each other; in a scene with them Ager subtly pokes fun at the *nynorsk* language movement. But a coolness comes over his friends, and he breaks off his partnership with Nielsen. One begins to suspect that Rachel is somehow involved. Life with her becomes a hell for Christian. Rachel admits to being able to cry on command and she

132

laughs at his having been taken in by her. That evening Christian takes his first drink, and he soon becomes a regular guest at the saloon. Rachel and Christian have a child named Olaf and he is totally absorbed in the boy; but one day he tips a lamp over and is burned to death, while Christian burns his hands badly trying to save him.

After the tragedy Rachel starts going to church, and this proves to be due to Karsten's reappearance, without his wife. Karsten becomes a regular visitor. One evening Christian finds him (or rather his coat) with Rachel and he realizes that her love has always been for Karsten rather than himself. With Nielsen's help he is able to leave Chicago and settle on some land in the West, where he builds his little shack.

The story narrated so far is constantly interrupted by scenes from the present situation in the shack. Christian ponders a good deal on his writing: he asks why he is making these notations, and he wonders whether he should continue these very personal notes, obviously of no interest to anyone but himself. He keeps tearing open old wounds: "But a fresh wound is greatly to be preferred to an old one that has gotten a scab over it and become infected." He interrupts his writing, when it becomes too difficult, to make trips into town. This is where he gets to know the pastor. They are both interested in music; the pastor is also a doctor on occasion. They get to talking and eventually the talk turns to religion; Christian is unable to believe in the inspiration of the Bible or in Christ's sacrifice. The pastor compares God's work to a symphony: a great thing made out of a very small motif. The pastor gives him a fine cigar on condition that he will just read one of the gospels straight through like a story.

Another strange character he meets in town is an elderly bachelor named Egidius, whose amusing dialect gives color to his talk. He had taken care of his parents until he was too old to get married: he was cheated out of his youth and so has remained forever youthful. Other prairie characters are presented in short vignettes: "a flock of shipwrecked persons washed up here; the world's billows have landed us on an inhospitable shore; but each of us has in his own way found the mooring we sought."

But Egidius, comic as he is, will play an essential part in bringing Christian's story to a happy end. One day, after a snowstorm, Egidius has called on two women who have settled in a shack on the other side of town; at the pastor's suggestion he has brought them needed supplies. Eventually, after Christian has written most of his story, it turns out that these two women are Christian's mother and his sister Anette, who have been looking for him. The two women, ignorant of Christian's adopted name, send Egidius out looking for Pedersens, and he takes Christian with him. Neither of them realizes that he is in effect looking for himself until they arrive at the women's residence, where the long-lost brother is greeted with delight. When Egidius expresses amusement at the idea of hunting for oneself, Christian sententiously replies, "Oh, I've been doing that much longer than you think."

When he now looks in the mirror, he can say to himself, "You look more like a human being now, Christian; you can go where you wish with those eyes." The pastor tells him: "You look like a man whose prayer has been answered," and when Christian denies having prayed for anything, he replies: "We understand a dog when it begs without its having to say a word." In the end, Christian decides to look up the scenes of his childhood, and he can again dream of the future.

This book is unquestionably Ager's most poetic work. It affords a fitting climax to a lifetime of literary effort. Although its structure is clearly too imitative to count as a great original contribution to literature, it carries in concentrated form a tribute to Ager's own childhood and to his emotional and intellectual life. It contains a sad story with tragic overtones, but in essence it is more thoughtful and pensive than tragic. It ends on an upbeat note, and one can only agree with Kilde's characterization of it as marked "by a maturity of understanding expressed in a developed artistic style." However, it is impossible to agree with Kilde in his judgment that it shows life as "ultimately tragic."[3] On its last page Ager wrote: "Now it is spring, and it is green, and what Egidius helped me plant has shot up beautifully. . . . My door is wide open, and through it comes a fragrance of spring and sprouting life."

Of the contemporary reviews one of the most spontaneous was by the Norwegian-American politician and writer Knut Wefald: "I have just finished reading Ager's new book, *Hundeøine*. I don't know if I can get to sleep tonight, for it has moved my heart powerfully. I have never read a book with such tenseness. . . . As I sit here alone on Thanksgiving, I am shaken through and through by the tragedy Ager has portrayed with such a tender hand."[4]

The reviewer in *Decorah-Posten*, signed S-d (Georg Strandvold), particularly admired the pastor's simile comparing God's creation with Beethoven's Fifth Symphony to illustrate how a great master can make something out of even a simple motif. He recommended the book highly, though he found fault with Christian's psychology and considered the conclusion improbable; he also nitpicked anglicisms in Ager's Norwegian.[5]

Reviewers in Norway were generally favorable. The critic for *Aftenposten* in Oslo, R. Grieg, praised its psychology, which expressed "the eternally human that will always retain its character." He found "the description of the poor childhood home to be delicate and delightful, often refreshing and full of humor, simple and unaffected, never sentimental." He saw the real content as "the story of how one who was deprived of all his happiness did not capitulate, but found a deeper significance in all that he had experienced." He concluded that "although there is much that is sad in *Hundeøine*, the book is never depressing. On the contrary, there is much about its spirit that is very liberating."[6]

The reviewer in *Morgenposten*, Stein Balstad, called it "one of the year's good books, not a great and remarkable literary work, but sober and trustworthy." "The book is wise, witty, ironical, and has many whimsical fancies." However, he finds some of the discussions overly solemn and lengthy; "the author assumes that the reader is very patient." But he admires the picture of the urban milieu and the gallery of persons one meets: "One is greatly enriched by having read it."[7]

An analysis by a Norwegian scholar, Arne Sunde, defends Ager's resolution of the novel's problem. He points out that it was based on Ager's view of culture and morality. To let Christian go down to destruction would have been to reject all the causes he had fought for in his life. But to "bring him back to lost values and his childhood home is in agreement with his political and religious views." "The emigrant must by no means lose contact with his own distinctive quality and his ethnic background."[8]

When the book appeared in English two years later as *I Sit Alone*, it was widely reviewed in the American press. While James Gray in the *Minneapolis Tribune* found it "a wholly admirable piece of work," Eugene Lohrke in the *New York Herald* found it "romantic and sentimental" and headed his review "oversensitive." "Its author cannot see the shoreline through the haze of his own self-pity." He admitted that there was in it "a sensitive feeling for all of the life it touches." The *Springfield Republican* in a long and sympathetic review noted that it "tends to become less of a novel and more of a religious and psychological treatise." He found it to Ager's credit "that he makes these homiletics so natural and so simply reverent in tone that they seem to play a necessary part in the development of the transformed Christian Pedersen." The *Milwaukee Journal* found in Mr. Ager "a writer of real talent and ability," and his book "a work of no little artistry."[9]

The reviews were mixed, as is apparent; the results in terms of sales were disappointing. In a letter of February, 1933, Ager wrote that it had been "a complete failure as far as sales are concerned, in spite of good reviews."[10]

In the very next year after *Hundeøine*, Ager gathered together nine of the short stories he had been writing and published them himself. He significantly titled them *Under forvandlingens tegn* (Under the Sign of Change).[11] The zodiacal allusion suggests that Ager was beginning to feel that change was an inexorable fate. The book was dedicated to son Roald Sneve, born 1913, his seventh child, described as "my youngest boy." In this book Ager for the first time adopted the modernized Norwegian orthography of 1907 instead of the Dano-Norwegian spelling he had learned as a child.

The collection might as well have been called "I Sit Alone" like the English

135

title of his novel, for it deals almost wholly with old people who feel lonely because of the generation gap between the immigrants and the native-born. While there are no masterpieces, there are many interesting reflections of Ager's thinking.

"Hun tok os paa fanget" (She Took Us On Her Lap) is a quotation from a well-known poem by Bjørnson about Norway as a nurturing mother. The story is about an elderly couple who are lonely as Christmas approaches and keep getting in each other's way. They are overwhelmed when their scattered children decide to visit them as a surprise to celebrate Christmas together.

"Den norske Nissen" (The Norwegian Elf) tells of Ole Torgersen, or "Ole Thompson, as it was written in the congregational protocol and at the farm store," whose cows do not thrive as well as they ought. The only one who knows the reason is his daughter Astrid, or "Esther, as she was called at school," who is especially fond of her mother's father, Grandpa Nordlie. He lives in the old log house, which the Thompsons have abandoned for a fine new mansion. His explanation, which Astrid adopts, is that the problem is caused by the Norwegian goblin, who misses having his Christmas porridge, as was his due in all Norwegian barns. Astrid sneaks a bit of porridge into the barn and Grandpa furnishes the money for a new barn, placed where the *nisse* wants it. The cattle begin thriving again, and Astrid goes off to St. Olaf College; she takes part in a Norwegian declamation contest, and wins by reciting the first chapter of Bjørnson's *Arne*, retold in her grandfather's dialect. In a humorous ending, the father stumbles with a pail of water that he threatens his daughter and father-in-law with, and they are both convinced that this too is the doing of the *nisse*.

"En mor" (A Mother) is the story of Mrs. Gina Gilbertson, who recalls her childhood in Buffalo county and the care her mother gave her there. Now living in town she decides to commemorate the anniversary of her wedding to her deceased husband by having a mock wedding and giving the children a hundred-dollar gold piece each. But the children all have other plans, and she is left alone. The neighbors notice her walking by: "She's getting old, Mrs. Gilbertson . . . Just look how she drags her feet and rolls her head; she's not especially old, but I suppose she has her problems."

"Assimileret – Et eventyr" (Assimilated – A Fairy Tale) is the story of a farmer who came from a foreign land and acquired great wealth and power; but his heirs, in desperation over his longevity, devise a scheme for using up his money until he is shrunk into insignificance. This is a slightly disguised parable about the fate of the Norwegian language which Ager sees as being impoverished by the writing of the history of Norwegian America.

"Hvor hjertene mødtes" (Where the Hearts Met) tells of a boy who travels abroad and keeps only one possession, love of his mother. But when he goes back home to see her, she is all dressed up so that he does not recognize her. They meet in a common urge to see the scenes of his childhood. The story reflects Ager's disappointment on seeing that his native country has become modernized.

"Et Nutidseventyr" (A Modern Fairytale) tells of the devil tempting a happy young wife to lie to her husband. She tells him she got a compliment from his employer. Their marriage is threatened by the husband's ungrounded jealousy until she decides to tell the truth and the devil is driven away.

The next two tales are drawn from biblical sources. "En Profet som stod paa sine Fødder" (A Prophet who Stood on his Feet) is about Ezekiel from the Old Testament and his resistance to assimilation in the Babylonian captivity. The fact that Ezekiel "stood on his feet" was enough to allow the two tribes that returned to Israel to "advance world peace and yield a greater contribution to world culture than any other people." "Vinduet som vendte mot Jerusalem" (The Window that Turned toward Jerusalem) is an application of the story of the prophet Daniel and his defiance of the empire of the Medes and Persians, which was possible because he kept Israel in sight through a window in his wall. The lions help his cause by eating the soothsayers instead of Daniel. Ager hereby hints at how he would like the prophets of doom for the Norwegian language in America to be treated.

The last story, "Norsk-Amerikaneren Peer Gynt," is a retelling and interpretation of Ibsen's *Peer Gynt* as typical of the Norwegian American. Peer is at bottom a farm boy who is attached to his mother and to his sweetheart, Solveig. But in the interval between Act III and Act IV he has, in Ager's view, lived in America and become the international vagrant of Act IV. He is materialistic and self-important throughout his African adventure, a true object of satire. The result of his experience is seen in Act V, where he returns to Norway to die: in the end his soul is saved by Solveig, "a symbol of Norwegian strength and faithfulness." Her love conquers and she saves him from the melting pot: "She represents the strongest element in Norwegian folk character."

These stories are nearly all expressions of Ager's own philosophy of ethnic self-assertion, an almost religious faith in the potentialities of Norwegian character as a leaven in American society.

In these years of 1929–1931, Ager had reason to feel that he did indeed "sit alone." His children were growing up, getting married and scattering. His friends in the movements for temperance and the Norwegian language were getting older and dying off. In 1929, he took over the entire ownership of *Reform*, abandoning the fiction that it was published by the Fremad stock company. He explained to his subscribers that "we could see the time coming when we could no longer gather a majority" of the stockholders. "It takes considerable capital to produce a competitive Norwegian-American newspaper now,

137

and it is a matter of course that with immigration almost stopped and the churches going over to English, it will get more difficult than ever to keep a Norwegian weekly going." "Laying my cards on the table, I must confess that it was not business considerations that made me undertake this. When one has worked over thirty-two years in a place, it is hard to tear oneself away. . . . I have received so many proofs of friendship and indulgence that I have felt as if I were in the midst of a large and close-knit family; it has been a work that has brought me a great feeling of happiness besides the necessary drudgery. When I have been offered better positions—better paying, I mean—then after a period of indecision I have not been able to bring myself to leave, as long as there was still a possibility of carrying on."[12]

Ager's life style had always been social and outgoing, as revealed in his editorials, his temperance agitation, his popular speeches, his short stories, and his novels. Perhaps it was a feeling of his own growing isolation that led him to write extensively about his polar opposite, the *nynorsk* poet Jon Norstog. Having settled in a remote and isolated spot in North Dakota, where his American-born wife supported him by working as Superintendent of Schools, he wrote epic and lyric poetry in his own brand of Norwegian. He not only wrote his books, but also printed and bound them, producing little gems of bookmaking that no one wanted to read.

In 1927, Ager reviewed *Livshorpa* (The Harp of Life), calling it "a handsome collection of poems" that gave him "an almost choking sense of something a little deformed or misshapen, something that one cannot rejoice about." He was annoyed at the title because it reminded him of the word "hurpe" (hag) and other ugly words.[13] In 1928, when he received a new book by Norstog called *Exodus*, he confessed that his books made him "fidget." "Just as he has in part made up his own language and done the technical or mechanical work of setting and printing his books himself, so he does not take his types from life but spins them out of himself. He has made himself independent of everything and everyone. That is dangerous. It can lead to the greatest heights, but more often it leads down into a hole."[14]

In reviewing *Exodus*, which for once was in prose, Ager took up the whole question of Norstog as a writer, which must have posed a baffling dilemma for the advocate of a Norwegian-American literature; he called it "Problemet Jon Norstog" (The Jon Norstog Problem) and devoted five issues to his article. This review may be the best literary essay Ager ever wrote, at once thoughtful and devastating as he tries to retell what was at best a very confused narrative. The title *Exodus* suggested that the novel dealt with emigration, but Ager struggled in vain to find its relevance. As he said, "The problem has got on my nerves." "On my bookshelf there are eighteen books by Norstog. No less than five thousand pages has he written and published here among us." "It is said that Norway was created by a natural eruption which made it self-contradictory, helter-skelter, formless, but very beautiful and varied." "Just so with Norstog's book: it seems to have come into being by eruption, and you can't look for straight lines. . . . Perhaps the time will come when such a book with its collection of unreal persons mirroring a real soul will be regarded as the summit of art."[15]

Ager was exasperated by Norstog, but he was also fascinated by him and drawn to him by his intransigence, which in a way matched his own: they were both independent thinkers. Ager was more interested in being understood than Norstog was. In commenting on an article in *Decorah-Posten* about the tendency of Norwegian Americans to treat their colleagues gently, he replied that he could not recall that anyone had encouraged O.A. Buslett when he started writing. "What we miss is understanding, derived from knowledge of ourselves and our own circumstances and possibilities." He noted that the only individual who had contributed positively to the development of Norwegian-American literature was the Honorable O.M. Oleson in Fort Dodge, Iowa, a merchant who had donated an annual prize of $100 for the best Norwegian book, awarded by the Norwegian Society.[16] He could have mentioned also his old friend J.J. Skørdalsvold, whom he helped to honor at a banquet in Minneapolis on the occasion of his seventy-seventh birthday, on November 6, 1930. Skørdalsvold had not only encouraged Ager personally, but had written many reviews of his books.[17]

But the man who meant the most to Ager in these years was Rølvaag, who was forging ahead of Ager in outward fame but was ever helpful to his literary plans. Their correspondence in these years was carried on in a bantering tone that reflects great mutual admiration. Ager was anxious about the reception of *Hundeøine* and wrote that "it is a comfort that you too are a little anxious about your *Tullinger* [*Pure Gold*]. . . . That is good for you. You've had altogether too much success and you need a beating more than I do; but it will no doubt turn out that I will get it after all and not you who would profit from it."[18] But when the English translation did appear, Ager wrote about it with respect: "It should remind all of us that such a gifted old people as ours cannot live by bread alone. . . . Our *To Tullinger* had no anchor either in the old country or the new, no love or care for either."[19]

When Rølvaag's book *Peder Seier* (*Peder Victorious*, in its English translation) appeared, St. Olaf College held a convocation in his honor. On that occasion Ager wrote: "He came with two empty hands, but he had fabulous energy and working capacity. Wherever he went, his personality found powerful expression. Majestic ideas, unyielding courage, a passionate need for self-development, these have made him a world figure. . . . He is and remains

139

the one among us who for the first time has called the attention of literary Americans to our national group."[20]

About his own *Hundeøine*, he wrote: "It is a very serious book and may suit the taste of the church people better than *Gamlelandets sønner*."[21] In response to Rølvaag's criticism of his conclusion, he wrote, "It would have been a simple matter to let him die there in his shack and have someone find his writings. But that would not have been in harmony with the view of life that the book's title presupposes. The 'dog's eyes' have had their prayer answered. Without that the story would have been degraded. . . . He understands that even his life has had a meaning."[22] Later Ager comes back twice to the problem of the conclusion. He could easily have changed the hero, "but that would have been outside the tone and plan of the book. I am quite religious in my way and I have formed an opinion about Our Lord and life: that as long as one is honest in one's ways and one's thinking, one will realize in the end that everything has been for the best. This is not exactly theology, but it is supported by the experience that life itself gives."[23]

In a reply to Ager's irritated comments about his reviewers, Rølvaag counsels him not to worry about them. "You know that you've brought a handsome child into the world." Contrary to the critics he insists that Ager's language is fine: "You do have some anglicisms, as you always have had, and why shouldn't you? I think it's a great art to take the words out of the mouths of people, just as they say them. And why shouldn't we Norwegian Americans have the right to weave in Norwegian-American expressions that are typical of our Norwegian speech? I swear that not two percent of us who speak Norwegian over here speak of the *veranda*; we say 'the porch.' " He tells Ager that he has sent an article about him to a Norwegian-American periodical, *Norden*. "I'm so far away from you that I got brave and dared say what I wanted: interpret it in the best sense—as a reprimand for having cast your sinful eyes on an innocent Nordland girl."[24] By this time Rølvaag was in Florida for his health.

In an undated letter from 1930, Rølvaag reported that the president of Harper's had been to see him, and "here I was holding forth about you for him until I began to get enthusiastic myself, and isn't that darn well done when you consider the topic?"[25] He advised him to send both books and suggested to Harper's that they should take *Hundeøine* first and then *Sons*.[26] Meanwhile Ager received a negative review of *Hundeøine* from Norway (*Tidens Tegn*): "The beast skins me alive, calling it a self-satisfied dilettante's work . . . It's a good thing I'm old; if I'd been young, it would have cooled my interest in keeping the language alive. It is just about impossible to keep one's language ear pure here if one is not lucky enough to be able to keep up with developments in this area in Norway."[27] Rølvaag comments on the importance of "connections." "If you for instance had spent the fall in Oslo drinking highballs with the so-called critics, you would no doubt have been taken more seriously than you were."[28]

In March Ager can report that a contract has been signed with Harper's for *Hundeøine*, but "I don't have the same opportunity as you to cooperate with my translator. I am in general in damnably poor shape. It is getting harder to keep a Norwegian newspaper going. . . . Our whole Norwegian movement is a huge process of begging. . . . But like my friend the prophet Ezekiel I believe that a remnant can be saved. . . . Soon you'll be coming north again, when the sunfish begin to thrust their snouts out of the water to look for you."[29] He is glad for the contract: "Now if things go badly, it's your fault; you fooled me into it."[30]

Having read Rølvaag's review in *Norden*, Ager thanks him but objects to the idea that the conflict is between the hero and Rachel. "It is rather a conflict (as in *Pilate*) between the 'Kingdom' that is visible and that which is not. The norms of value that we know are turned on their heads." "Our friend 'Bjarne Blehr' was right in saying that the man, the protagonist of *Hundeøine*, had to get into contact with American practical religion to get hold of himself. I simply could not have drawn a Norwegian Lutheran minister who was gentle enough to handle such a human being. It is all too true that the book could have been better if I had had time for a revision; but I had to get it off in time. . . . I am particularly glad for your saying what you thought: even if we are good friends, we can say what we think anyway. That is a higher degree of friendship."[31]

Harper's engaged a well-known translator of Scandinavian literature, Charles Wharton Stork, to do Ager's book. He complimented Ager extravagantly, saying that "it was a great delight and inspiration to translate your book, which in my opinion is the best novel written in America up to now."[32] Ager commented to Rølvaag that Stork's translation "was not bad," but his knowledge of Norwegian was limited. "It's Swedish that he knows: all through the book he translates *pike* [girl] as 'boy,' confusing it with Swedish *pojke*."[33]

Ager learned that Rølvaag was going to Florida for the winter of 1930 and advised him to look up his sister, Camilla Cameron, "who has no equal in all the world."[34] Rølvaag jokingly regretted Stork's letter: "The result will be that you won't digest your *lutefisk* properly. . . . Celebrate Christmas with moderation. I wish I had a bottle of *good* whisky!" Obviously, this was a deliberate tease of the old temperance man.[35] In his next letter Ager warns Rølvaag to watch out for alligators; they are crazy for Nordlendings, but he didn't worry about sharks, "for they wouldn't touch one even if you smeared butter and syrup on him."[36]

In March Ager reported to Rølvaag on an almost comic annoyance with the

141

book. Augsburg Publishing House, the church publisher in Minneapolis, had refused to handle it unless three "unnecessary" paragraphs in chapter 23 were omitted.[37] For once in his writing Ager had ventured a short passage about sexual relations, first in referring to the "healthy physical basis" of Christian's and Rachel's marriage. He had written that it was "almost degrading" that two people could disagree in the daytime and yet decide to agree at night. He was revolted at the idea that a woman who hated or was indifferent to a man could still "make herself a sexual outlet for him." She even did so willingly: "People are also a kind of animal."[38]

To Rølvaag Ager fumed. He assumed that there was some hidden motive; he countered that even the Bible had "unnecessary passages." "I could have answered Adsem more pregnantly in just three words, but it is one of my little victories over myself that I write as nicely as I do. I purposely write to you about my worries, for you have had too good a time down there together with Al Capone and other elegant folk. It will be good for you to get something to annoy you."[39] In the end Ager agreed on a compromise whereby certain phrases were modified: "sexual outlet" became "submit to wifehood" and the reference to man as an animal was deleted. The real content of the passage was left untouched and Lutheran sensibilities were unruffled.

Rølvaag wrote back to say that he would have answered a straight-out no. The correction, he thought, was not aimed at Ager, but at his (Rølvaag's) having gotten *To tullinger* translated by Harper's as *Pure Gold*. He reported that last fall the Augsburg Publishing House had tried to junk all the Norwegian-American books in their collection. "I am going to tell them to *go to hell* (that isn't swearing when you smuggle it in in English)." He commends the translation of *Hundeøine*, but notes that he would have made changes "in order to bring out more strongly its fervent pulse beats. The warm intimacy has been quite a bit bleached out."[40]

Ager remained conservative about such matters. He had occasion to congratulate Rølvaag on his new book *Den signede dag* (The Blessed Day), which he found much better than his *Peder Victorious*. But he wished he would eliminate a scene in which Peder and Susie retreat to the barn; it reminded him too much of Hamsun's "creatures of nature."[41] Rølvaag defended the scene and said he thought it was probably the best he had written. "Susie is both afraid of Peter and fond of him at the same time. Her nature is to be a person of moods and a sexual animal when the spell comes upon her. . . . For her the important thing is to overcome and to disarm him." He expressed appreciation for Ager's advice, knowing that it was well meant. As for his health, he felt that "the stay down here has done me no good."[42]

When Ager knew that Rølvaag was back in Northfield, he invited him to his cottage on Lake Chetek. They had a joshing exchange of letters, but

Rølvaag suggested the visit be postponed until the weather was cooler.[43] In what seems to have been his last letter to Rølvaag Ager reported that "we have had the two worst years in my existence here. I was a fool to take over the responsibility for the business. The bad times are making themselves felt and the banks are closed." "I hope the book sells, or will sell. But the times will put obstacles in the way of its sale also. People have begun to hang on to their pennies as never before. Hope you are careful about your health; listen to what the doctor and your wife tell you and don't turn a deaf ear when they remind you of your depravity and your willfullness."[44]

Rølvaag's ailment, under the shadow of which he had written his last two books, overcame him on November 5, 1931; the cause was diagnosed as angina pectoris. Ager's sympathetic review of *Den signede dag*, which was translated as *Their Fathers' God*, did not appear until nearly a month later. He remarks that it was a miracle that Rølvaag could write such a book in the midst of his illness. "Without doubt he intended to continue with one more book. His introducing the girl from Nordland indicates that. We know at once that when she returned to Norway, she would have been the wife for Peder."[45] As it was, Ager wrote an introduction to a collection of Rølvaag's short stories, *Fortællinger og skildringer* (Stories and Sketches), published in 1932.

Rølvaag's widow wrote to Ager, asking him on behalf of Rølvaag's biographers for the correspondence between them. He replied agreeably, but remarked: "We had our own way of writing, which might appear childish and silly to others. We scrawled away whatever occurred to us. . . . When I now took them out to read them again, it struck me as something treasonable that I would betray his trust. Can you believe it, I was just about in tears as I sat with those letters."[46] Rølvaag's death ended a lifetime of cooperative endeavor in the service of the Norwegian cause. Henceforth, Ager would be lonelier than ever. Now he did indeed "sit alone."

15

Last Years: 1931–1941

DURING THE LAST DECADE of his life Ager continued to edit and publish *Reform*. It was a desperate decade, with not only the Depression, but also the passing of his subscribers and friends and the general decline of interest in the cause of the Norwegian language. He became, if not the last man, at least the last warrior on the bastion of Norwegianness in America. The last years were lighted by some bright spots, which will be recorded in due course: his last visit to the homeland and his last published volume. Ager's sixties were characterized by many lasts.

The first and worst blow was Rølvaag's sudden if not entirely unexpected death. At the funeral, Ager was especially moved when he entered Rølvaag's study: "I had been in his upstairs study several times before, but this was the first time I had noticed that he had my photograph, framed and under glass, on his wall. . . . It was sad, terribly sad."[1] In his introductory essay to Rølvaag's posthumous volume, he characterized him as one who remained childlike all his life.[2]

Despite the Depression, Ager was still actively trying to promote Norwegian enterprises, for example a book club and a Norwegian language magazine.[3] He saw that the Norwegian cause was at a crossroads: "The old man is in retirement and the children are going around to collect money for a suitable funeral." Yet he believed that a renaissance was still possible. During the decade, he received many tributes, including an article by Skørdalsvold in *Norden*[4] and a greeting from Ludvig Saxe in *Nordmanns-Forbundet* on the occasion of his sixty-fifth birthday: "Is there in the whole Norwegian press any writer who is more distinctive, who has a more personal style, who has so much of value to give his readers as he?"[5] *Nordisk Tidende* in Brooklyn also praised him: he was "one of the most interesting Norwegians in America

144

. . . a full-blooded human being." "Fortunate is that man who at his age can look back on his life and activities and know that he has succeeded in saving his self-respect in our somewhat muddied waters."[6]

Such well-intentioned tributes did not save him from disappointments. One of the hardest blows must have been the repeal, on December 3, 1933, of the Eighteenth Amendment. Also, he submitted *Det vældige navn* to his publisher in Norway without result, and neither an English translation of this book nor his Norwegian book club nor his Norwegian magazine fared any better. In 1935, he modernized the language of some short stories, but the manuscript remains unpublished. His closest friend, probation officer John Gaustad, died on April 29, 1935. Ager would later tell his daughter Hildur, "There hasn't been one day since John died that I have not mourned for him."[7]

His contacts with the Norsemen's League, however, led to a pleasant if strenuous interlude: his last visit to Norway. In return for his expenses, he was invited to give a series of lectures; to his family's relief, his second daughter Valborg accompanied him. "It was easy to forget to exchange a soiled collar, shirt, or handkerchief for a clean one."[8] It is a sign of Ager's acquiescence to English that his travelogue this time was not only printed in Norwegian in *Reform* but also in the Eau Claire *Leader* in English. He titled the series, with an allusion to his favorite American, Mark Twain, the "Marvelous Adventures of Two Innocents Abroad." The trip lasted from September 22 to November 21.[9]

Before sailing from New York he visited the Century of Progress in Chicago, the city of Washington, and New York's Brooklyn Norwegian colony. He was interested in the many scientific marvels at the Chicago fair, including a Ford that talked, "a very human Ford." He had long admired Lincoln and in Washington he saw his impressive memorial: "Here no one but Lincoln is to be heard. . . . Nothing is to disturb the exalted calm that rests on Lincoln's name." In Brooklyn he visited an active Norwegian group, the Bondeungdomslag (Farm Youth League), an offshoot of similar groups in Norway; he noted without comment that their language was *nynorsk*.

They sailed from New York on the *Bergensfjord* of the Norwegian America Line; he observed that contrary to the situation in 1914 the ship was almost empty, with only 125 passengers, no doubt because of the season. He also contrasted the stiff hierarchy on the English boat in 1900 with the obvious democracy of the *Bergensfjord*. He was pleased to meet Gustav Henriksen, then the head of the Norwegian America Line, which in Ager's opinion "is the most solid and happy enterprise for joining our million emigrants with the three millions of Norway."

An attempt by an Oslo journalist to interview and sketch him was waved off. "Write nothing about me," Ager told him. "I've been in America half a century

Ager family picture taken about 1935. From left, back row: Magne, Solveig, Valborg, Roald, Eyvind; front row: Gudrun, Hildur, Waldemar, Gurolle, Borghild. Trygve is not present.

and have experienced nothing remarkable. Others are there for two months or two years and have incredible experiences . . . I haven't made any epoch-making inventions, I haven't been in the films, I haven't even murdered anybody, I don't like to murder, least of all a fellow journalist." The sketch remained incomplete and was printed just as it was, showing only his nose and moustache.[10]

His lecture tour took him down the west coast of the Oslofjord and across to his birthplace Fredrikstad. Then he made his way by the Bergen railroad to western Norway. From there he traveled down the west coast and around to the east. Back in Oslo he headed north on the Dovre railroad over the mountains to Trondheim and points farther north. All in all he gave something like forty lectures in thirty days.

In Oslo he found "everything so new and overwhelming that it almost takes my breath away." After twenty years' absence all had changed, with new functionalist architecture. He philosophized over the new Folketeater built by the Labor Party, "a threatening class symbol, a huge fist raised opposite the old jail, which looks down from the heights in a supercilious and bitter way with its clock eye." He admired the cleaned-up Aker River and did not even dare

146

Waldemar Ager with granddaughter Barbara Bergh. She wrote: I know now that his contributions to the community were important, but as a little girl, he just seemed like a kind old man who would sit and smoke a pipe while he told me stories." (From Glimpses into My Grandfather's Scrapbook, *by Barbara Bergh).*

tell his daughter what it had looked like in his youth. He noted the comparative absence of automobiles and the lack of traffic regulations. He found no evidence of poverty. In southern Norway he glimpsed the great author Knut Hamsun riding a bus unnoticed. In Trondheim he inspected the cathedral, which was being restored. In Oslo he visited Idar Handagard, as he had in 1900 and 1914. In a note, he thanked him for his hospitality to him and his daughter and commented that now he is back in the "daily struggle." "One newspaper after the other is going to the devil and soon it will no doubt be our turn."[11]

In his childhood home in Gressvik "there was no traffic regulation, no police, no crime, no liquor or cards." Those who wanted to sin had to cross the bay to Fredrikstad. "It is strange about one's own home; the children grow up and realize that the parents have struggled for this home . . . for the children's sake. They grow fond of it and no matter how many times it changes owners in later years, it is theirs for life. Such children are never rootless." He concluded his letters from Norway with a deeply felt peroration: "One can trade, exchange, and obtain much in life; but mother is and remains mother, and her children are and remain hers whether or not they recognize her as mother . . . It is easier for children to forget their mother than for the mother to forget her children . . . Those who do so are as a rule poor citizens whether at home or abroad. No country gains anything from them while they live and in heaven there is no place for them when they die." Today Ager's home bears a plaque and the road is named "Waldemar Ager's Way" (Waldemar Agers Vei).

Ager's last trip to Norway was a highly emotional occasion for him. In his reports he offered little criticism, only praise and admiration for the progress the country had made. While he jested about coming back, he clearly felt that this was a final farewell.

Before leaving he gave a talk in the Bergen Museum on the general topic of "The Bridge between Norwegians on Both Sides of the Atlantic." He "gave a lively description" of the struggles of Norwegian immigrants to better their lot in America. He suggested that they had won respect through their industry, but also through the fame of violinist Ole Bull, their contribution to the Civil War, and the recognition of Leif Ericson as the discoverer of America.[12]

Back in Eau Claire he was again faced with problems of Americanization. In January, 1935, the First Norwegian Lutheran Church of that city adopted an entirely new constitution under the name of First Lutheran Church. When the congregation celebrated its seventieth anniversary, the historical pamphlet was in English and a single afternoon service was all that remained of Norwegian. This Ager persistently attended, though he did not cluster with the other members in front, but sat alone in the church balcony. In September, 1935, he wrote his son Trygve about an offer to move to Minneapolis: "What

148

keeps us here, more than anything else, is our job printing, which is independent of the language and is making good progress." He found relief in the cottage at Lake Chetek: "It's a blessed thing to be able to rove around there and fuss with food and kerosene lamps and break things without getting scolded and spill ashes on the floor without any fear or trembling, and even to sit there with your nose in the air, secure in the knowledge that no one but God Himself has seen you, and your conscience is there to testify that even God thinks such things are all right as long as your wife isn't there to see it."[13]

Ager once explained to son Trygve the platform tricks with which he spiced his talks. "I've discovered," he said, "that a public speaker can 'play' his audience much as a musician plays a big pipe organ. First, of course, you must win your listeners over — get them with you. So you tell them a story or two, get them chuckling and really enjoying themselves. Then you shift to something serious, enough to sort of open the curtains to your real message. The audience, with a few signs of restlessness or inattention, will quickly let you know when it's time to turn back to something humorous — or to an anecdote with a strong element of suspense where you actually feel your listeners hanging on every word. Next, probably something serious, even sad, pursuing it until you see eyes moistening and handkerchiefs being raised to the mouth or eyes. That's your sign to turn to something humorous again, giving the people with the handkerchiefs a chance to find relief in laughter. And so on and on. Meanwhile you're delivering your message in short, digestible doses, but saving your strongest appeal for the very end."[14]

This sensible, if somewhat cynical, account of speechmaking, probably reflects Ager's actual practice in addressing his innumerable audiences. One amusing speech that remains in manuscript is an undated one, obviously delivered in English to a group of librarians, perhaps the Library Commission of Eau Claire, of which Ager was a longtime member. It was titled "The Library of the Future," and is a teasing account of possible advances in the storing and distribution of books. He begins by noting that he would have preferred to speak of the librarian, "since he or she is a human being and is constantly rubbing up against the authors on one side and the reading public on the other." Contrary to his own youthful experience with books, people no longer read books as they used to. They are busy studying books, as they might enjoy a restaurant's fine menu instead of ordering a meal. It should be possible to invent a stew, with librarians as the cooks. The talking machine offers another possibility, with books on rolls, to be borrowed in wheelbarrows. The possibility should be explored of ethereal vibrations which the librarian would conduct by wire from author to reader. It should even be possible to inject books, just as surgeons can remove parts of the brain, making librarians into "pill-administering functionaries." Some speak of a "sixth sense" that could be introduced just by rubbing someone's forehead. Trained librarians would do the rubbing, which brought him back to the librarians he started with, who are forever rubbing up against authors and public and "transmitting knowledge from one to the other."[15]

In 1938, Ager prepared his last collection of short stories and called it *Skyldfolk og andre* (Kinfolk and Others).[16] He dedicated this book to Hildur, his eighth child, born in 1915. The book contains eight stories.[17]

"Det hvide Kors i Skogen" (The White Cross in the Woods), the first story in the volume, tells of an ex-typographer, Joakim Roaldsen, who has become a vagrant in America. He has learned to avoid work and has begged a parson's coat in solid black; when he is thrown off a train in a remote Wisconsin community, he is taken for a preacher in the first saloon he enters. When he admits to being Norwegian, an American man married to a Norwegian woman forcibly takes him home to preach a sermon and do ministerial services. He dares not admit that he is not a minister and performs a service to the great satisfaction of the would-be parishioners. When a forest fire breaks out Jens Ruelson (as they call him) helps them all to escape and himself dies, leaving only a white cross in the woods.

"Det blev en Raad tilsist" (A Way was Found at Last) is about a boy and a girl who grow up together. Their families expect them to marry, but somehow each marries someone else. They are constantly quarreling, though they will not allow others to criticize them. The two couples move away together and Per continues his rivalry with Anne Elizabeth. He has seven children, but she has none. After a time their mates die and they could marry, but a sharp remark by her drives him away. Only a visit by his parents brings them together, children and all.

"Veien til Lykken" (The Road to Happiness) tells of a young man named Olaf who is miserable on Christmas Eve because his sweetheart has rejected him on account of his drinking. He decides to try making someone happy and has a hard time finding anyone who needs help. But then he finds a boy whose mother has been run over; he helps the boy find his mother, and in the hospital her nurse turns out to be his old sweetheart.

"Undesirable" is the story of a young Norwegian girl who gets a good job with an American family. She is so well treated by them that she begins to feel like a member of the family. She rejects offers of marriage and stays on with the couple until they are old and feeble and she herself has become slightly demented. In the end younger relatives claim the estate and she is deported back to Norway as an "undesirable alien."

"Sjel tilsalgs" (Mussels for Sale) is about a man who visits Norway and goes with a boating party out to some islands. Two of the group go looking for water and run across an old couple who have been in America. The old woman expresses her impatience with being back in Norway; they have lived in Chicago and Tacoma and do not feel happy either here or there. One of the men philosophizes about nostalgia; it is not so much a question of geography as of missing one's childhood. "People do not realize that it is their own youth, or their own best manhood years, that they have moved away from." Twenty years later the narrator remembers the episode and the sign, which in Norwegian can also be read as "soul for sale."

"Juledrømmen som brast" (The Shattered Dream of Christmas) is a rather bitter story about an old couple whose seven children are scattered all over the country. But they have decided to come home for Christmas, and the old folks dream of similar occasions with the children in earlier years when they were home in Norway. But the American children get so absorbed in discussing baseball and bridge that they forget the old folks. The father goes to bed and the mother cries in the kitchen.

"Det kunne slompe" (It Could Happen) is about a pastor's wife whose husband neglects her for his work. In desperation she thinks of leaving with a friendly engineer; but in the end she stays with her husband because they have both been to a shoemaker who has a cryptic way of responding "it could happen" to any problem. The phrase becomes a subtle indicator of the possibilities in life that are frequently overlooked. It is a potentially humorous story.

"Arven" (The Inheritance) is the ironic story of Mrs. Torplie, who has been caring for her old bachelor roomer Hans for many years. She emphasizes how much she has done for him and she is tearful because after his death the chest he had promised her is empty. But when a lawyer comes and tells her she will be well off, she discovers that the valuable securities old Hans had willed her have been cut up by her children. Because of her ignorance she gets only a small inheritance instead of a fortune.

These stories are all about quirks of human nature, oddities or absurd stupidities that get in the way of human accomplishment. They read well and have a resigned tone, characterizing his Norwegian Americans as caught up in the psychological problems of immigration.

As always, his friend Skørdalsvold was ready with praise for the collection. He characterized the first story, "The White Cross in the Woods," as a masterpiece. As a whole, he was glad to see that there was none of the "empty, boring affectation (*jaaleri*) that we find in so many authors in our time."[18]

Reform was in serious financial trouble, but Ager kept with it, doing most of the work himself, along with a linotypist from Eleva, Wisconsin, one Elton Johnson. In writing to Professor Olav Midttun in Oslo, to thank him for a birthday greeting, he described the situation: "Conditions are distressing for Norwegian newspapers here now; but we have struggled our way through. . . . We can still make a stir when either Mr. Hambro [the president of the

Storting] or the Crown Prince and his wife come over. But it is more like the squirming of a half-dead fish when you touch it."[19]

On April 9, 1940, the German war machine rolled over Norway without warning and occupied it for what would be five dismal years. To Ager it must have seemed like the ultimate catastrophe. He had just received the St. Olaf Medal established the previous year by King Haakon VII, for his promotion of knowledge about Norway and solidarity between Norway and the emigrated Norwegians in America, when the king had to flee and go into exile in England. Ager would not live to see the liberation of Norway.

A cordial exchange of letters between President Lars W. Boe of St. Olaf College and "Dr. Ager" began with Boe's chiding him for charging too little for a St. Olaf advertisement in his newspaper. He told him "you have at least one reader who appreciates the 'salt' in your philosophy and outlook." He said he read Ager's newspaper with greater interest than any other. In his payment he added ten cents for a "good ten-cent cigar." Ager accepted the money but pointed out that he did not know just what effect such a cigar would have on a printer "spiritually and otherwise" so he spent only half of it on a cigar and the other half on a cup of coffee. He went on to wish that he could have had a genuine vacation. "I do believe I could have written a real book. Working piecemeal in evenings with no place to sit down in solitude is trying. When I wrote *Hundeøine* I was surrounded by two high-school girls, one son in teacher's college, one in grade school, one grown-up girl and her boy friend, a radio, and a dog that wasn't grown up and was therefore bothersome." "But your letter was a sort of tonic. I have no one here now that I can talk with and discuss my own faults and — principally of course — other people's. At times I am not sure whether anybody reads the newspaper or not." In further letters President Boe noted that he put on the Litt. D. "because we gave it to you and I notice that you never use it." To this Ager replied that it stood him in good stead in Norway, where "it made up for lack of dignity, weight, height, and looks."[20]

On May 17, 1941, Ager gave his last Seventeenth of May address, to a small Norwegian congregation in Hawkins, Wisconsin. After his speech, a freewill offering was collected and sent to the American organization known as Norway Relief. On June 27 he addressed a group of emigrants from Østerdal, a valley close to his birthplace, Fredrikstad.

His last two editorials were about the war. "The Last Kaiser" recalled the emperors overthrown in World War I, all preferable to what followed them: "The Czar was better than Stalin and William was better than Hitler." "What has been won or can be won by the present war is no doubt nothing. It does not seem that the sacrifice and sufferings have ever been justified by the results."[21] "The war goes on and people are busy killing each other." "There

152

Monument on Ager's grave in Lakeview Cemetery, Eau Claire. "Erected to the memory of Waldemar T. Ager by his many friends, associates and countrymen."

is poison in nearly all that we read or hear." "Most of the history we read is about war. But few recall why the wars began." "There have been so many excuses for war." "People must some day recognize that international crime does exist." "In our world, where might is right among the nations, a huge fist that represented a common international conscience would be something the Lord could use in his service."[22]

On June 28 he complained of feeling miserable and was taken to Luther Hospital in Eau Claire. He proved to have cancer of the colon, and on Friday, August 1, 1941, he died.

Ager's funeral was held in Eau Claire's First Lutheran Church and was attended by a large number of mourners, including President Lars W. Boe of St. Olaf College. The usual eulogies were pronounced by the pastors, one in English and one in Norwegian. As one speaker put it, "He was not always right, but he was always honest." Obituaries in the local newspapers and the Norwegian-American press were numerous and detailed, all complimentary

153

to his life and personality. He was a great and good man, much loved and admired, not least for his unfailing modesty. Friends and admirers gathered funds for an imposing monument in Lakeview Cemetery, which was dedicated in November, 1945. The inscription reads: "Editor, author, lecturer, publisher of 'Reform,' a distinguished interpreter of Norwegian heritage and cultural traditions."

Reform was kept alive only until September 18, 1941, when his heirs shut it down. As he had predicted, when he died the newspaper died. "*Reform* was Ager and Ager was *Reform*."[23]

The Eau Claire Library Board provided a memorial plaque which was placed near the main entrance to the library building. Gurolle Ager survived her husband by ten years and was cared for by her son Roald: she died on December 25, 1951. According to son Trygve, she woke up from a deep sleep just before she died and said, "I did the best I could with the little I had to do with." He felt that here she had succinctly expressed the essence of a life of family service.

Perspective

THE NORWEGIAN-AMERICAN editors who were still alive to memorialize Ager at his death were only too well aware that with his passing an era was over. Voices were raised to keep *Reform* alive, but the heirs wisely recognized that not only could no one replace him, but the day of Norwegian-American journalism was past. *Reform* clung to life only because of Ager's dogged determination, which still left him at his death a year short of his fifty-year goal. All other small newspapers were gone and even the large ones were falling by the wayside. *Skandinaven* closed its doors in 1941 and *Minneapolis Tidende* in 1935. *Decorah-Posten* would expire in 1972.[1] *Nordisk Tidende* on the East Coast and *Washington Posten* on the West Coast survived, only by heroic effort, under the altered titles of *Norway Times* and *Western Viking*, and for a time there were successor newspapers in Chicago and Minneapolis. But as Karsten Roedder, columnist in *Nordisk Tidende*, wrote after Ager's death: "Norwegianness in America is coming to an end." He philosophized a bit about the fact that Norwegian immigrants were primarily concerned with making a living and that literary culture was a product of economic surplus. "Their newspapers pale and die because the immigrant pales and dies."[2]

This was of course in full accord with Ager's gloomier predictions. He had hoped that new generations would arise to carry the torch, retaining and developing their heritage like the Jews, whose example he never tired of citing. From his own experiences as an immigrant in the flood tide of the 1880s he projected an ideal pluralistic America that would leave space and freedom for a variety of languages and cultures, all feeding into a larger unity. It was somehow a new Europe, with all the nationalities and ethnic groups intact, but without the hates and rivalries, the bitter wars and massacres that soaked nearly every foot of European soil. This was the vision that sustained Ager's life and

155

work, a noble vision that in the end proved to be just that—a vision. Like many an idealistic advocate, he lost his case, but he won his glory.

That glory is still not entirely dimmed. There are still teachers of Norwegian in various academic institutions in the northern and western United States who seek to spread knowledge of the Norwegian language and culture to their American students. There are summer camps that cultivate the language among children of Norwegian ancestry, and publications in which one can read of current events in Norway. The Sons of Norway flourishes in the northern states and has even spread its tentacles to Norway; one of its programs includes courses in Norwegian. Above all the Norwegian-American Historical Association in Northfield and Vesterheim, the Norwegian-American Museum in Decorah are living resources for knowledge about the Norwegian-American past. Ager would have sniffed at much of this and declared that it was all well and good, but it was not the living tradition he had envisioned. It was all history, a celebration of the past.

But the past *is* history. The crises that America has endured in its various booms and depressions, not to mention two world wars and the constant threat of a third, have altered the face of the whole world. But one can still look back on Ager's world and learn something of value for the present.

Various writers have explored Ager's contribution from special points of view, most of which have been considered in the present study. Two of the most perceptive are American scholars, both with Eau Claire antecedents, Clarence Kilde and Kenneth Smemo. Only the fact that neither one has planned a whole book on the subject emboldened the present writer to undertake this volume.

Smemo's three articles on Ager constitute excellent studies with many illuminating insights. He neatly summarizes Ager's goals in three points: to eliminate alcohol from American life; to preserve the Norwegian language among the immigrants and their descendants; and to inspire a Norwegian-American literature. Baldly stated, these ideals were certainly the mainsprings of Ager's life and career. Since in the end all three failed, the logical conclusion is that Ager's life was a failure. Smemo claims that "his causes were all doomed to failure," and calls him the "Norwegian-American Sisyphus," in allusion to the classical figure who "was condemned to spend eternity pushing a heavy stone up a hill only to have it constantly roll back down again."[3]

Kilde, who has dealt primarily with Ager's last years, sees him as a figure in a Greek tragedy, "a great and good man" who "had a tragic flaw in his character: he was unable to compromise." "Fate, in the form of inevitably changing circumstances, brought his life down to an unhappy, indeed a sad ending in the dark decade of his declining years."[4]

Both of these studies are fine analyses of Ager's life and character, deeply

156

sympathetic assessments. No one can overlook Ager's failure to achieve the goals he set for himself. However, there are other points of view which one can adopt in considering Ager's life work. One could argue that the literary character most like Ager is Don Quixote, the hero of lost causes, who spent his life vainly fighting windmills. Cervantes made of his hero one of the great figures of world literature. The fact that Ager was an ironic humorist in the tradition of Mark Twain kept him from being either a Sisyphus or an Agamemnon. He knew that his battles were in vain, but he enjoyed the fight. As he once put it, "I have to have something to love or hate." He loved temperance and Norwegian culture, and he hated drinking and assimilation, but he loved controversy more. In fact, fighting against the inevitable has long been regarded as the very hallmark of the hero. In his modest sphere, Ager had qualities that allied him with that noble tradition.

Hence, Ager's life can be seen as neither unhappy, fruitless, nor tragic. This study has tried to show that he led a fruitful and satisfying life. He carried on activities that were of incalculable benefit not only to his own group but to America as a whole. He was surely one of the most outstanding Norwegians ever to settle in the United States.

Ager fell short of becoming the greatest author among Norwegian Americans: that distinction was reserved for his friend Rølvaag. But his writing is well worth more attention than it has received. He may not have been the greatest mind among them: that may have been Thorstein Veblen. But he did have a very sharp mind and a flawless memory that he could call on both night and day. He did not achieve the fame of Rasmus B. Anderson, or the political status of Knute Nelson, or even the popularity of the writer and lecturer Peer Strømme. But he is easily the most significant humanist among Norwegians in America.

The three ideals listed above by Smemo were all *ideals of culture*. He strove for sobriety because Norwegian immigrants were wasting their potential on the nearest and cheapest drug. His temperance societies were organizations that emphasized worthwhile cultural activities to replace the seductive atmosphere of the saloon. Only by staying sober could Norwegians climb the ladder of American success. He worked for the Norwegian language because it was a precious bond between parents and children. It carried with it centuries of tradition and kept mothers and fathers from becoming "foreigners" despised by their own children. Otherwise, nothing awaited the second generation but adopting Anglo-Saxon ways before they were ready to absorb them.

Finally, he wanted a Norwegian-American literature because he regarded literature as the highest cultural expression of any group. Here he had in mind, for instance, the example of the Icelanders, who had borne a most precious treasure with them out of Norway to their remote North Atlantic island. He believed there was an unbreakable bond between language and literature, being well aware that no language can be adequately rendered into another. A literature of their own would be the ultimate cultural achievement of Norwegians in America.

Through a lifetime he single-handedly created a sense of cultural unity among Norwegian Americans; he gave the group the concept of a Norwegian America that stands as its historical monument. From Norway he had learned, in Ibsen's words, "to hold aloft the banner of the ideal." In America he had absorbed the spirit of freedom, of personal achievement, the "American dream." He read both American and Norwegian literature and embodied aspects of both in his writing. Out of the miscellaneous raw material of immigrant life he welded a conscious body of persons whose institutions and ideal goals went beyond the purely material. As the quintessential Norwegian American he was not typical, and he kept up a lifetime love-and-hate relationship with his countrymen. Because he could look at them with irony, he was neither a tragic nor an unhappy figure. He led a long and useful life, doing what he wanted to do, fighting all the way. Waldemar Ager amply deserves the lines from the poet Johan Sebastian Welhaven that Kilde cited as an ideal description of him:

> Kan du, igjennem din Strid og din Daad
> redde det barnlige Skjær til det Sidste,
> da har du Regnbuen over din Graad,
> da har du Glorien over din Kiste.

> (If through your strife and your fears,
> Your childlike heart you can save,
> You will gain a rainbow over your tears,
> And a halo of glory over your grave.)[5]

Notes

Introduction

1. Theodore C. Blegen, *Norwegian Migration to America: The American Transition* (Northfield, Minnesota, 1940), 589–590.

Chapter 1

1. Ole Brunshus Olson, born in Oslo in 1857, customarily abbreviated his name; friends affectionately expanded it to Ole Broder Olson.

2. Minutes in Ager collection, Norwegian-American Historical Association (NAHA) archives, dated June 23, 1892.

3. *Reform*, December, 1897.

4. Pamphlet titled "The Norwegian Danish Grand Temple," in Ager collection, NAHA. The poem in Norwegian reads

> "Man kan læse, man kan samle
> Ind fra alle Verdens Bøger —
> Efter Kundskab grandske, famle,
> Dog vor Grandsken bare øger
> Længslen efter hvad vi søger, —
> Sandhed, Skjønhed: ja derefter
> Vildt vi jager for at ta dem
> Naar vi ei har mere Kræfter
> Er vi kanske langt ifra dem.
> Ingen vil det; Ingen ved det —
> Jeg har gjort det, — jeg er kjed det."

5. Waldemar Ager, *Paa drikkeondets konto* (Eau Claire, 1894).

6. Olson, introduction, *Paa drikkeondets konto*. In Norwegian it is

"Om ikke jeg ved, hvad jeg evner—
En Ting er mig ganske klar:
Jeg faar ikke Fred, før jeg stævner
Til Kamp med de Vaaben, jeg har."

7. The verse in Norwegian is as follows:

"Smukke Kvinder ham rakte
Bægeret fyldt med perlende Vin,
Han vægred sig før han smagte,
Og tog forsigtig og sagte
Imod Lasten det første Trin."

8. A. H. Winsnes, *Norsk litteraturhistorie*, 5 (Oslo, 1937), 385.

9. Excerpts in *Reform*, January 15, 1895.

10. J. J. Skørdalsvold, in *Reform*, November 27, 1894.

11. "Idar," in *Menneskevennen* (Oslo), September 25, 1897. The writer was Idar Handagard.

12. Ager to O. A. Buslett, December 1, 1894, in Ager collection, NAHA.

13. Ager to Buslett, February 13, 1900.

Chapter 2

1. Ager, *Reform*, January 24, 1935; also in English in *The Daily Telegram* (Eau Claire).

2. Ager, *Reform*, January 24, 1935. Ager is the author of all citations from *Reform* unless otherwise indicated.

3. Ager, *I strømmen* (Eau Claire, 1899).

4. Ager, *Hundeøine* (Oslo, 1929), trans. by Charles Wharton Stork as *I Sit Alone* (New York, 1931).

5. *Reform*, May 17, 1923.

6. Andrew Hansen, in *Reform*, February, 1914.

7. Peer Strømme, "Norsk-amerikanske forfattere—Waldemar Ager," in *Symra*, 3 (1907), 138.

8. *Reform*, December 31, 1889.

9. Pamphlet in Ager collection. The Norwegian text follows:

"Din Kamp ved vi gjælder den gode Sag,
Et Maal maa du da hae' for Øie.
O maatte vi Fienden da se en Dag,
I Stöv for dit Banner sig böie.
Da naar du træder din sidste Dands.
Din Isse prydes med en Laurbærkrands."

10. Ager, "Paa de berusende Drikkes Konto," in *Templarbladet*, 1:7–9 (April-June, 1891).

Notes

Chapter 3

1. *Reform*, April 31, 1895.

2. *Reform*, March 24, 1896.

3. "The Emperor's New Clothes," in *Reform*, August 4, 1896.

4. For further information about Tveitmoe, see Lloyd Hustvedt, "O. A. Tveitmoe: Labor Leader," in *Norwegian-American Studies*, 30 (Northfield, Minnesota, 1985), 3–54.

5. Johannes B. Wist, ed., *Norsk-amerikanernes festskrift* (Decorah, Iowa, 1914), 127–128.

6. *Reform*, July 6, 1897.

7. *Reform*, September 7, 1897.

8. *Reform*, March 15, 1897.

9. *Reform*, November 16, 1897.

10. Hustvedt, *Rasmus Bjørn Anderson: Pioneer Scholar* (Northfield, Minnesota, 1966), 259–260.

11. *Reform*, October 31, 1899.

12. *Reform*, December 5, 1899.

13. Ager, *Afholdssmuler fra boghylden* (Eau Claire, 1901).

14. Reviews reprinted in *Reform*, December 1, 1901.

15. *Reform*, August 2, 1899.

16. *Reform*, September 12, 26, 1899.

17. Hildur Ager Nicolai, trans., *The White Cross in the Woods* (n.p., 1982), 95–96.

18. Clarence Kilde, interviews with Ager children, 1975–1976. Notes in NAHA archives.

19. Nicolai, *The White Cross*.

Chapter 4

1. *Reform*, November 13, 1900.

2. *Reform*, October 12, 1907 – March 3, 1908.

3. Handagard, "Wm. Ager som forfatter," in *Menneskevennen*, reprinted in *Reform*, June 26, 1900.

Chapter 5

1. *Reform*, June 19–July 31, 1900.

2. Ager, *Nordmanns-Forbundet*, December, 1934, 353.

3. Ager to Handagard, September 28, 1900.

4. Ager to Handagard, November 7, 1900.

5. Ager to Handagard, December 24, 1900.

6. Handagard, "Vor sag og dens digtere," in *Afholdsvennens Aarbog 1903* (Oslo, 1903), 10–15.

7. Ager, handwritten autobiography in Handagard collection, in possession of his daughter, Herborg Handagard, Oslo.

Chapter 6

1. *Reform*, October 2, 1900.

2. *Reform*, January 15, 1901.

3. *Reform*, February 5, 1901.

4. Ager to Buslett, March 23, 1900.

5. Ager to Buslett, August 19, 1900.

6. *Reform*, November 27, 1900.

7. T. K. Thorvilson, in *Reform*, August 20, 1901.

8. *Reform*, August 27, 1901.

9. Thorvilson, in *Reform*, January 21, 1902.

10. O. M. Norlie, *Norsk lutherske prester i Amerika 1843–1915* (Minneapolis, 1915), 187.

11. *Reform*, April 29, 1902.

12. Henrik Voldal, in *Reform*, May 6, 1902.

13. Ager to Handagard, April 30, 1902.

14. Ager to Handagard, December 17, 1902.

15. *Reform*, February 3, 1903.

16. A selection of articles from *Kvartalskrift* that deal with pluralism and assimilation has been published by the Norwegian-American Historical Association as *Cultural Pluralism* versus *Assimilation: The Views of Waldemar Ager*, ed. Odd S. Lovoll (Northfield, Minnesota, 1977).

17. Johannes B. Wist, in *Kvartalskrift*, January, 1906, 6.

18. *Reform*, August 30, 1904.

19. *Reform*, September 27, 1904.

20. Ager, "Vore kulturelle muligheter," in *Kvartalskrift*, April, 1905, 2–10. Reprinted in Lovoll, *Cultural Pluralism*, 46–54, trans. by Sigvald Stoylen.

Chapter 7

1. *Reform*, November 14, 1905.

2. *Reform*, April 23, 1907.

3. Ager, *Fortællinger for Eyvind* (Eau Claire, 1905). Translated by J. J. Skørdalsvold as *When You Are Tired of Playing* (Eau Claire, 1907).

4. S. O. Møst, in *Reform*, October 4, 1905.

5. Ager to Buslett, March 21, 1908.

6. Møst, in *Reform*, October 4, 1905.

7. Ager, *Hverdagsfolk*, (Eau Claire, 1908).

8. *Kvartalskrift*, May, 1919, 16–19.

9. Ager, "Om at bevare vort Morsmaal," in *Kvartalskrift*, October, 1905, 14–29. Reprinted in Lovoll, *Cultural Pluralism*, 55–63, trans. by Sigvald Stoylen.

10. J. N. Kildahl, in *Reform*, September 3, 1907.

11. Ager, "Det viktigste," in *Kvartalskrift*, January, 1908, 4–12. Reprinted in Lovoll, *Cultural Pluralism*, 68–76, trans. by Leif E. Hansen as "The Language is Most Important."

12. *Reform*, December 18, 1906.
13. *Reform*, April 17–May 1, 1906.
14. Peer Strømme, in *Symra*, 3 (1907), 137–147.

Chapter 8

1. Ager, *Kristus for Pilatus. En norsk-amerikansk fortælling* (Eau Claire, 1910), translated as *Christ before Pilate* (Minneapolis, 1924).
2. The name may have been suggested by a Fredrikstad family named Velde.
3. The large church in Eau Claire, to which Ager's family belonged, was the First Norwegian Lutheran Church, founded in 1864. In Ager's day it was a congregation of the United Norwegian Lutheran Church. The high-church congregation was the smaller Our Savior's of the Norwegian Synod, founded in 1876.
4. Ager to Arne Garborg, December 5, 1910, in University of Oslo library.
5. *Reform*, February 28, 1911.
6. Buslett, in *Reform*, February 7, 1911.
7. *Reform*, March 21, 1911.
8. Agnes M. Wergeland to Ager, April 2, 1913.
9. Dr. Christian Johnson to Ager, April 2, 1913.
10. J. L. Nydahl to Ager, sometime in 1913.
11. O. E. Rølvaag to Ager, December 15, 1910.
12. *Reform*, January 9, 1912.
13. Handagard, in *Morgenposten* (Oslo), reprinted in *Reform*, January 9, 1912.
14. *Reform*, January 9, 1912.
15. *Reform*, July 23, 1912.
16. O. M. Olesen to Ager, December 2, 1912.

Chapter 9

1. Ager, in *Symra*, 7 (1911), 214–224.
2. *Reform*, June 4, 1913.
3. *Reform*, December 5, 1911.
4. *Reform*, December 19, 1911.
5. *Reform*, January 2, 1912.
6. Ager, in *Symra*, 7: 166–192.
7. Ager, in *Symra*, 7: 191.
8. Ager, in *Symra*, 8 (1912), 214–224.
9. *Symra*, 9 (1913), 46–54, 110–115, 171–173.
10. *Reform*, January 13–April 21, 1914.
11. Ager, *Fortællinger og skisser* (Eau Claire, 1913).
12. Ager, "Før og nu," in *Nordmanns-Forbundet*, 27 (1934) 353–355.
13. *Norge i Amerika*, vol. 5 of *Boken om Norge* (Christiania, 1915).
14. *Reform*, July 7, 14, 1914; *Kvartalskrift*, 10 (1914), 105–127, and 11 (1915), 2–12, 34–49.
15. *Reform*, July 7, 1914.

16. *Reform*, July 14, 1914.

17. Ager, in Wist, *Norsk-amerikanernes festskrift*, 292–306.

18. Handagard, "Waldemar Ager," in *Fem folkedigtere* (Trondheim, 1915), 75–105.

19. *Reform*, December 14, 1915.

20. Ager, *Oberst Heg og hans gutter* (Eau Claire, 1916).

21. Ager to Buslett, March 8, 1911.

22. Ager to Buslett, January 5, 1915.

Chapter 10

1. A manuscript translation by Harry T. Cleven is in the NAHA archives.

2. Ager to Buslett, September 22, 1916.

3. Ager, *Paa veien til smeltepotten* (Eau Claire, 1917).

4. Israel Zangwill, *The Melting Pot* (New York, 1908), 33.

5. Skørdalsvold, in *Folkebladet*, reprinted in *Reform*, December 18, 1917.

6. *Washington-Posten*, reprinted in *Reform*, December 18, 1917.

7. Ager to Carl G. O. Hansen, November 15, 1917.

8. Ager to Buslett, September 26, 1917.

Chapter 11

1. Magnus Swenson to Ager, September 11, 1917, in Ager papers, NAHA.

2. Ager to Swenson, undated, in Ager papers.

3. For an outline of his career, see Olaf Hougen, "Magnus Swenson, Inventor and Engineer," in *Norwegian-American Studies and Records*, 10 (1938), 152–173.

4. Ager, *Udvalgte fortællinger* (Minneapolis, 1918).

5. Ager, "Den store Udjævning," in *Kvartalskrift*, 13 (1917), 73–89; 14 (1918), 100–115; 15 (1919), 37–50; and 16 (1920), 9–16.

6. Ager, "Den store Udjævning," translated by Liv Dahl as "The Great Leveling," in Lovoll, *Cultural Pluralism*, 101–116.

7. Ager, "Forholdet til Staten," translated by Carl H. Chrislock as "The Citizen and the State," in Lovoll, *Cultural Pluralism*, 117–129.

8. *Reform*, January 15, 1918.

9. *Reform*, March 15, 1918.

10. *Reform*, March 25, 1919.

11. *Reform*, February 25, 1919.

12. Letter by Louis J. Kernen in *Reform*, March 10, 1919.

13. Eau Claire *Leader*, March 24, 1919.

14. *Reform*, March 25, 1919.

15. *Skandinaven*, April 4, 1919.

16. Eau Claire *Leader*, August 2, 1941.

17. Ager to Camilla Cameron, March 31, 1920.

18. *Reform*, July 15, 1919.

19. *Reform*, October 5, 1920.

20. *Reform*, December 14, 1920.

21. *Reform*, January 4, 1921. The book was translated by Sivert Erdahl and the author and published by Harper's in 1930 as *Pure Gold*.

22. *Reform*, January 3, 1922.

23. *Reform*, December 28, 1920.

24. *Reform*, June 7, 1921.

25. Ager, *Ny samling. Fortællinger og skisser* (Eau Claire, 1921).

26. Skørdalsvold, in *Reform*, March, 1922.

27. Wist, in *Decorah-Posten*, reprinted in *Reform*, January 31, 1922.

Chapter 12

1. Sigurd Folkestad, in *Reform*, February 14, 1922.

2. Ager, in *Smaalenslaget i Amerika—Aarbok* (St. Paul, Minnesota, 1922), 5.

3. *Reform*, May 4, 1922.

4. Haugen, *The Norwegian Language in America* (2nd ed., Bloomington, 1969), 258–259.

5. *Reform*, September 28, 1922.

6. *Reform*, December 14, 1922.

7. *Reform*, December 6, 1923.

8. *Reform*, December 14, 1922.

9. *Reform*, January 25, 1923.

10. *Reform*, January 11, 18, 1923.

11. Bjarne Blehr, in *Duluth Skandinav*, December 23, 1922.

12. *Reform*, January 11, 18, 1923.

13. *Reform*, February 15, 1923.

14. *Reform*, March 1, 1923.

15. *Reform*, May 3, 1923.

16. *Reform*, May 17, 1923.

17. *Reform*, June 1, 1923.

18. *Reform*, August 19, 1923.

19. *Reform*, August 2, 1923.

20. *Reform*, October 18, 1923.

21. *Reform*, November 15, 1923.

22. Ager, *Det vældige navn* (Eau Claire, 1923).

23. Skørdalsvold, in *Reform*, January 24, 1924.

24. Buslett, in *Skandinaven*, quoted in *Reform*, December 27, 1923.

25. Olav Lie, in *Reform*, July 24, 1924.

26. Rølvaag, in *Reform*, January 3, 1924.

27. "Jens K. Hansen," in *Reform*, June 7, 1924.

28. Ager to Buslett, May 7, 1921.

29. "En gammel Lærerinde," in *Reform*, January 4, 1922.

Chapter 13

1. *Reform*, January 3, 1924.

2. *Reform*, October 30, 1924. See also Ager, in *Nordmanns-Forbundet*, 25 (1932), 294–297.

3. Ager, undated speech.

4. *Reform*, November 6, 1924.

5. *Reform*, June 12, 1924.

6. *Reform*, October 6, 1925.

7. *Reform*, July 9, 1925.

8. *Reform*, July 30, 1925.

9. *Reform*, November 27, 1923.

10. *Reform*, November 5, 1924.

11. *Reform*, January 15, 1925.

12. *Reform*, February 5, 1925, reprinted in *Norse-American Centennial 1825–1925* (Minneapolis, 1925), 12–13.

13. *Reform*, May 21, 1925.

14. Rølvaag, in *Reform*, July 2, 1925.

15. *Reform*, February 25, 1924.

16. *Reform*, January 8, 1925.

17. *Reform*, September 3, 1925.

18. *Reform*, April 8, 1926.

19. Ager, *Gamlelandets sønner* (Oslo, 1926). Translated by Trygve M. Ager as *Sons of the Old Country* (Lincoln, Nebraska, 1983).

20. *Reform*, March 10, 1927.

21. D. G. Ristad, in *Decorah-Posten*, 1927.

22. Hans Olav, in *Nordisk Tidende*, October 7, 1926.

23. Handagard, in *Porsgrunns Dagblad*, December 16, 1926.

24. Rølvaag, in *Skandinaven*, November 24, 1926.

25. Øyvind T. Gulliksen, "In Defense of a Norwegian-American Culture: Waldemar Ager's *Sons of the Old Country*," in *American Studies in Scandinavia*, 19 (1987), 39–52.

26. *Reform*, February 23, 1928.

27. Ager to Rølvaag, December 14, 1928. The Ager-Rølvaag correspondence is in the NAHA archives.

28. Ager to Rølvaag, March 12, 1929.

29. Ager to Rølvaag, March 28, 1929.

30. *Reform*, February 14, 1929.

31. *Reform*, February 23, 1928.

32. *Reform*, February 23, 1928.

33. Ager, "En gammel Kjæmpe," in *Nordmanns-Forbundet*, 23 (1930), 408–411.

34. Folkestad, in *Nordmanns-Forbundet*, 22 (1929), 156–157.

Chapter 14

1. Ager, *Hundeøine* (Oslo, 1929). Translated by Charles Wharton Stork as *I Sit Alone* (New York, 1931).

2. Clarence Kilde, "Dark Decade: The Declining Years of Waldemar Ager," in *Norwegian-American Studies*, 28 (1979), 177.

3. Kilde, "Tragedy in the Life and Writings of Waldemar Ager, Norwegian immigrant, author and editor, 1869-1941" (M.A. thesis, University of Minnesota, 1978), 177-178.

4. Knud Wefald, in *Normanden*, December, 1929.

5. Georg Strandvold, in *Decorah-Posten*, November 12, 1929, reprinted in *Reform*, November 21, 1929.

6. R. Grieg, in *Aftenposten*, November 2, 1929, reprinted in *Reform*, November 21, 1929.

7. Stein Balstad, in *Morgenposten*, November 12, 1929.

8. Arne Sunde, *Heime men borte: Ein analyse av 7 norsk-amerikanske romanar* (Bergen, 1984), 82.

9. Reviews reprinted in *Reform*, May 28, 1931.

10. Trygve Ager scrapbook, cited in Kilde, "Dark Decade," 180.

11. Ager, *Under forvandlingens tegn* (Eau Claire, 1930).

12. *Reform*, May 9, 1929.

13. *Reform*, April 7, 1927.

14. *Reform*, April 19, 1928.

15. *Reform*, October 19-November 27, 1930.

16. *Reform*, April 10, 1930.

17. *Reform*, November 6, 1930.

18. Ager to Rølvaag, undated.

19. *Reform*, May 1, 1930.

20. *Reform*, January 31, 1929.

21. *Reform*, October 23, 1929.

22. *Reform*, November 29, 1929.

23. *Reform*, January 10, 1930.

24. Rølvaag to Ager, undated. Ager's wife, like Rølvaag, was from Nordland.

25. Undated letter from Rølvaag to Ager, 1930.

26. Rølvaag to Ager, February 13, 1930.

27. Ager to Rølvaag, February 7, 1930.

28. Undated letter from Rølvaag to Ager.

29. Ager to Rølvaag, March 18, 1930.

30. Ager to Rølvaag, April 4, 1930.

31. Ager to Rølvaag, undated. Bjarne Blehr was a reviewer for a Duluth newspaper who had written what Ager considered a particularly stupid review of Ager's writing.

32. Charles Wharton Stork to Ager, December, 1930.

33. Ager to Rølvaag, November 21, 1930.

34. Ager to Rølvaag, December 18, 1930.

35. Rølvaag to Ager, December 22, 1930.

36. Undated letter from Ager to Rølvaag.
37. Ager to Rølvaag, March, 1931.
38. Undated letter from Alfred Adsem to Ager.
39. Ager to Rølvaag, undated.
40. Undated letter from Rølvaag to Ager.
41. Ager to Rølvaag, April 4, 1931.
42. Rølvaag to Ager, April 10, 1931.
43. Ager to Rølvaag, July 18, 1931; Rølvaag to Ager, August 10, 1931.
44. Ager to Rølvaag, October, 1931.
45. *Reform*, December 3, 1931.
46. Ager to Jennie Rølvaag, November 12, 1932.

Chapter 15

1. Ager to Trygve Ager, in Trygve Ager's scrapbook.
2. Ager, introduction to Rølvaag, *Fortællinger og skildringer* (Minneapolis, 1931), 7–23.
3. Ager to J.N. Kildahl, December 19, 1930.
4. Skørdalsvold, "Man of Many Minds," in *Norden*, July, 1931.
5. Ludvig Saxe, in *Nordmanns-Forbundet*, 27 (1934), 153.
6. *Nordisk Tidende*, March, 1934.
7. Kilde, interview with Hildur Ager Nicolai, March 23, 1977.
8. Kilde, "Tragedy in the Life and Writings of Waldemar Ager," 182.
9. His accounts of the trip appeared in *Reform*, October 18, 1934 – February 28, 1935.
10. Undated clipping from *Dagbladet* (Oslo), ca. September 29, 1934.
11. Ager to Handagard, December 7, 1934.
12. *Morgenavisen* (Bergen), November 26, 1934.
13. Ager to Trygve Ager, September, 1935.
14. Trygve Ager scrapbook.
15. Ager, undated manuscript in NAHA archives.
16. Ager, *Skyldfolk og andre* (Eau Claire, 1938).
17. Hildur Ager Nicolai translated these stories and had them published privately in 1983 as *The White Cross in the Woods and Other Norwegian Immigrant Stories*. Her English title is based on the first story in the book. The volume also contains biographical material and a number of pictures.
18. Skørdalsvold, in *Reform*, November 3, 1938.
19. Ager to Olav Midttun, May 26, 1939, in University library, Oslo. The reference is to a visit by Carl Joachim Hambro and Crown Prince Olav and his consort Märtha.
20. Boe-Ager correspondence, October 7, 8, 22, November 30, December 6, 1940, in the St. Olaf College Archives.
21. *Reform*, June 12, 1941.
22. *Reform*, June 19, 1941.
23. J. O. Evjen, in *Reform*, August 1, 1941.

Perspective

1. Lovoll, *The Promise of America* (Minneapolis, 1984), 209.

2. Karsten Roedder, in *Nordisk Tidende*, August 14, 1941.

3. Kenneth Smemo, "Waldemar Ager: Norwegian-American Sisyphus," in Dorothy Skårdal and Ingrid Kongslien, eds., *Essays on Norwegian-American Literature and History* (Oslo, 1986), 141.

4. Kilde, "Dark Decade: The Declining Years of Waldemar Ager," 162.

5. Quoted in Kilde, "Dark Decade," 189.

Bibliography

1. Stories and Sketches by Ager, with selected reviews

"Paa de berusende drikkes konto." *Templarbladet* (Milwaukee), 1 (April-June, 1891), 7–9.

Paa drikkeondets konto. Fortællinger og vers. Eau Claire, Wisconsin, 1894. Reprinted 1897, 1898, 1909.

    Contents: "Blade af en Dagbog"; "Johannes (En Randtegning)"; "Manden med de brede Skuldre (Sujet for et Arbeiderforedrag)"; "Den sidste Kveld"; "En af de 60 Tusinde"; "To"; "Lille Johnnys Juleaften"; "Af Hensyn til Milten."

    Reviews: J. J. Skørdalsvold, *Reform*, November 27, 1894; others reprinted in *Reform*, January 16 and March 5, 1895.

I strømmen. Fortælling. Illustrated by Ben Blessum. Eau Claire, 1899.

    Reprinted 1908, and in *Reform*, October 12, 1907–March 24, 1908.

    Reviews: O. A. Buslett, *Reform*, March 27, 1900; others reprinted in *Reform*, November 13, 1900.

Afholdssmuler fra boghylden. Eau Claire, 1901.

    Contents: "Falstaff—Jeppe paa Berget"; "Vin-Poeter"; "Livsglæden—Faust"; "Vinløv i Haaret"; "Rosmersholm"; "Arveligheden—Gjengangere"; "En Folkefiende"; "Hvo, som gaar foran"; "Markisens Skuldre"; "Et Parti Billiard"; "Den amerikanske Saloon"; "Moderne Korstog"; "Kjøbmanden i Venedig"; "Wm. Hogarth"; "Trætte Mænd—Wulffie og Comp."; "En gammel Tekst"; "Tidselskjægplukkeren."

Fortællinger for Eyvind. Eau Claire, 1905. Reprinted 1907, 1909, Trondheim, 1911.

Translated by J. J. Skørdalsvold, *When You Are Tired of Playing*. Eau Claire, 1907.

    Contents: "Tidlig Vaar og sen Høst"; "To Brødre"; "Skjøde-hunden"; "En hjemsøgt Stad"; "En Fiskehistorie"; "Korsets Tegn"; "Et Spørgsmaalstegn": "Hvorfor? Fordi—"; "Præmie-frøet"; "Den Stygge Jerven"; "Bror min"; "En En-

170

foldig spurgte i sin Enfoldighed"; "Et Eventyr om 'Reform' "; "Den gamle Kone med det graa Sjal"; "Saloon-Interiør"; "Et Stykke af et vindfældt Træ."
Review: S.O. Møst, *Reform*, October 4, 1904.

Hverdagsfolk. Eau Claire, 1908.
Contents: "Hvorledes Magnus blev beskjæmmet"; "Det slukkede Blik"; "En Teddybjørn"; "Løst fra alt"; "Et Stjerneskud"; "Naar Græker møder Græker"; " 'Norskie' "; "Han saa liden og unanselig ud"; "En Skjæbne (Et Øiebliks-billede)."
Reviews: Fr . . . v, *Kvartalskrift*, January, 1909, 16–19; Laurits Stavnheim, *Nordisk Tidende*, May 7, 1908; Haldor Hanson, *Idun*, 1.2 (October, 1908) 26.

Kristus for Pilatus. En norsk-amerikansk fortælling. Eau Claire, 1910; Norwegian edition, titled *Presten Conrad Walther Welde. En norsk-amerikansk fortælling*. Christiania, 1911. Reprinted in *Reform*, January 7–July 1, 1926. Translated by J. J. Skørdalsvold as *Christ before Pilate. An American Story*. Minneapolis, 1924.
Reviews: J. B. Wist, *Decorah-Posten*, December 13, 1910; D. G. Ristad, *Decorah-Posten*, May 12, 1910; H(aldor) H(anson), *Skandinaven*, December 14, 1910; Oscar Gundersen, *Kvartalskrift*, April 7, 1911, 9–11; E. Josephsen, *Symra*, 1912, 125–127; Ola Perstølen, *Syttende Mai*, January 28, 1911; Inge Debes, *20. Aarhundre 11*, (Christiania, 1912), 96; E. Kr. Johnsen, *Lutheraneren*, 17 (1911), 307.

"Den gamle prest," in *Jul i Vesterheimen* (Minneapolis, 1911).

Fortællinger og skisser. Eau Claire, 1913.
Contents: "Borte! – Hjemme!"; "Lars"; "Nu kommer jeg, Mor"; "Et gammelt Koncertprogram"; "Den gamle Prest"; "Hvad Skolemesteren fortalte"; "Et Drømmebillede, Humoresk"; "Johan Arndt og Mor hans"; "To tomme Hænder."

"Norsk-Amerikanernes Deltagelse i Afholdsarbeidet i de Forenede Stater." In *Afholds-folkets festskrift, 1914* (Eau Claire, 1914), 5–25

"Den sidste Kveld," "Et Stjerneskud," "En Ligtale." In *Anthologi til en samfundside*, ed. Idar Handagard. Trondheim, 1915.

Paa veien til smeltepotten. Eau Claire, 1917. Reprinted in *Reform*, January 9–July 24, 1917.
Reviews: J. J. Skørdalsvold, *Folkebladet*, November 28, 1917; J. B. Wist, *Decorah-Posten*, November 27, 1917; E. Kr. Johnsen, *Lutheraneren*, 1 (1917), 753–754; F. G. Gade, *Nordmanns-Forbundet*, 12 (1919), 363–364.

Udvalgte fortællinger, Minneapolis, 1918.
Contents listed in text.

"Der fandtes ikke Ondt i ham," In *Jul i Vesterland*, ed. Olav Redal (Minot, North Dakota, 1920).

Ny samling fortællinger og skisser. Eau Claire, 1921.
Contents: "Hvorledes Ægteparret fik Nattero"; "En Fortælling om tre Trold"; "Da Graagaasen trak mod syd"; "John McEstees Vuggesang"; "Ungdom"; "Et Minde fra Forbudskampen"; "Der fandtes ikke Ondt i ham"; "Hans Hustru"; "En Kveldsstund paa 'Driven' "; "Ellefson og Ingvold."
Reviews: "Arnljot" [J. B. Wist], *Decorah-Posten*, January 31, 1922; J. J.

Immigrant Idealist

Skørdalsvold, *Reform*, March 28, 1922; C. J. Eastvold, *Lutheraneren*, 6 (1922), 179; F. L. Trønsdal, *Lutheraneren*, 6 (1922) 1166–1167.

"Aaffer kommer du 'nte da, Jaala," In *Jul i Vesterheimen*, Minneapolis, (1922).

Det vældige navn. Et drømmebillede fra verdenskrigen. Eau Claire, 1923.

    Reviews: O. A. Buslett, *Reform*, December 27, 1923; O.E. Rølvaag, *Reform*, January 3, 1924; J. J. Skørdalsvold, *Reform*, January 24, 1924; Olav Lee, *Lutheraneren*, 8 (1924), 882; I. Dørrum, *Decorah-Posten*, January 4, 1924; John Storseth, *Washington-Posten*, March 7, 1924.

"Et Barndomsminde." In *Jul i Vesterheimen* (Minneapolis, 1925).

"Den norske Nissen." In *Sønner av Norge, Julenummer*, 1925, 38–41.

Gamlelandets sønner. Oslo, 1926. Translated by Trygve M. Ager as *Sons of the Old Country*, Lincoln, Nebraska, 1983. Reprinted in *Ved Arnen*, October 18, 1927–February 3, 1928.

    Reviews: D. G. Ristad, *Skandinaven*, January 12, 1926; Franklin Petersen, *Nordisk Tidende*, September 23, 1926; Hans Olav, *Nordisk Tidende*, October 7, 1926; O. E. Rølvaag, *Skandinaven*, November 24, 1926; Idar Handagard, *Porsgrunns Dagblad*, December 16, 1926.

Hundeøine. Oslo, 1929. Translated by Charles Wharton Stork as *I Sit Alone*, New York, 1931.

    Reviews: C. J. Hambro, *Morgenbladet*, (Oslo), reprinted *Minneapolis Tidende*, December 12, 1929; G(eorg) S(trandvold), *Decorah-Posten*, November 12, 1929, February 18, 1930; Hans Olav, *Nordisk Tidende*, November 28, 1929; O.E. Rølvaag, *Norden*, 2.1 (1930), 15–16; Knud Wefald, *Normanden*, December, 1929.

"Et Nutidseventyr." In *Jul i Vesterheimen*, 1929.

Under forvandlingens tegn. Fortællinger og saadant. Eau Claire, 1930.

    Contents: "Hun tok os i Fanget"; "Den norske Nissen"; "En Mor"; "Assimileret"; "Hvor Hjertene mødtes"; "Et Nutids Eventyr"; "En Profet som stod paa sine Fødder"; "Vinduet som vendte mod Jerusalem"; "Norsk-Amerikaneren Peer Gynt."

"Det blev en råd til sist." In *Nordmanns-Forbundets Julenummer*, 1931.

"Sjel tilsalgs." In *Jul i Vesterheimen*, (Minneapolis, 1935).

Skyldfolk og andre. Eau Claire, 1938.

    Contents: "Det hvide Kors i Skogen"; "Det blev en Raad tilsist"; "Veien til Lykken"; " 'Undesirable' "; "Sjel tilsalgs"; "Juledrømmen som brast"; "Det kunne slompe"; "Arven."

    Review: J. J. Skørdalsvold, *Reform*, November 3, 1938. Translated by Hildur Ager Nicolai as *The White Cross in the Woods and Other Norwegian Immigrant Stories*. Privately printed, 1982.

2. Publications Edited by Ager

Templarbladet, Milwaukee, Wisconsin, 1891–1894.

Sangbog for afholdsforeninger (with J. J. Skørdalsvold), Eau Claire, 1901.

Reform, Eau Claire, 1903–1941.

Bibliography

Kvartalskrift, Eau Claire, 1905–1922.
Norge i Amerika, vol. 5 of *Boken om Norge*, Christiania, 1915.
Oberst Heg og hans gutter, Eau Claire, 1916.
Smaalenslaget i Amerika, Aarbog. St. Paul, Minnesota, 1922.

3. Books and Articles about Ager

Andersen, Arlow W. *The Norwegian-Americans*. Boston, 1975.
Andersen, Thor M. *Norway in America* (Oslo, 1983), 21–24.
Barstad, Johanna. *Litteratur om utvandringen fra Norge til Nord-Amerika*. A bibliography based on the catalog of the Norwegian-American Collection, University of Oslo Library.
Beck, Richard. "Norwegian-American Literature." In G. Bach, ed., *The History of Scandinavian Literature* (New York, 1938), 74–84.
Blegen, Theodore C. *Norwegian Migration to America*, 2 (Northfield, Minnesota, 1940), 585–596.
Brevik, Sigrid. " 'The Sensitive Soul' in the Fiction of Ole E. Rølvaag and Waldemar Ager." Cand. philol. thesis, University of Oslo, 1982.
Chrislock, Carl H. "Introduction: The Historical Context." In Odd S. Lovoll, ed., *Cultural Pluralism vs. Assimilation*, (Northfield, Minnesota, 1977), 3–37.
———. *Ethnicity Challenged: The Upper Midwest Norwegian-American Experience in World War I*. Northfield, 1981.
Culver, Barbara Bergh. "Glimpses into my Grandfather's Scrapbooks," student paper reprinted in Hildur Ager Nicolai, ed., *The White Cross in the Woods* (1982), 71–87.
Folkestad, Sigurd. "Waldemar Ager." *Nordmanns-Forbundet*, 1929, 156.
Gulliksen, Øyvind T. "In Defense of a Norwegian-American Culture: Waldemar Ager's *Sons of the Old Country*." *American Studies in Scandinavia*, 19 (1987), 39–52.
Handagard, Idar, "Wm. Ager som forfatter." *Reform*, June 26, 1900, reprinted from *Menneskevennen* (Christiania).
———. "Vor sag og dens digtere." *Afholdsvennens Aarbog 1903*. Christiania, 1903.
———. "Waldemar Ager, en norsk-amerikansk forfatter." *Dagens Nyt*, April 29, 1911.
———. "Norsk-amerikansk litteratur." *Dagens Nyt*, November 30, 1911; *Morgenposten*, December 13, 1911.
———. "Waldemar Ager." In *Fem Folkedigtere* (Trondheim, 1915), 75–105. Reprinted in *Afholdsdagbladet* (Aarhus), December 16, 17, 1915.
———. "Waldemar Ager." *Drammens Tidende*, May 20, 1925.
———. "To norsk-amerikanske digtere I–II." *Arbeiderbladet*, August 10, 11, 1925. Also in *Dagen*, August 19, 1925; *Telemark Kommunistblad*, October 7, 1926; *Nordmanns-Forbundet*, 21 (March, 1928), 96–98.
———. "*Gamlelandets sønner*, Waldemar Agers sidste bog om det utflyttede Norge." *Porsgrunds Dagblad*. December 16, 1926.
Hasås, Sigurd. "Avholdssaken og norskdommens dikter i Amerika." *Afholdsspørsmålet* (Oslo), 14 (1962), 193–214.

Immigrant Idealist

Haugen, Einar. *The Norwegian Language in America: a Study in Bilingual Behavior*. 2nd ed. Bloomington, 1969.

——. *Norsk i Amerika*. Oslo, 1939, 1975.

——. *Ole Edvart Rölvaag*. Boston, 1983.

——. Taped interview with Eyvind Ager, June 15, 1987.

Hjellum, John. "Waldemar Ager," in "Hvem er hvem blandt Nordmænd i Amerika?" *Skandinaven* (Chicago), April 1, 1927.

Hoidahl, Aagot D. "Norwegian-American Fiction since 1880." *Norwegian-American Studies and Records*, 5 (Northfield, 1930), 61–83.

Hustvedt, Lloyd. *Rasmus Bjørn Anderson: Pioneer Scholar*. Northfield, 1966.

Johnson, Simon. "Skjønlitterære sysler blandt norsk-amerikanerne." *Decorah-Posten*, February 24, March 3, 10, 1939.

Jorgenson, Theodore and Nora O. Solum. *Ole Edvart Rölvaag: A Biography*. New York, 1939.

Kilde, Clarence. "Tragedy in the Life and Writings of Waldemar Ager, Norwegian immigrant, author and editor. 1869–1941." (M.A. thesis, University of Minnesota, 1978.)

——. "Dark Decade: The Declining Years of Waldemar Ager." *Norwegian-American Studies*, 28 (1979), 157–191.

——. Cultural Pluralism Versus Assimilation in the Writings of Waldemar Ager." Student paper at University of Minnesota, March 15, 1976.

——. "Editor Ager a Norwegian Advocate." *Our Story 1776–1976*, 5 (Eau Claire, 1976), 152.

——. Interviews with Ager children, 1975–1976: Gudrun Bergh; Solveig Best; Eyvind. Notes in NAHA Archives.

Lovoll, Odd S. *A Folk Epic: The* Bygdelag *in America*. Boston, 1975.

——. *Cultural Pluralism versus Assimilation: The Views of Waldemar Ager*. Northfield, 1977.

——. *The Promise of America: A History of the Norwegian-American People*. Minneapolis, 1984. Norwegian version: *Det løfterike landet*. Oslo, 1983.

——. Introduction, Ager, *Sons of the Old Country*, translated by Trygve Ager (Lincoln, Nebraska, 1983), v–xiv.

Nicolai, Hildur Ager, trans. and ed. *The White Cross in the Woods and Other Norwegian Immigrant Stories*. Privately printed, 1982. Translation of *Skyldfolk og andre*, with pictures and information about Ager's life and family.

Øverland, Orm. "Waldemar Ager, *Sons of the Old Country*." *American Studies in Scandinavia*, 17.2 (1985), 77–78.

Rynning, Øivind. "The Impact of English on American Norwegian: A Study of Linguistic Interference on the Writings of Waldemar Ager." (Cand. phil. thesis, University of Oslo, 1975.)

Saxe, Ludvig. "Waldemar Ager." *Nordmanns-Forbundet*, 1934, 153; 1939, 118; 1941, 205.

Skårdal, Dorothy Burton. *The Divided Heart*. Lincoln, Nebraska, 1974.

Skørdalsvold, J.J. "Man of Many Minds." *Norden* (Chicago), July, 1931, 6–10.

Bibliography

Smemo, Kenneth. "The Immigrant as Reformer: The Case of the Norwegian American." Paper presented at meeting of Organization of American Historians, Chicago, 1974.

——. "The Norwegian Ethnic Experience and the Literature of Waldemar Ager." In Harald Næss, ed., *Norwegian Influence in the Upper Midwest* (Duluth, Minnesota, 1976), 59–64.

——. "Waldemar Theodore Ager 1869–1941." In Lovoll, ed., *Cultural Pluralism versus Assimilation*, 130–136.

——. "Waldemar Ager: Norwegian-American Sisyphus". In Dorothy Skårdal and Ingeborg Kongslien, eds., *Essays on Norwegian-American Literature and History* (Oslo, 1986), 141–159.

Strømme, Peer. "Norsk-amerikanske forfattere – Waldemar Ager." *Symra*, 3 (1907), 137–147.

Sunde, Arne. *Heime, men borte: Ein analyse av 7 norsk-amerikanske romanar*. Bergen, 1984.

Thorson, Gerald H. "America is not Norway: The Story of the Norwegian-American Novel." (Ph.D. dissertation, Columbia University, 1957.)

——. "Pressed Flowers and Still-Running Brooks: Norwegian-American Literature." In *Ethnic Literatures since 1776: The Many Voices of America*. Proceedings of the Comparative Literature Symposium, Texas Technological University, 1978, part 2, 375–394.

Ullnæss, Sverre P.N. "Waldemar Ager – Gressvik-gutt som kjempet for norsk kultur i USA." *Fredrikstad Blad*, March 25, 1975.

Wist, Johannes B. *Norsk-amerikanernes festskrift*. Decorah, Iowa, 1914.

Unsigned Articles:

Biographical notes, *Symra*, 1905, 199; obituary, Eau Claire *Leader-Telegram*, August 1, 1941, editorial August 2, 1941; obituary, *Decorah-Posten*, August 5, 1941; *Who's Who in America*, 1915 and later editions; *Scandinavian-American Fraternity*, 40.12 (August, 1941), 3.

Index

Immigrant Idealist

"En Profet som stod paa sine Fødder" (A Prophet Who Stood on his Feet), short story, 137

Quale, Sigvald declamation contests, 128
Qualley, R. N., of Sons of Norway, 116
Quo Vadis, Polish novel translated by Ager, 27, 28

Reform 12, 75 (*ills.*); history of, 2, 10, 98, 116, 128, 151, 154, 155; Ager as printer and business manager for, 7, 10, 24, 25; reviews and articles by others in, 8, 14, 119; its print shop, 11; Ager's writings in, 22, 25–27, 29–32, 39, 47, 51, 54, 55, 64, 73, 82, 88, 110, 145; Ager as editor of, 50, 54, 137, 144, 151; short story about, 59
Relling, I. T., Chicago bookseller and editor, 22
Republikaneren, 38
Revyen (Chicago), 60
Ristad, D. G., Norwegian-American pastor and literary man, 109, 123
Rodhuggeren (Fergus Falls, Minnesota), 25
Roedder, Karsten, columnist in *Nordisk Tidende*, 155
Rolfsen, Nordahl, Norwegian author of school readers, 81
Rølvaag, Jennie (Mrs. O. E.), 143
Rølvaag, Ole Edvart, reviews of Ager's books, 70–71, 114, 124; Ager's reviews of his books, 103–104, 109, 117–118; friendship with Ager, 110, 124–127, 139–143; comparison *Gamlelandets sønner* and *Giants in the Earth*, 120–121; Ager on, 139–140, 144; death, 143; reputation, 157
Rønning, N. N., Norwegian-American author, 109
Roosevelt, Theodore, 84

St. Olaf College, and Rølvaag, 70, 117; Ager addresses students, 110; Ager given honorary degree by, 125–127; and President Boe, 152, 153
"Saloon Interiør," short story, 59
Saxe, Ludvig, journalist, 144
Scandia (Chicago), 14, 38
Shakespeare, William, 28, 29, 64
Sienkiewicz, Henryk, Polish author, 27
Siljan, Lars, editor of *Normanden*, 101
"Sjel tilsalgs" (Mussels for Sale), short story, 150–151
Skandinaven (Chicago), history, 2, 22, 155;

Ager attacks, 47; Ager visits, 110; review of *Det vældige navn*, 113
"En Skjæbne" (A Fate), short story, 62–63
"Skjødehunden" (The Lapdog), short story, 56
Skørdalsvold, J. J., temperance advocate and literary man, reviews of Ager's works, 14, 95, 107, 113, 151; translation of *Kristus for Pilatus*, 116; birthday celebration, 139; article on Ager, 144
Skyldfolk og andre, 150–151
Slettedahl, P. J., advocate of assimilation, 100
"Det slukkede Blik" (The Light that Went Out), short story, 61, 98
Smemo, Kenneth, expert on Ager, 156, 157
Sneve, O. S., poet and temperance advocate, 75, 77
Social-Demokraten (Oslo), 71
Sons of Norway, 33, 73, 77, 111, 116, 156
Sons of the Old Country, see *Gamlelandets sønner*
"Et Spørgsmaalstegn" (A Question Mark), short story, 57
Springfield Republican (Illinois), 135
"Et Stjerneskud" (A Shooting Star), short story, 62, 98
Stork, Charles Wharton, translator, 129, 141
Strandvold, Georg, journalist with *Decorah-Posten*, 134
Strømme, Peer, Norwegian-American author and editor, as writer, 3, 157; on Ager, 22, 64; reviews of Ager's books by, 29, 38
"Den stygge Jerven" (The Nasty Wolverine), short story, 58
"Et Stykke af et vindfældt Træ" (A Piece of a Windfelled Tree), short story, 59–60
Sunde, Arne, Norwegian literary historian, 135
Sundheim, A. M., editor of *Vesterheimen*, Christmas annual, 76
Superior Tidende (Wisconsin), 29
Swenson, Magnus, Norwegian-American industrialist, 97–98
Symra (Decorah, Iowa), 63, 75, 76, 77, 83

"En Teddy-Bjørn" (A Teddy Bear), short story, 61, 98
Temperance, societies, 7–9, 22–24; and *Reform*, 9–10; in Ager's fiction, 11–14, 23–24, 37, 39, 55–60; journals, 22; in Ager's articles, 28–29, 47; and Handagard, 45–46; Prohibition and Repeal, 98, 145; as one of Ager's ideals, 156–157
Templarbladet (Milwaukee), 23–24

182